MAKING THE BIBLE FRENCH

JEANETTE L. PATTERSON

Making the Bible French

The *Bible historiale* and the Medieval Lay Reader

UNIVERSITY OF TORONTO PRESS
Toronto Buffalo London

© University of Toronto Press 2022
Toronto Buffalo London
utorontopress.com
Printed in the U.S.A.

ISBN 978-1-4875-0888-3 (cloth)
ISBN 978-1-4875-3920-7 (EPUB)
ISBN 978-1-4875-3919-1 (PDF)

Library and Archives Canada Cataloguing in Publication

Title: Making the Bible French : the Bible historiale and the medieval lay reader / Jeanette L. Patterson.
Names: Patterson, Jeanette, author.
Description: Includes bibliographical references and index.
Identifiers: Canadiana (print) 20210285532 | Canadiana (ebook) 20210285621 | ISBN 9781487508883 (cloth) | ISBN 9781487539207 (EPUB) | ISBN 9781487539191 (PDF)
Subjects: LCSH: Moulins, Guyart des, approximately 1251–approximately 1297. | LCSH: Bible – Translating – France – History – To 1500. | LCSH: Bible. French – Versions – History – To 1500. | LCSH: Bible – Criticism, Narrative. | LCSH: Narration in the Bible. | LCSH: Lay readers – France – History – To 1500.
Classification: LCC BS460.F7 P38 2022 | DDC 220.5/41090902 – dc23

We wish to acknowledge the land on which the University of Toronto Press operates. This land is the traditional territory of the Wendat, the Anishnaabeg, the Haudenosaunee, the Métis, and the Mississaugas of the Credit First Nation.

University of Toronto Press acknowledges the financial support of the Government of Canada, the Canada Council for the Arts, and the Ontario Arts Council, an agency of the Government of Ontario, for its publishing activities.

Contents

Figures

Acknowledgments

This volume is not the work of a solitary mind, but a product of the help and support of many friends, colleagues, and institutions, without whom I could not have brought it to publication.

First, I must thank the people and entities that made my research possible in the first place, through funding and other kinds of research support and access to materials. Research for this book was supported by funding from the Mellon Foundation (for a related digital project); the American Council of Learned Societies; the Medieval Academy of America's Charles T. Wood Dissertation Grant; and the French Embassy, whose Chateaubriand Fellowship supported a year in Paris doing indispensable primary source research. I am grateful to my present institution, Binghamton University, for its support of my research through funding for travel, research, and publication costs, research-related course releases, and special opportunities through Harpur College, the Institute for Advanced Studies in the Humanities, and the Dr. Nuala McGann Drescher Leave Program co-funded by New York State United University Professions. I also thank my previous institutions that have provided various forms of support to pursue this project: Johns Hopkins University, Princeton University, and the University of Virginia. Finally, I wish to express my gratitude to all of the librarians, curators, and other staff who provided assistance, access to materials, and answers to questions at all of the libraries whose collections I consulted, as well as those who have digitized and curated digital images of *Bible historiale* books at those libraries: the Bibliothèque nationale de France (Richelieu and Arsenal), the British Library, the Walters Art Gallery, the US Library of Congress, the Pierpont Morgan Library, the Bibliothèque royale de Belgique, the Bibliothèque municipale de Montpellier, and the Vatican Library. Among these librarians and curators, Will Noel deserves special mention for introducing me to the *Bible historiale* during his time at the

Walters Art Gallery and mine in graduate school at Johns Hopkins, and thanks for answering my many questions at the early stages of my project.

Second, I want to thank all of the people who helped make this book better. This begins with my dissertation committee, especially my advisor, Stephen Nichols, and co-reader, Deborah McGrady, under whose supervision the seeds of this project developed, and who have both continued to be reliable, outstanding mentors and dear friends. I am incredibly grateful to my Binghamton University colleague Marilynn Desmond, who generously read drafts of every chapter in this book and provided invaluable feedback that improved the clarity of my arguments, and whose advice, kindness, and support have been of the utmost value. I extend my warmest thanks to my editor, Suzanne Rancourt; my talented and meticulous copyeditor, Emily Reiner; and the two peer reviewers whose thoughtful, thorough, and insightful reading of my work greatly strengthened the book's organization and bibliography and nudged me to push my ideas further. This project has also benefited from the collective feedback of colleagues in faculty seminars and workshops, including the spring 2018 IASH faculty seminar and the spring 2019 NEH grant-writing workshop, for which I thank my fellow participants. I would equally like to thank all of the colleagues who have invited me to participate in their conference sessions, to collaborate on projects, or to present my work (especially repeat offenders Jeanette Beer and Xavier-Laurent Salvador), as well as the audience members at my talks, students in my classes, and colleagues in conversation, whose questions and comments gave me new directions to think about.

Finally, I extend my profound and heartfelt gratitude to all of the friends and family who have encouraged and motivated me, tolerated my erratic and sometimes obsessive work habits, and offered love and moral support. Special thanks to my parents for always supporting my academic pursuits and nerdy interests and showing interest in my work. Among the many people whose friendship has kept me going, I especially want to thank Doreen Densky for many a late-night phone call and much-needed weekend retreat, Kathleen Hruska for keeping me grounded through graduate school, my Kalamazoo crew, Rachel Geer and Ellie Voss, for all the dancing and virtual wine hours, Bridget Whearty for innumerable acts of friendship and commiseration, and Olivia Holmes for getting me out of the house and out of my own head during the COVID-19 pandemic. Thanks, more broadly, to all my fabulous friends and colleagues in Romance Languages, CEMERS, and TRIP at Binghamton, and to the long list of friends in and out of academia, throughout the world, who've been there for me. Last but not least, I thank my cats Kipling and Sappho for their unwavering encouragement and for reminding me when it is time to stop working to eat, play, cuddle, or sleep.

MAKING THE BIBLE FRENCH

Introduction

All writing is translation;
and conversely translation, after all, is writing.

Robert Pinsky[1]

The Bible (if we can speak of it in the singular) has always filled numerous functions. Its text forms the cornerstone of multiple theologies and philosophical anthropologies, proposing an account of God's relationship with that cherished but rebellious species made in his image. Its foundation narratives have historically served an essential role in establishing ethnic, cultural, and religious identities. The Hebrew Bible connected a diasporic community through the genealogies and stories of the early Israelites. The Christian New Testament helped to establish the early church by articulating a faith-based identity that set out to transcend or even supplant geographic, linguistic, tribal, and genealogical affiliations (even if, in practice, predominantly Christian societies have also wielded the Bible to assert national identities or defend social hierarchies). The Bible continues to provide a legal, social, and moral code that defines the boundaries of licit and illicit conduct, community-inclusive and community-exclusive actions. Its cohesive social functions are reinforced in the religious rituals founded on its text. Moreover, the artfully constructed stories, poems, psalms, and proverbs in the Bible constitute a complex body of literature whose influence remains inescapably legible throughout the artistic production of the cultures it has touched.

Medieval Christianity looked to the Bible for theological, moral, historical, and even scientific truth value, but also maintained a pervasive interest in its literariness. This reading of the text as simultaneously "truthful" and "literary" contrasts with the resistance some modern readers of faith have shown towards self-described "literary" approaches to reading the Bible, which these modern readers deem to be a secular pursuit at odds with religious Bible study.[2] As Robert Alter puts it, using the same techniques usually applied to literary fiction to read the Bible requires modern audiences to rethink what literature is, and "conversely, that we develop a somewhat more troublesome understanding of what a religious document might be."[3] This book examines what the Bible's literariness meant for readers of the late thirteenth-century French Bible translation known as the *Bible historiale*. As the examples in this book show, the *Bible historiale* adopts textual modes adapted to readers for whom literary and religious approaches to and reasons for reading narrative texts were tightly intertwined. Employing strategies of transla-tion, commentary, and narration borrowed from contexts as diverse as scholastic study, vernacular preaching, and secular fiction, its translator produced one of the most popular, most widely copied French-language texts of the later Middle Ages.

In 1291, in the northern French village of Aire-sur-la-Lys, the priest and canon Guyart des Moulins began a composite French translation of the historical books of the Latin Vulgate Bible interspersed with *histoires,* or chapters from Peter Comestor's *Historia scholastica* meant to help read-ers interpret biblical narrative texts in both the cultural context of their original source and within the framework of dominant contemporary church norms and beliefs. According to his prologue, Guyart's intention was to "faire laies personnes entendre les histoires des escriptures anci-ennes" ("help laypeople understand the histories of the ancient scrip-tures," Paris, Bibliothèque nationale de France, MS fr. 155, fol. 1 [BnF fr. 155]).[4] Completed four years later, with a prologue added in 1297, Guyart's *Bible historiale* was not the first Bible translation into French, but with at least 144 surviving manuscript volumes and over twenty early print editions, it was the most widely disseminated and most influen-tial French-language Bible translation for over two hundred years.[5] With its close attention to cultural context and its interrogation of narrative cause and effect, Guyart's historical approach to translating and explicat-ing the Bible held particular value for lay readers in positions of secular power who had access to one of its deluxe manuscripts.[6] This French Bible was meant to shape their understanding of their place in the world and in salvation history. Over time, high-profile patrons such as those within the French royal family also took an active role in shaping what the *Bible historiale* would become, as its manuscripts were customized and expanded and committed to print. Soon after its composition, book-makers began expanding *Bible historiale* manuscripts to include books of the Bible that Guyart did not translate, adding material from a second, slightly earlier French translation known as the *Bible du XIIIᵉ siècle* or *Old*

French Bible. This convention of combining the two translations in various permutations (sometimes with other texts as well) produced a modular, variable text whose customizations reflected individualized as well as culture-specific readings of the Bible.

Making the Bible French: The Bible historiale *and the Medieval Lay Reader* demonstrates how Guyart's first-person authorial voice narrates his choices in compiling, annotating, and translating the biblical text in response to the imagined expectations of his implied reader. Anticipating the questions of a hypothetical lay reader, the translator-narrator creates a space for an actual reader to inhabit and interact with the text. To foster such interaction, the translation employs the literary strategies of fictional narrative to aid readers' visualization of biblical stories and to encourage readers' identification with the stories' characters in ways that parallel other medieval literary and art forms. In addition to examining how the translation itself employs these strategies, I also trace how individual manuscript copies of the work adapt them for new intended readers, and how these manuscript interventions reflect changing ideas about their target readers, about translation, and about the Bible itself.

Previous studies of the *Bible historiale* have primarily focused on its visual programs, the linguistic features of its translation, the ownership and provenance of its manuscripts, or its intertextual networks (e.g., sources, citations, and "influence"). All of these considerations intersect with my own, and I owe a great deal to the work of my predecessors who have catalogued *Bible historiale* manuscripts, identified their artists, authors, and readers, and paved the way for further research on the text. The present work differs from most prior scholarship in its approach to the *Bible historiale*'s textual tradition. Following upon the contributions made by scholars of medieval translation such as Rita Copeland, Jeanette Beer, Ruth Evans, and Zrinka Stahuljak, I dispense with essentialist taxonomies of translation to parse out how Guyart's work simultaneously operates both as a translation and as a literary text in its own right. I treat the *Bible historiale* as a self-consciously constructed text that engages creatively with the preoccupations of its cultural moment, in conversation with overtly fictional literature and in direct response to the perceived needs, literacies, and literary tastes and expectations of its target audience. I show, for example, that the translator's strategic addition of sensory details and fictionalized elements encourages imaginative speculation, and that he rearranges and reframes biblical episodes to maximize their aesthetic potential in conformity with narrative conventions of verisimilitude, all aimed at bolstering the Bible's claims to truth and readers' capacity for belief. I trace how the translation, with its framework of commentary driven by the interventions of its first-person translator, constructs a space for actual readers to inhabit as they navigate the text following the translator-narrator's instructive guidance. Compared to other Bible formats similarly aimed at a primary readership of lay aristocrats (such as the *Bible moralisée*, so named to contrast its methods with the *Bible historiale*), I argue that the *Bible historiale* cultivates a specific kind of literacy predicated on patience and modeled on a scholastic practice of asking productive questions of the text.

The *Bible historiale*'s sizeable manuscript corpus opens a two-hundred-year window into medieval modes of thought across a range of domains: Christian religious practice; biblical exegesis; moral, political, and natural philosophy; historiography; translation; art; and narrative aesthetics. It also engages in debates surrounding social issues of interest to modern scholars, such as gender, race, ecology, and what it means to be human. Until now, the *Bible historiale* has remained on the margins of scholarly conversations on these topics, and largely absent from histories of translation as well as from surveys of medieval European literatures. As more of its manuscripts are digitized and made available to the public through the Bibliothèque nationale de France's *Gallica*, the British Library's digitized manuscript collection, and other online repositories, the increasing visibility of the *Bible historiale* promises to bring it into dialogue with other influential texts of the Middle Ages and with the questions medievalists ask of them. The present book aims to initiate some of those conversations by looking at how the *Bible historiale*'s choices in translation, compilation, and manuscript presentation adapt biblical sources to the changing cultural values, literacies, and aesthetics of its target readership.

Constructing the Lay Reader

The title of this book, *Making the Bible French: The* Bible historiale *and the Medieval Lay Reader*, highlights the cultural impact of the translation and its reception as a function of the translated text's relationship to its intended or implied readership. Much has been made in recent scholarship of "vernacular" texts and translations in the Middle Ages, in some cases at least rhetorically granting languages an agency of their own, separate from the heterogenous groups of people who used those languages. The political, religious, social, and literary ramifications of medieval diglossia – the way languages and their designated uses perpetuate social hierarchies within some multilingual societies – are certainly pertinent to medieval translation and to the *Bible historiale*.[7] Being "illettré" – meaning, in the Middle Ages, illiterate *in Latin* – meant depending on the mediation of Latin-literate clergy for access to knowledge.

This dependence afforded the Latin-educated clerical class a powerful gatekeeping function that affected how translations were made, valued, and used. Meanwhile, this diglossia also shaped the perception of translation because the power attached to Latin literacy was projected onto Latin itself: since knowledge of Latin granted institutional authority over sacred texts, the language itself was invested with authority and an aura of holiness. Some of Guyart's translation choices reflect such attitudes about language: he posits, for example, that the words of consecration for the rite of the Eucharist would not effectuate transubstantiation in French as they do in Latin, and he always quotes Jesus in Latin before translating his words into French.[8] While vernacular translation is sometimes credited with subverting or eroding diglossic language hierarchies and the power of the elite clerical class they sustained (and it can have that effect, intentionally or not), sociolinguistic subversion does not figure as an explicit goal of Guyart's translation. On the contrary, his translation practices and discourse uphold the higher authority of Latin and the laity's reliance on clerical mediation even if the *Bible historiale* ultimately contributed, alongside other major French texts and translations, to the gradual elevation in status and expanded social functions of the French language.

In any event, the *Bible historiale* does not define itself or its purpose primarily by its language, but by its target readership. Far from conceiving translation as a transaction that operates between languages in the abstract, the translator of the *Bible historiale* explicitly begins with its readers, whom the translator defines not as French people or French speakers, but as "laies personnes." This distinction is meaningful to our understanding of his choices, even if there is a good deal of overlap between the broad category of "laypeople" and the broad category of people who, in the late Middle Ages, read texts in French, whether or not they also read Latin. It is the primary target audience's status as laity, juxtaposed against Guyart's subject-position as a priest, that together shape the translation and its framing. That positionality allows him to construct a deferential role for his implied reader, thus inviting actual lay readers, regardless of their positions of secular authority, to adopt a humbler attitude towards the text as they would towards the religious authority of their flesh and blood chaplain or priest. My use of "positionality" in this context refers not only to Guyart's literal profession, but also to all of the ways that his experience as a priest have socialized him to interact with laypeople, how his social and ideological affiliations inflected that communication, and, conversely, how lay Christians in medieval French-speaking communities would have been socialized to perceive and interact with priests.[9]

My arguments concerning the "lay reader's" relationship to the *Bible historiale* are less focused on actual, known readers than on how the text represents and addresses its potential readers. Most of the evidence I examine about readers of the *Bible historiale* comes from the text and its paratexts: from Guyart's own statements and from those of scribes, as well as the ways in which the text and its manuscript recensions react to perceived, anticipated, or explicitly known reader preferences and behaviours. Occasionally, individual readers do leave direct evidence of some aspect of their reading, such as annotations in a manuscript or quotations from or references to the *Bible historiale* in other texts or contexts, but that evidence is scant and does not always lend itself to straightforward, confident conclusions.[10] To distinguish what is known about actual readers of the *Bible historiale* from how the text portrays, caters to, and engages with its readers as imagined by Guyart, later scribes and editors, or their narrating avatars, I prefer Wolfgang Iser's term "implied reader" to describe how an authorial voice in the text constructs a fictional dialogue with a hypothetical reader, which in turn assigns actual readers a role to play in reading the text.[11]

Translating and Rewriting

Even as a prose translation that promises a *mot a mot* ("word-for-word") rendering of its Latin sources, Guyart's text and each of its many manuscript and early print reworkings "rewrite" the Bible in the specific sense that André Lefevere uses that term in his *Translation, Rewriting, and the Manipulation of Literary Fame*. Lefevere's model of rewriting challenges the assumptions behind the strict categorical boundaries around translation, namely that if translation is "literal" and "faithful" to the source text, it is objective, unmanipulated, and unideological. Starting from the position that literary translation can never be any of these things, he proposes a heuristic for understanding the cultural scripts and systems that affect the intra- and intercultural reception of texts, situating translation among the many ways that "professional" readers repackage texts for a larger audience of "non-professional" (or lay) readers in alignment with their own ideologies and poetics. In his words,

> Inside the literary system the professionals are the critics, reviewers, teachers, translators. They will occasionally repress certain works of literature that are all too blatantly opposed to the dominant concept of what literature should (be allowed to) be – its poetics – and of what society should (be allowed to) be – ideology. But they will much more frequently rewrite works of literature until they are deemed acceptable to the poetics and ideology of a certain time and place.[12]

Lefevere's approach to rewriting and its discursive underpinnings is especially apt for medieval Latin–based cultures in which clerical authors, translators, scholars, and exegetes had substantial control over non-Latin-literate readers' access to cultural knowledge and where manuscript transmission invites re-evaluation, with each new copy, of the source copy's translation, compilation, and paratextual framing. In his choices as to which parts of the Bible he translates (and doesn't), how he translates, how he adapts biblical narratives to medieval poetics, and how he frames them to privilege some interpretations over others, Guyart des Moulins engages in all of the activities Lefevere counts as rewriting: "translation, historiography, anthologization, criticism and editing" and, in a few places, the creative licence of fictionalized adaptation.[13] His "rewriting" of his source text(s), as well as later scribes' and editors' "rewritings" of his translation, do not make the *Bible historiale* any less of a translation, nor do they imply irreverence for, or falsification of, their biblical source. Rather, these "rewritings" reveal how much Guyart's project both bends to and helps shape the prevailing world views and literary preferences of his time and culture. The rewritings also shed light on how the text and its manuscripts respond to constraints imposed by what Lefevere calls "patronage," which would include not only the unnamed "friend" Guyart credits with commissioning his work, but the other actors and institutions – most notably the church, but also individual makers and purchasers of new manuscripts – who held power over the favourable reception, status, and continued copying of his work.[14] The large degree of variation in its manuscript tradition testifies to copyists' sensitivity to changing cultural contexts as well as the different priorities of individual manuscript owners.

Readers of the *Bible historiale* are coded first as lay readers, and second, as readers of French, both of which characteristics shape the rewriting that happens in translation. When I say the *Bible historiale* "makes the Bible French," I refer to multiple ways the translation and aspects of its manuscript presentation adapt and appropriate biblical texts to new, "French" linguistic, cultural, and ideological contexts. First, the translation brings the cultural and textual norms expressed in both the Latin Vulgate and its anterior ancient Hebrew and Greek sources closer to those of medieval French-speaking cultures and the vernacular literature they produced. Second, the text and its manuscripts perform various degrees of politically motivated appropriations of holy texts and lands as rightfully "belonging" to Christians over Jews and Muslims and, at times, according a special place to the French monarchy in biblical history.

In the centuries following Guyart's initial composition of the *Bible historiale,* people involved in making, selling, and cataloguing books increasingly foregrounded its French language and "Frenchness." Many late medieval inventories of manuscripts as well as the covers of some manuscript copies and early print editions of the *Bible historiale* replace that title (given by Guyart) with something like "Bible in French" ("Bible en françois"), shifting the focus from the translation's historical framing (chosen as a function of the reader's lay status) to its language. In the nineteenth century, philologist Samuel Berger titled the first book on the *Bible historiale* and other medieval French-language prose Bible translations *La Bible française au moyen âge: Étude sur les plus anciennes versions de la Bible écrites en prose de langue d'oïl.* By attributing an essential "Frenchness" to the collective objects of his study, in his shift from "Bible en français" to "Bible française," he inscribes the medieval translations in a tradition of national philology that elides and idealizes the relationship between language, culture, and national identity.[15] I do not endorse this aspect of Berger's study, but mention it here to illustrate what I see as a trajectory through which not only Bible translations themselves but also the critical discourse about those translations continually "rewrite" the Bible's place within a culture and history through the lenses of dominant poetics and ideology. The *Bible historiale* and its medieval manuscript transmission participate in this discourse insofar as its translation is framed by a significant amount of metacommentary about its choices in relation to the past, present, and future reception of biblical texts in the target culture. In its efforts to make biblical narrative relatable and relevant to its French-language readers, the *Bible historiale* makes the Bible French in ways both benign (inserting shared cultural references and adopting conventions of French-language literature) and malevolent (using the Bible to promote or justify violent oppression and conquest). To make the Bible French at the end of the thirteenth century is to bring the Bible more fully into dialogue with French language and literature and their associated ways of thinking about the world. The chapters that follow investigate how that cultural specificity manifests itself in Guyart's translation project and in its reader-customized manuscript iterations.

Guyart's own words about his interventions, echoed by some scribes' justifications for their own modifications, most often explain those choices as a function of the target reader, or rather, a culturally conditioned mental image of the *Bible historiale*'s target readership. Notions about the prior knowledge, experience, and beliefs of hypothetical French-language lay readers drive choices small and large: whether to use adaptation or explanatory paraphrase or a gloss to explain an unfamiliar cultural reference; what must be added, left out, or euphemized to avoid offending readers' sensibilities; the selection and arrangement of textual contents; the manuscript layout and illustration program. I demonstrate how the translation and its manuscripts construct their implied readers through their most visible editorial and translation choices, with special focus on those instances where the translator or scribe senses that a departure from the source text(s), whether from the Latin Bible and *Historia scholastica* or from a manuscript exemplar, is particularly bold and interrupts to identify and justify it. Each chapter of this book focuses on a different aspect or example of such interventions in light of their relationship to the reader.

The first chapter ("Making the French Bible, or Making the Bible French") introduces and contextualizes Guyart's translation project and its manuscript tradition while also challenging prevalent misconceptions about the history of Bible translation. It examines an important central facet of the translation that informs all of the chapters that follow: namely how the translation, its framework of commentary, and the interventions of its first-person translator work to construct the subject-position of the reader as a function of the text, constructing a space for actual readers to inhabit and navigate the text with the translator-narrator's instructive guidance. Finally, it traces how later manuscript expansions and recensions adapt the contents and structure of the *Bible historiale* in response to changing ideas about vernacular Bibles and their readers.

Chapters 2 and 3 focus on two different aspects of how the *Bible historiale* engages with literary norms and expectations to enhance the aesthetic and persuasive force of biblical narrative. Guyart presents biblical truth not as inherent in the translated text, but as a recreative process that requires the translator to delight readers' imaginations, earn their trust, and inspire their will to believe. Paradoxically, this process of negotiating narrative truth owes much to medieval norms of fictional narrative. The *Bible historiale*, even where it is a relatively close translation of the Vulgate, takes on the aspect of a faith-dependent literary endeavour in which it is imperative that the *vrai* be made *vraisemblable*, the truth be made to resemble itself through the mimetic ruses of fiction. Chapter 2, "Telling It Right: Confronting Reader Resistance," examines how Guyart utilizes narrative structure and literary form, paratexts (glosses, diagrams, illustrations), and extratextual references to geographical locations and shared cultural references to bring the Bible into the world its reader inhabits and recognizes. I show how Guyart's translation accomplishes this through a dialogue built into the text that helps readers establish connections between the biblical text and their lived experiences. Finally, I discuss how some manuscript copies reinforce connections between the French Bible and French literary traditions as well as how miscellanies juxtaposing parts of the *Bible historiale* with other genres of literature repurpose biblical narrative to support a variety of reading programs.

Chapter 3, "Soothing Listeners' Ears: Narrative Aesthetics and Poetic Faith," examines a different kind of literary engagement with the Bible, namely the use of a set of apocryphal biblical legends which are identified as such in the translation, but ostensibly included for their moral and aesthetic value. These stories of "anti-saints" and the peregrinations of the True Cross function simultaneously as mnemonic aids to remember emblematic biblical events and figures and, on an exegetical level, as shortcuts to understanding allegorical interpretations in which Old Testament episodes prefigure New Testament ones. Emphasizing the difference between the authoritative truth of the canonical Bible and the pleasing but fictional apocryphal stories, the translator notes supplied by Guyart ultimately accord readers the authority to choose what to believe in the apocryphal stories and even to decide how they end. The stories construct what I call "narrative truth" through readers' active co-creation of a story that resonates with what they feel and desire to be true: a story that punishes the villains in proportion to their crimes and manifests in a concrete, satisfying way the ineffable truth of God's justice.

In chapters 4 and 5, I shift my focus to the tension that emerges between two competing drives present in medieval lay Bibles: one, to engage their readers' active imaginative participation with the same interpretive freedom seen in fictional literature (as seen in chapters 2 and 3); and the other, to constrict or silence readers' questions. These two chapters coalesce around the idea of "patience" as both a moral and a hermeneutic ideal for the lay reader, who must be trained how to read the Bible with humility and disciplined curiosity, to know when to ask questions and when to defer to clerical authority. In chapter 4, "*Les paroles dont je vous ay fait mention*: The *Bible historiale*'s Two Books of Job," I examine the translator's self-censorship of the Book of Job (as well as some other theologically fraught or otherwise taboo topics) as a means of controlling or even suppressing interpretation on the part of his readers. I then trace the strategies in some manuscripts to reconcile Guyart's "patient," silenced Job with the one who laments, disputes, and interprets his fate in the full translated text, which was often added alongside Guyart's abridged version.

Chapter 5, "The Patient Reader," further considers "patience" as a set of reading attitudes, behaviours, and strategies that define the ideal reader of the *Bible historiale*. Following from a scribe's comment that reading the *Bible historiale* requires more "patience" than reading the *Bible moralisée*, I compare the reading practices elicited by each in order to define "patience" as both a particular kind of literacy that the

Bible historiale cultivates and as an implied moral good promised to its regular practitioners. Readerly patience emerges as a cluster of practices that includes self-discipline, a student-like deference to the translator's authority, and a heightened awareness of self and of time. Based on this multifaceted definition, I examine how manuscripts of the *Bible historiale* both demand and encourage patient reading through their narrative structure, their manuscript formats, and their visual programs. Finally, the conclusion brings similar questions to bear on current discussions of reading technologies, formats, and practices and their implications for the longer history of Bible reading and rewriting. Drawing from contemporary as well as medieval examples of Bible formats and from recent work on the hermeneutics of textual technologies, I explore how text formats and technologies develop in parallel with and in response to what readers already do with texts even as they innovate new ways to represent them.

Jerome's Latin Vulgate translation carried the weight of institutional authority in Latin-based Christianity throughout the Middle Ages. However, the later Middle Ages saw an increasing demand for written vernacular translations of the Bible both for preaching and for a growing population of vernacular-literate lay readers with access to manuscript books. Their reasons for reading the Bible, their ways of reading or listening to it, and their capacity for interpreting it in a manner congruent with established orthodoxy would all have differed from those of biblical scholars and clergy. As the next chapter shows, the *Bible historiale* became for French what the Vulgate was for Latin: the most authoritative and most widely copied translation, and also the most adaptable, thanks to its modular structure that allowed for adding, removing, or replacing units of text/gloss without destroying the compilation's coherence. This adaptability guaranteed the longevity of the *Bible historiale* as a preferred base translation, and its resulting manuscript corpus tells a story of changing ideas about vernacular French Bibles and what they should do for their readers.

Citing the *Bible historiale*: Some Final Notes on My Methods and Assumptions

Some realities of medieval authorship and manuscript culture – and especially of working with a vast and varied manuscript tradition for which no complete "standard" edition exists – present both opportunities and challenges due to incompatibilities with modern scholarly conventions of citing authors and texts. Some of my own choices in addressing these quandaries, as well as the assumptions and intentions underlying these choices, merit explanation, especially for those "professional readers" who might be reading this book as a starting point for their own primary source scholarship on the *Bible historiale.*

Even notwithstanding the already complicated question of authorship in translation, Guyart is only the first of many actors involved in making the *Bible historiale* what it would become, and it would be misleading to identify the *Bible historiale* as exclusively his creation. All of the insights that "new" or "material" philology brought to the study of medieval manuscript culture – concepts such as variance, *mouvance*, and manuscript intentionality, as well as the rejection of print-based notions of authorship and the stability of texts – apply to the *Bible historiale* and its complicated manuscript tradition.[16] All references herein to Guyart as the author of text quoted from manuscripts or as the agent of specific translation choices should therefore be understood to bear an invisible asterisk or caveat, since it is never possible to know with absolute certainty which details of the *Bible historiale* text as represented in any given manuscript copy originated with Guyart and which were introduced or modified by a scribe at some later stage in transmission. In other words, "Guyart" is shorthand for an ambiguous, fuzzy authorial figure that coalesces around common features among manuscripts and a strong first-person voice in the text, but that is never fully identical with the real author because no surviving manuscript can be confirmed as identical to what he wrote. For that matter, no surviving manuscript is identical to any other: not only do visual and material aspects of the manuscripts differ considerably from each other, but their textual contents vary as well, from small orthographic or semantic variants (e.g., substituting one synonym for another based on regional lexical variation or linguistic change over time), to the insertion or substitution of other French-language versions of whole biblical books, as well as many possibilities in between (e.g., adding or subtracting glosses, adding editorial commentary through rubrics, etc.). Meaningful differences among manuscripts and changing patterns or trends in manuscript production are explicit concerns of the chapters to follow; however, even when these differences recede into the background in order to foreground, for example, narrative features of "the text," that text should be understood as variable and subject to manipulation and change.

There is no complete modern edition of the *Bible historiale.* Xavier-Laurent Salvador has created a partial digital edition of a single manuscript copy, Paris, Bibliothèque de l'Arsenal, MS 5059 (Ars. 5059), but as a partial edition, it lacks many of the materials cited herein, and it does not account for the large degree of variation among manuscripts.[17] Relying on a widely available edition for quotations would offer some advantages in terms of finding common ground for citation and reference. So far, scholars working on the *Bible historiale* have identified very different criteria for choosing a manuscript to quote from or as a base text for a partial edition: it could be the manuscript copy deemed to be closest to the "original," or the one that has the "best" language, is the most "complete," the most legible, or that is the most geographically convenient. However, the lack of a centre within the vast, diverse corpus of *Bible historiale* manuscripts offers a perspective that may be lost if and when an edition sets a standard. Therefore, I have chosen to exploit that opportunity by working with and quoting from a representative sampling of manuscripts that capture several different stages and trends in the production of the *Bible historiale* and a number of different strategies adopted by scribes, artists, and *libraires* in response to perceived insufficiencies of their source copies or to consumer demands. The need to consult multiple copies became necessary to my project because of the types of questions I ask.

As I have not chosen a base copy, my quotations come from a number of manuscripts. In most cases, quoted text would be similar among most manuscripts; when that is not the case – when I quote a manuscript for its unusual commentary or rendering of a portion of text, or where I quote a version that is representative of most copies but still find noteworthy variations among manuscripts – I explain those contexts in the text and/or notes. Manuscripts that serve to illustrate a particular point are described the first time they are mentioned; some manuscripts recur in several chapters as subjects of analysis. I have provided an appendix at the end of the book summarizing the dates, contents, and some other salient features of those manuscripts most frequently and extensively discussed herein.

This brings me to one last point about scholarly conventions for describing the *Bible historiale*. Samuel Berger's classification system for manuscripts, as laid out in his 1884 *La Bible française au Moyen Âge*, is widely accepted as a shorthand for identifying a manuscript's contents.[18] I have not consistently maintained his distinction between the *Bible historiale* and the *Bible historiale complétée*, a distinction made based on the inclusion of books from a second, near-contemporary translation he calls the *Bible du XIIIe siècle*, a point to be explained in chapter 1. I made this decision in part because Berger's categories often become blurred, especially in late fourteenth- and fifteenth-century witnesses, and partly because it is misleading (and needlessly cumbersome) to treat the *Bible historiale* and its "*complétée*" versions as two distinct projects when the manuscripts themselves do not identify them as such. Indeed, even the versions Berger classifies as *non-complétée* are usually supplemented, to a smaller degree, from extraneous sources as well. While I will occasionally refer to Berger's system, unless otherwise indicated, my use of the term *Bible historiale* includes all manuscript and early print versions in any combination containing the usually hybrid Bible-*Historia* translations attributable to Guyart.

1 Making the French Bible, or Making the Bible French

Be ye not many masters, my brethren,
knowing that you receive the greater judgment.

James 3:1[1]

Many modern histories of Bible translation focus on the well-known touchstones of Saint Jerome's late fourth-century translation, known as the Latin Vulgate, and Martin Luther's German translation, published in 1534. However, during the millennium in between these two culturally significant translations, Christians produced a vast number of translations and adaptations of the Bible, from individual books to complete canonical collections, in Ge'ez (Ethiopic), Coptic, Persian, Syriac, and Arabic, as well as most European vernacular languages. These latter versions, most of which are indirect translations based on Jerome's Latin Vulgate, circulated in various media, in verse and in prose, and in languages including multiple varieties of French, English, German, Dutch, Spanish, Mozarabic, Italian, Romanian, Polish, and Czech.[2] The number of medieval vernacular Bible translations is difficult even to estimate, given the large extent of internal variation among manuscript copies, fragmentary and ephemeral instances of translation, and the many attested (and unattested) translations that have been lost. Their authors and audiences counted clerics, religious, and laypeople, mainstream Catholic and Eastern Orthodox Christians, as well as members of minority and dissident religious groups.[3] In addition to the numerous large-scale textual translations, vernacular biblical quotations, commentaries, narratives, allegories, and tropes found their way into sacred and secular literature and art, into oral preaching, onto household objects, and even onto the walls and vaulted ceilings of medieval churches, as in the example of the recently restored fourteenth-century church of Saint-Jacques in Merléac, France.[4] In short, the Middle Ages were a period of vibrant translation activity during which the norms of Bible translation were fluid and adapted to context, purpose, and readership.

To match the diversity of reading and listening audiences, their varied needs, and their varied levels of literacy and of access to manuscript books, medieval vernacular Bible translations varied in their approaches to translation, their sources of commentary, their material and generic forms, and their modes of transmission. Translating the Bible from Latin into vernacular languages, for a primary target readership of laypeople, required more than a choice between "word-for-word" or "sense-for-sense" translation (as evoked by Jerome, although this oft-quoted formula belies the nuances of his actual theory and practice of Bible translation).[5] Making the Bible French required considerable intervention based on what a linguistically and culturally French Bible should *do* for its target audience, which would necessarily diverge in some ways from the Latin Bible's functions in its clerical and ritual contexts. In modern critical terminology, we might say that the most successful medieval translations – the ones that were widely copied and used, embraced by readers and church authorities alike – are those governed by the target-text *skopos*, as defined by translation scholars Katharina Reiss and Hans Vermeer.[6] That is, concerns about lexical, formal, or even functional equivalency between source and target texts are secondary to an overarching sense of the text's purpose for its anticipated target audience. This purpose, as conceived by the translator and other agents involved in the production and dissemination of translated texts (patrons, scribes, artists, booksellers), will shape the entire translation program as well as its paratexts: text selection; comprehension aids and textual framing; linguistic features such as semantics, syntax and style; the physical form, medium, or genre of the target-language text; and even how the translation is packaged, marketed, and distributed.

From the end of the thirteenth to the first decades of the sixteenth century, the predominant French translation of the Bible would have been Guyart des Moulins's 1295 *Bible historiale*, a compiled translation of a large part of the Latin Vulgate and of Peter Comestor's late twelfth-century commentary known as the *Historia scholastica*. Guyart's *Bible historiale* survives alone or in combination with other translations in over a hundred manuscript copies and multiple print editions, and it inspired similar "historical" translations into English, Dutch, German, and several other languages during the fourteenth and fifteenth centuries.[7] The present chapter introduces the *Bible historiale* in the context of its cultural moment and follow its manuscript transformations as a function of changing priorities of its readership. I begin by elucidating how some misperceptions about the pre-Reformation history of Bible translation have led to mischaracterizations of the *Bible historiale* and have thus limited the critical lenses through which it has been studied. By confronting and analyzing the sources of those misperceptions, I also wish to give my readers important context for understanding specifically medieval points of debate concerning vernacular Bible translation and how the *Bible historiale* tradition responds to them. Then I introduce, in broad strokes (to be developed in more detail in later chapters), Guyart des Moulins's translation strategies as shaped by the translator's understanding of who will read his translation, how, and why. More specifically, I show how Guyart weaves into his translation a rhetoric of presence that makes his mediation visible and asserts his authoritative role with respect to his readers. Finally, I trace how the *Bible historiale*'s varied manuscript and print forms both reflect and drive changing cultural perceptions about the French Bible, its status, and what it should do for its target readership.

The Myth of Censorship

Despite its large number of surviving manuscript copies, the *Bible historiale* is frequently mischaracterized, especially in English-language scholarship, when it is acknowledged at all. Some reasons for these misunderstandings are self-perpetuating: there exists no complete edition of the text, and its complex manuscript tradition is difficult to grasp from secondary sources alone, even when those sources are accurate. Although there have been relatively few detailed studies of its text, it is well known enough that scholars frequently reference it without clearly defining it, and incomplete or inaccurate descriptions of it spread via secondary citation. These conditions have occasionally resulted in flatly erroneous characterizations of its contents that, for example, conflate the *Bible historiale* with other French Bible traditions (such as the similarly titled, but very different, *Bible moralisée*) or misidentify it as only a translation of the *Historia scholastica* without acknowledging its biblical contents.[8] More commonly still, preconceived notions about what does and does not qualify as "translation" or as "Bible" have paved the way for dismissive treatments of the *Bible historiale* and its cultural impact, even when its contents are better understood. For example, medieval book historians H.M. and M.A. Rouse, in reference to a *"Bible en romans"* listed in an inventory, cast doubt on that medieval characterization of the book by suggesting that it was "perhaps really a Bible, but more likely Guiart des Moulins's *Bible historiale*."[9] Describing the *Bible historiale* as not "really a Bible" is hard to justify, whether based on its contents, on its translation style, or on how medieval scribes, clergy, and readers referred to it. But it is a common perception that not only misrepresents the *Bible historiale*, but also reflects faulty assumptions about medieval Bible translation and its religious contexts.

The exaggerated spectre of "Dark Age" censorship figures prominently among the loaded narratives that have limited the study of medieval Bible translation. Inasmuch as the stories we tell about the past often say more about our present or aspirational selves than about the people and events they purport to represent, the would-be heirs of the Protestant Reformation and the Renaissance have largely defined Early Modern Europe as the site of origin for such modern Anglo-Protestant ideals as the individualized humanistic pursuit of knowledge.[10] In this narrative, the Middle Ages embody the opposite: radical repression, ignorance, and enforced conformity.[11] It may come as little surprise to find such reductive histories repeated uncritically in mass-market media targeted at Protestant Christian audiences keen to stake their identities on a vindicating narrative. For example, a pamphlet produced by the evangelical Christian organization Bibles for America asserts that "the truths in the Bible gradually became lost or misunderstood" during the Middle Ages, and "the Bible was even locked away so that the common people could not read it," until the sixteenth century, when "God began to recover the lost truths of the Bible."[12] Taking the shape of a Christian cycle of fall and redemption, this narrative manufactures ancient origins for its brand of Protestantism. The narrative metonymically attaches its identity to a fictionalized history of the Bible that hinges on two key events: the writing of the Bible and its purported resurrection. The story's appeal to divine intervention recalls older accounts that served to grant authority to premodern Bible translations such as the Septuagint and Jerome's and even echoes the arguments of some modern proponents of the King James Version.[13] Meanwhile, its familiar portrait of the Middle Ages as a period during which knowledge was suppressed or corrupted aligns the text's target community with a genealogy of truth-seekers that includes the apostles and the Reformers, but excludes the Catholic Church, the implied but never named impersonal agent of the Bible's long imprisonment.

The history of the Bible as told in the Bibles for America pamphlet is an extreme example, and one that lacks scholarly credibility. However, the underlying assumptions of this trope, which casts the pre-Reformation Latin Church as a strict gatekeeper or even a conspiratorial destroyer of knowledge, find corroboration in a long history of scholarship that ignores, mischaracterizes, or dismisses medieval Bible translation.[14] The trope expresses itself differently according to scholars' differing rhetorical aims and fields of study, but it has had an outsized influence even outside of scholarship with an explicitly Protestant or modernist point of view.

Despite the central place it has given to Bible translation, and despite recent translation scholars' willingness to embrace more expansive definitions of translation, the field of translation studies has tended to either gloss over the Middle Ages or to portray the entire period between Jerome and Luther as a naive or repressive foil against which modern translation arises. For instance, the influential translation scholar Douglas Robinson, known for his theoretical histories of translation, cavalierly remarks in his 1996 *Translation and Taboo* that "Bible translation was tabooed, banned, and prohibited both tacitly and by law for over a thousand years."[15] Based on a somewhat disingenuous reading of translation concerns expressed by Aelfric in the tenth century and Thomas More in the sixteenth, he concludes with the following false choice between "medieval" and "Protestant" translation:[16] "Do you protect your own anxieties by protecting others from 'dangerous' knowledge, as the medieval church did? Or do you, like 'Protestants' from the fourteenth-century Lollards to the sixteenth-century Reformers, disseminate your institutionalized prophylactics to everyone in the form, say, of carefully regulated Bible translations accompanied by catechistic teaching?"[17] As it happened, the medieval church did not, on the whole, seek to "protect" the laity from knowledge of the Bible. And it was not only "Protestants" and their anticlerical precursors who translated the Bible before (or, for that matter, during) the Reformation. While translation could and did sometimes serve to challenge church and university hegemony over the interpretation and dissemination of biblical texts, it could also work to assert or leverage that control or to negotiate relations between ecclesiastical and secular power (such as the French royal family, who commissioned and collected many French Bible manuscripts). Medieval as well as Reformation-era translators employed strategies that speak at times to both of the impulses Robinson cites as representing the incommensurable goals of either side (hoarding knowledge versus institutionalized teaching), and that also sometimes defy both impulses, exposing rifts in the underlying assumptions of this model.

Even medievalists have not been immune to a narrative that, by centring the Reformation as its endpoint, overstates the association of earlier vernacular Bible translation efforts with heresy or anticlerical subversion and assumes these efforts to be subject to institutional censorship. While commonplace assumptions of widespread suppression of Bible translation arise from unfamiliarity with relevant sources and scholarship, there is also a significant thread of specialist scholarship that misrepresents the state of medieval vernacular Bible translation. This misrepresentation is based either on an overly narrow definition of "translation" or of "Bible" (a point to which I shall return) or on overgeneralized interpretations of medieval sources documenting efforts to restrict or control translation. A brief re-evaluation of some of these sources and the prominent scholarly arguments made about them can help us not only to put to rest lingering myths, but also to better understand how church concerns about medieval lay vernacular readership of the Bible did influence church-sanctioned translations such as the *Bible historiale*.

Reassessing the Evidence: The Exception and the Rule

In some cases, medieval as well as Reformation-era church authorities did in fact restrict translation in an attempt to curb the influence of individuals and movements perceived as threats to the church's hegemony over its sacred texts and sacraments. An early controversy that scholars sometimes cite as evidence of a long-standing de facto papal ban on all Bible translations from Latin into vernacular languages comes up in a correspondence between the Bishop of Metz and Pope Innocent III at the end of the twelfth century. In 1199, the bishop wrote to the pope for advice concerning groups of laypeople who had obtained French translations of biblical texts and Christian commentaries and were holding meetings to discuss them. The bishop's letters do not survive, but in his replies (which do), Innocent quotes or paraphrases his correspondent as he responds to the bishop's concerns point by point. He reiterates the bishop's dilemma thus:

> Our venerable brother the Bishop of Metz has communicated to us in his letters how in the diocese of the city of Metz, a great number of lay men and women are driven by an immoderate desire to have the Gospels, the Epistles of Paul, the Psalms, the *Moralia in Job*, and several other books of scripture translated for them into the French language [*Gallico sermone*]. Indeed, such translations are readily made available to them (if only this were done prudently!), for the purpose of holding secret assemblies where lay men and women dare to debate and to take turns preaching to one another.[18]

As it progresses, Innocent's letter, perhaps quoting the bishop's, describes an increasingly chaotic scene in which unruly readers shout at one another, mock priests, and reject their input, altogether "behaving like heretics." The exaggerated language of the description channels the bishop's anxieties over how, in a worst-case scenario, a vernacular-literate lay public might use Bible translations and commentary to perform their own exegesis and subvert church authority.

Some scholars have credibly linked the lay reading groups, described in Innocent's 1199 letters, to Waldensians, members of a growing movement that advocated lay preaching and religious life independent of church orders.[19] Margaret Deanesly's 1920 book *The Lollard Bible and Other Medieval Biblical Versions,* which was instrumental in defining the conversation about medieval English Bible translation for decades to follow, takes this reasonable conjecture several steps further.[20] Identifying the lay reading groups mentioned in the letters with an incident described in a chronicle by Alberic of Trois-Fontaines that resulted in suspected Waldensians' books being confiscated and destroyed, she concludes that the incident set precedent for a general church policy to ban Bible translations for lay readers and to associate translation with heresy for centuries to come. Armed with this foregone conclusion, she cursorily dismisses the numerous uncontroversial translations made in the thirteenth and fourteenth centuries, in English, French, and other languages, as anomalies that were made only for "royal personages," had minimal influence, and weren't really Bible translations anyway.[21] She lists the *Bible historiale* among these, but inaccurately describes it as translating only the *Historia scholastica* and not the Bible itself.

In a 1985 article, Leonard Boyle challenged Deanesly's selective reading of the letters, and with it, her (and others') more far-reaching claims about a medieval church that inherently distrusted translation.[22] He interpreted the pope's response to the group's activities not as a ban on translation, but as a more measured approach to understanding the circumstances, practices, and motivations of both translators and readers of translations. Recognizing the inevitability of translation, Innocent III saw not a threat but an opportunity to engage a lay demographic that was becoming increasingly literate in vernacular languages. He did not condemn the laity's interest in reading the Bible in any language; on the contrary, he praised would-be lay readers' "desire of understanding the Holy Scriptures" as "something not to be reprimanded but rather to be encouraged" so long as they remained open to the clergy's guidance in interpreting what they read.[23] Boyle (rightly, I believe) concluded that

> what [Innocent] is arguing against is not translations of Scripture or even preaching and reading the Scriptures, but, oddly as it may seem in light of what Deanesly and others say, against those who maintain (as some bishops and preachers did) that the "holy things" of Scripture and the "pearls" were only for the elect. To Innocent, on the contrary, the "holy things" and the "pearls" are for all without exception who willingly and gratefully accept

them, but they are not to be given to those who do not revere the Scriptures and the sacraments of the Church – who are heretics.[24]

A second document sometimes cited as evidence of medieval church hostility to translation comes much later, from England: Archbishop Thomas Arundel's 1407–9 Constitutions at Oxford, which prohibited the production and use of English Bible translations that had not been authorized by the church. Some modern commentators have read the section on translation, Article 7, as a ban on English Bible translation in response to the Middle English Bible, which many have attributed to John Wycliffe or his followers. However, Arundel's language clearly accommodates the possibility of church-approved translations, both past and future. According to the article, a translator was not to make new translations "on his own authority" (*auctoritate sua*), which implies that an external authority (i.e., church sponsorship or approval) could make translations licit, and readers were not to read translations or theological works without the approval of a local diocesan or provincial council (which, again, is not an outright ban).[25] Moreover, recent work by scholars including Henry Ansgar Kelly and Fiona Somerset, among others, has called into question prior claims about the Lollard or "Wycliffite" religious leanings of the Middle English Bible's authors and readers, as well as just how "banned" or "heretical" it was.[26]

By the end of the fifteenth century, complete medieval translations of the Bible from the Latin Vulgate into most European vernacular languages circulated widely not just in manuscripts but also in print, with royal privilege (or formal permission to print) and at least tacit church approval.[27] It was only during the mid-sixteenth century that anxieties about the spread of Protestantism combined with new textual-critical debates about competing source texts (the Greek New Testament, newly available to the Latin West via Byzantine refugees, versus Jerome's Latin Vulgate) prompted the church, at the Council of Trent, to codify more restrictive policies governing the authorization of Catholic Bible translations and the conditions of lay access to them.[28]

While premodern translation controversies have occasionally been cited as evidence of widespread church prohibitions on translation, or to portray all medieval Bible translators as subversive proto-Reformers, the evidence resists such facile generalizations. Neither Innocent III nor any pope after him ever banned Bible translation outright.[29] With that said, the thirteenth to sixteenth centuries were punctuated by occasional formal restrictions concerning translated scriptures and commentaries in a particular place, language, or community in response to perceived threats to established dogma or church authority. Some notable examples include edicts restricting translation in Toulouse in 1229, Tarragona in 1234, and Beziers in 1246, based on the activities of Cathars and Waldensians in Languedoc and Catalonia.[30] As Frans van Liere remarks in his 2014 *Introduction to the Medieval Bible*: "On the one hand, there are a number of edicts and injunctions against the translating of the Bible into the vernacular, and against the use of such Bibles. On the other hand, no text was more widespread and popular than the Bible in its many vernacular versions, and many of these do not seem to have raised an eyebrow from the ecclesiastical authorities."[31] Or as Wim François more bluntly puts it: "Often it has been stated that the Catholic Church was very reluctant towards, if not opposed to, the laity's reading of the Bible in the vernacular. This may for example be true with regard to the Roman authorities and their Counter-Reformation reflex in the second half of the sixteenth century, but it should be considered a blunt and uncritical generalization when taking the entire late medieval and early modern Church history into account."[32]

In short, the attitudes of church leaders towards translation varied according to the translation in question as well as to the allegiances and goals of its translators and users, but as a rule, Latin Christianity embraced translation from about 1100 to 1500.[33] Vernacular-language Bibles, Gospel harmonies, and psalters, as well as oral preaching, narrative art depicting biblical stories, and what Rita Copeland calls "secondary" translations (e.g., mystery plays, biblical epics, and romances) offered valid aids to religious education, a means to promote church interests with secular rulers, and spiritually edifying alternatives to secular literature.[34] Formal restrictions on translation were, in contrast, exceptions to that rule, arising from specific circumstances that made expanding lay access to biblical material through translation seem more threatening than beneficial to the church's aim of administering mainstream Christian doctrines and practices of the time, or to maintaining its power as the central authority of religious life. When we set aside the presumption of medieval institutional hostility towards translation by default, we see instead a vibrant debate about the specifics of what Bible translations should do for individual lay readers as well as for the interests of church and secular powers.

The *Bible historiale* as One Translation among Many

The large number and variety of medieval vernacular Bible translations represent many different approaches to framing biblical material for primarily lay audiences. Such translations served a multitude of purposes: from the religious education and devotional needs of wealthy patrons, to entertainment, to leveraging biblical authority for political influence. In the *langues d'oïl*, the languages of northern France, Flanders, and the English aristocracy, Bible translation and adaptation flourished beginning in the twelfth century. Verse Bibles, or biblical romances, included, among others, Herman de Valenciennes's late twelfth-century *Li romanz de Dieu et de sa mere* and the Bibles of Jehan Malkaraume and Macé de la Charité, both written around 1300.[35] The thirteenth century saw several partial and full prose translations into French, including the Acre Bible, an Old Testament translation from the 1250s associated with Saint Louis and his crusader colony in Acre; the mid-thirteenth-century *Bible du XIIIe siècle* or *Old French Bible*, which according to Clive Sneddon was a complete translation of the Latin Vulgate likely made by Dominicans; and finally, Guyart des Moulins's *Bible historiale*.[36] French kings commissioned at least two other translations: the unfinished Jean de Sy Bible, undertaken for Jean II but most likely abandoned either during his captivity or after his death in 1264, and Raoul de Presles's 1375 complete glossed translation of the Latin Vulgate Bible for Charles V.[37] This list is not exhaustive. Psalters and other individual books of the Bible, including the Apocalypse, the Book of Job, the Song of Songs, and composite narratives of the Gospels, circulated independently in translation, in verse and in prose, as did a large number of "abridged" Bibles and collections of selected verses for use as breviaries, lectionaries, and quotable *florilegia*.[38] French-language biblical texts and commentaries enjoyed wide circulation among aristocratic lay bibliophiles, and they were a staple in royal and monastic libraries. With the advent of print and the late medieval practice of making personal handwritten miscellanies that frequently included books of the Bible alongside devotional texts, French-language Bibles and Bible extracts also passed through the hands of an urban, merchant-class audience. As Sabrina Corbellini and Margriet Hoogvliet have argued, this practice inscribed those readers' active engagement with the texts.[39] Written translations as well as spontaneous oral translation would have also reached a wider and more socio-economically diverse public through preaching.

As far as medieval readers, makers, and collectors of French-language biblical manuscripts were concerned, almost any biblical compilation was simply a "Bible" or a "Bible in French" ("Bible en francoiz" or "en romanz").[40] They did not, for the most part, share some modern scholars' hesitation over where to draw the line, for example, between a Bible translation and related categories such as "paraphrase," "adaptation," "biblical extracts with commentary," or "biblical literature." As Jeanette Beer has argued, the rigid application of such anachronistic distinctions fails to represent medieval understandings and practices of translation, "categoriz[ing] a millennium of translative vitality as one thousand years of non-translation."[41] Moreover, as Margriet Hoogvliet has argued, some scholars' insistence on such distinctions has contributed to both the under-representation of medieval Bible translation in scholarship and the perpetuation of a weak version of the locked-away Bible myth, according to which the pre-Reformation Catholic Church allowed limited lay access to isolated Bible stories and commentaries, but rarely "real" translations (as defined, anachronistically, by the post-Council of Trent canon and modern norms of translation).[42] As Hoogvliet goes on to show, the widespread coexistence of fragmentary translations, translations with commentaries, and versified and illustrated Bible stories speaks to the variety of purposes and preferences of medieval readers, and not, as some have claimed, a concerted effort by the church to limit lay readership of the Bible to harmless "substitutes."

The diverse criteria defining a "Bible in French" for those who commissioned, made, owned, and read them depended on the Bibles' target audiences and use. Readers' stated and implied reasons for and ways of reading French-language Bibles varied, some overlapping with common clerical uses of the Bible and some not. A Bible, or selections thereof, could educate readers in religious doctrine, history, natural philosophy, moral virtues, or even basic literacy. It could shed light on current social and political crises through historical typology or moral allegory. It could prepare readers for war, for ethical leadership, for marriage, or for death. Its stories could entertain, offer models for moral action, or serve to illustrate arguments or support ideologies. Evidence including prologues, readers' annotations, and documented recommendations by priests and counselors suggests all of the above as prescribed or actual uses of French Bibles.[43] As it became the predominant French-language version of the Bible, the *Bible historiale* tradition adapted to serve these various functions and uses; conversely, the adaptability of its modular structure and paratextual supports likely helped assure its prominent status and relative longevity as a preferred translation.

In the fourteenth and fifteenth centuries, the designation "Bible in French" could refer to many different things, but statistically, a majority of volumes thus described would have contained part or all of Guyart des Moulins's translation known as the *Bible historiale.* Guyart, a priest and canon at the collegiate church of Saint Pierre d'Aire-sur-la-Lys, worked on his translation from 1291–5 (1294 in the old system), as he relates in his prologue, which he added to a minimally revised edition of the translation after being elected dean of his chapter in 1297. His translation survives, in part or in full, and in various combinations with other translations and texts, in well over a hundred manuscript copies, and was printed more than twenty times in Paris and Lyon between 1496 and 1546.[44] Guyart des Moulins's *Bible historiale*, in all its permutations, was by far the dominant Bible in French for over two hundred years and is counted among the most widely owned books of any kind in French throughout the later Middle Ages. Its long-lasting favour must have owed much to its versatility of use, its reader-conscious approach to translation, and the adaptability of its manuscript tradition to changing perceptions and priorities among readers. I attempt, in the following sections, to demonstrate these features of the *Bible historiale* translation and manuscript tradition, and finally, to explore how its manuscript transformations respond to (and likely influence, in turn) changing reader expectations about the French Bible. First of all, however, let us define what is meant, in the first place, by a *Bible historiale*.[45]

Defining Guyart des Moulins's *Bible historiale*

Guyart's prologue assigns his work the title *Bible historiale*, which neatly encapsulates his project to translate a Bible focused on history, with the goal, as he defines it, to "faire laies personnes entendre les histoires des escriptures anciennes" ("help laypeople understand the histories of the ancient scriptures," BnF fr. 155). "*Historiale*" means, of course, "historical"; it also refers specifically to his main source of commentary: Peter Comestor's *Historia scholastica* (including the *Historia evangelica*, the title given to the part of that work dedicated to the Gospels), which provides nearly half of the content of Guyart's translation as well as a template for the work's overall structure, choice of contents, and didactic program.[46] Guyart's selective translation of the Vulgate was mostly limited to those historical books of the Bible selected for commentary in the *Historia*. Guyart explains his general approach in selecting, arranging, and translating his material thus:

> Ci doit on savoir que j'ai translaté les livres historiaus de la bible selonc le texte de la bible et selonc histoires les escolastres si com devant est dit. Si ai escrit le texte de la bible primerement de grosse lettre et puis apres en ordenné les histoires de plus deliee lettre .i. poi et quant il i a poi a esposer par histoires je les ai mises en gloze et ai poursuivi mon ouvrage en ceste maniere jusques en la fin. (BnF fr. 155, fol. 1v)
>
> (Let it be known that I translated the historical books of the Bible according to the text of the Bible and according to the *Historia scholastica* as mentioned previously. I wrote the text of the Bible first in large letters and then arranged the histories [i.e., corresponding chapters from the *Historia scholastica*] after in slightly smaller letters, and when there is little

explanation in the *Historia,* I put it in glosses and followed this procedure until the end.)

To wit, Guyart's compilation included, in order: a two-part prologue (Guyart's and his translation of Comestor's), Genesis, Exodus, Leviticus, Numbers, Deuteronomy, Joshua, Judges, Ruth, 1–4 Kings, Proverbs (abridged), "Petit" (abridged) Job, Tobit (or Tobias), Jeremiah, Ezekiel, Daniel (sometimes titled separately "Susanne" and "Daniel"), Judith, Esther, 1–2 Maccabees, John Hyrcanus (intertestamental material from Flavius Josephus via Comestor), a Gospel harmony (Comestor's *Historia evangelica* intercalated with extracts from all four Gospels), Acts, and a set of apocryphal narratives derived from *The Golden Legend* and Latin legends of the True Cross.[47]

Most of the books follow the process described in his prologue, alternating chapters of the Bible with corresponding chapters from the *Historia scholastica* (titled *histoires*), with shorter comments from Comestor or other sources (including Guyart's own interpretations) put in glosses (*gloses,*) or, if referring to non-biblical historical events, a subcategory of gloss labeled *incidents*. Guyart departs from his alternating Bible/*histoire* format in some books; for example, his version of Leviticus mostly translates Comestor, whose commentary on that book already summarizes large parts of the biblical text. Job and Proverbs receive no *histoires* in Guyart's translation because Comestor did not treat them in his *Historia scholastica*. Manuscript formatting conventions for the *Bible historiale* change over time, moving away from the format Guyart envisions in his prologue: some early copies do put the *histoires* in smaller letters as he specifies, and those manuscripts also tend to place the glosses and *incidents* in the margins, keyed to the text with symbols (see Figure 1.1). However, most copies made after the mid-fourteenth century present text, *histoires,* and glosses all in the main columns of text (of which there are usually two), in script of uniform size, differentiated only by the rubrics that introduce each segment by type (*glose … texte, histoire … texte*).

Both the layout and the contents of *Bible historiale* manuscripts diverge significantly from the translation that Guyart produced. Between the years of its composition from 1291 to 1295 and its enshrinement in print two centuries later as part of the first complete printed Bible translation in French under King Charles VIII, the *Bible historiale* was anything but a stable, standardized text. It is not always useful to separate Guyart's "original" composition from its later additions when discussing the manuscript tradition and its readers, who would not necessarily have been aware of the composite work's sources and stages of development. However, in order to understand the internal logic of Guyart's project

Figure 1.1 Folio containing Comestor's prologue, Genesis 1:1–4, and some corresponding *histoires* and glosses, in a manuscript following Guyart's stated format of large letters for biblical text, and smaller letters for *histoires*, marginal glosses, and *incidents*. Sections are delimited by rubric titles and decorated initials; rubrics also signal Latin quotations. Sigla key glosses to their textual referents. BnF fr. 155, fol. 2r. Source: gallica.bnf.fr/BnF.

as well as the motivating factors behind its manuscript recensions, it is worth examining Guyart's vision, his choice of texts to include, and his approach to translation before tracing how and why later manuscript copies revise and expand his work to fit the changing priorities of new generations of readers.

Je qui translatay: Medieval Translation as Mediation

Guyart's own practices of compilation, paired with his tendency to render his compilation and translation decisions visible to end readers (the lay readers for whom it is primarily intended, like end users in software terminology) as well as to intermediary readers such as scribes through translator notes, set in motion the dynamic processes of textual production that invited later expansions of his work. Meanwhile, his self-conscious reflection on his choices offers insight into medieval debates about the purposes, methods, and limitations of translation. The translator's purposeful, visible mediation of biblical narrative, embodied by his use of the first-person *je* (largely or entirely absent from other translations), is part of what makes Guyart des Moulins's *Bible historiale* uniquely successful as both a church-approved translation and one that appealed to readers for several generations.

The translator's editorial voice intervenes frequently to explain his choices in terms of the translation's purpose for its intended audience. Each of these explicit interventions to defend the inclusion, exclusion, or modification of a unit of source text (e.g., a book of the Bible, a chapter of commentary, an apocryphal episode), invites re-evaluation in each new copy. The inclusion of *the Historia scholastica*, an extensive commentary program on the historical sense of the text, suggests an opening to add moral and allegorical glosses within the same framework. Its layered structure of biblical text, gloss, and *histoires* self-consciously taps into the generative possibilities of texts, both in terms of how Latin texts accumulated interpretive commentary, glossing, and debate, in line with contemporary practices of university scholarship and education, and, at the same time, the endless potential of popular vernacular narratives to take on a life of their own in continuations, responses, rewritings, and literary debates.

Recognizing that the laity's primary vernacular contact with the Bible was through preaching, Guyart also draws upon his pastoral and instructive duties as a priest to create an engaging, authoritative narrative persona that mediates a kind of dialogue between the reader, the biblical text, and a host of exegetical authorities; between contemporary French-speaking territories and ancient Judaea; and between a lay reading culture and one formed by Latin scholastic exegetical practices. Anticipating readers' questions as well as their competencies, tastes, and expectations, which were shaped by contemporary French narrative norms from other literary and historical genres, he produces a translation that foregrounds his mediation and his textual interventions in a very visible manner. Contrary to the (illusory) modern ideal of the self-effacing, invisible translator, one is struck by Guyart des Moulins's rhetoric of presence.[48] From his self-referential interjections of "je qui translatay" ("I who translated") to his direct appeals to "vous qui lisez" ("you who are reading"), the narrating translator asserts himself, if only as a construction of the text, as speaking, in the flesh, in the presence of his readers.

As Rita Copeland has shown, medieval theories of translation, influenced by rhetorical models from Roman antiquity, viewed interlingual and intercultural mediation as conceptually intertwined with and dependent upon the exegetical mediation between a text and its meaning.[49] The medieval translator (*interpres* in Latin), as defined by Isidore of Seville's seventh century encyclopedia, the *Etymologies*, is one situated "between the parts, midway between two languages" as well as one who stands "between God, whom he interprets, and men, to whom he reveals the divine mysteries, because that which he carries over is between."[50] Preaching and translation thus shared a special kinship, and the vernacular sermon was twice an *interpretatio. Interpretatio* and its more specifically linguistic counterpart *translatio* partially overlap in meaning and in metaphorical connotations: both terms could refer to interlingual translation, and both evoke the concept of a mediating figure, positioned between source text and target reader, who defines the terms of the reader's access to and experience of the text. A translator such as Guyart seems to slide effortlessly between his translating and preaching functions, not only rendering the text in a language accessible to his stated target audience of "laies personnes," but also contextualizing the text in such a way that they could relate to it, particularly through its relationship to the symbolism of church ritual.[51]

If the Latin etymology of words for translation and related activities – *interpretatio, translatio/transferre* – emphasizes tangible metaphors in which a mediating agent "stands between" languages (in Isidore's definition) or "carries across" meaning, so too do vernacular words and metaphors for translation invoke the active and corporeal presence of the translator. However, while scholars of translation including Zrinka Stahuljak and Maria Tymoczko have called attention to the problematic assumptions and implications of the Latin terms *translatio/transferre* for theorizing translation, medieval vernacular metaphors for translation reveal multiple modes of conceptualizing the work, and art, of translation.[52]

Guyart defines his work as a translator in two prologues: a general prologue introducing the translation, and an addendum to Comestor's prologue to the *Historia scholastica*, in which he briefly compares his goals for his audience of laypeople to those outlined by Comestor for his scholastic target readership of students, clerics, and preachers. In laying out his task, Guyart uses the French cognate *translater*, "to carry from one place to another," but also describes his activity in such artisanal and authorial terms as "finding" (*trouver*) material that "lay" (*giser*) inert in Latin or in the Bible and "extracting it from" or "pulling it out of" (*traire, tirer*) Latin. He writes that he will "put" (*mettre*), add or assemble (*ajouster*), "compose" or "arrange" (*ordener*) it into "*romans*" – meaning "French," which reinforces the French language's association with its most distinctive literary form of expression, the romance. The idea of storytelling is further echoed by his choice of referring to his own translator's voice as narrating the Latin Bible, "as I tell it" (*ainsi com je raconte*). Guyart's tactile metaphors – uncovering raw material, pulling out pieces of it, remolding and rearranging them within a new linguistic and cultural context, and filing or polishing the final product – suggest an ethos of translation-as-rebuilding. This ethos has less to do with illusory ideals of transparent reproduction than with conventional ways of thinking about a range of artistic and rhetorical activities that were less clearly delineated in the Middle Ages than today. These tactile expressions for translation can be found in his prologue, for example:

> […] je n'i ai riens mis ne ajousté fors pure verité si com je l'ai trouvé el latin de la bible et des *hystoires les escolastres*, et qui les voudroit regarder on i pourroit certainement prouver la pure verité de toutes ces translacions comment ge les ai trait du latin mot a mot ainsi com je le raconte. (BnF fr. 155, fol. 1r)
>
> (I have neither placed nor added anything here but pure truth as I found it in the Latin of the Bible and of the *Historia scholastica*, and whoever might wish to look at them could prove with certainty the pure truth of all of these translations and how I pulled them out of the Latin word for word as I tell it.)

"*Traire*" counts "translation" among its many possible meanings, but as Stahuljak notes regarding the use of the related "*retraire*" (recount or withdraw) to describe translation in the *Roman de Troie*, it connotes tension and fragmentation rather than transporting whole meanings.[53] The word "*trouver*" is commonly used to denote lyric composition, and "*ordener*" can refer to many different forms of verbal and artistic arrangement. Neither creating *ex nihilo* nor mechanically reproducing a source, Guyart describes his work as refashioning Latin knowledge from multiple sources into a French text that is made of the same materials but takes a new form and is transformed in the process. Extending the sculpting or building metaphor, he invites skilled readers, fellow clerics and scribes with knowledge of Latin and the Bible, to polish the rough edges of his work – any mistakes in need of correction – with the "file of their minds":

> Si pri a touz clers entandant escriptures qui cest ouvrage liront que s'il i treuvent a corriger que la lime de leur sens vueille limer mon rude engin et corrigier. (BnF fr. 155, fol. 1v)
>
>   (So I ask all clerics who understand scriptures who will read this work, if they find anything to correct, that they should polish my rude skill with the file of their minds and correct it.)[54]

Guyart's mediation in the *Bible historiale* occurs not only through the act of translation, but also explicitly on a metanarrative level, identifiable in the voice of the narrating translator figure. This "je qui translatay" ("I who translated") – a recurrent phrase that occurs in the main text, glosses, *histoires,* and rubrics to distinguish his voice from those of biblical authors, their Latin translator Jerome, and Comestor – asserts the translator's presence as the conduit (and, at times, barrier) between the reader and the source text to which the translator grants and controls access.[55] The verbally reconstructed translator directly addresses an implied reader ("ainsi comme vous verrez" ["as you will see"]) as he narrates the diegetic action, its interpretation by authorities ("ce dit le maistre en histoires" ["says the Master of Histories"]), his own movement within a story's plot ("si iray avant en l'histoire" ["so I will skip ahead in the story"]), and readers' anticipated response ("s'en semblera l'istoire miex ordenee" ["the story will seem better organized this way"]). This first-person voice details the translator's work as he consults, processes, organizes, translates, and interprets source texts ("voell je ci metre aucunes choses que je trouvai en hystoires" ["I want to insert here some things I found in the *Historia {scholastica}*"]). Through this extradiegetic layer that makes visible the mediating translator/compiler's interaction with both the source text(s) and the target text in preparation, one has the sense of witnessing the translation process. It is as if we are there with Guyart, privy to his internal deliberations about his translation choices and compositional processes.

Translation thus conceived is like reading the Bible "out loud," as it were, working in real time through its potential meanings and associations and the challenges of its translation. One has the impression of reading with a storyteller-priest whose constantly asserted presence guides, instructs, and anticipates questions. At times, he digresses from the text at hand (and excuses himself for doing so), invites the reader's physical participation in moving ahead or back in the book, directs attention to a gloss or diagram, or pauses to pray. The translator's identity and embodiment as a preacher (and the readers' as members of an actively engaged congregation) is also visualized in author portraits in some *Bible historiale* manuscripts, as Xavier-Laurent Salvador has noted:

> Le manuscrit [Paris, Bibliothèque de l'Arsenal] 5057 de la Bible historiale de Guyart-des-Moulins porte en préfiguration du récit une icône représentant le prêtre en chaire et un groupe de fidèles l'écoutant. Mais on sait que les ambiances des Églises ne sont pas silencieuses, que les fidèles interviennent et que les sermons, en langue vulgaire, servent plus souvent à frapper les esprits plutôt qu'à enseigner une vérité doctrinale, peut-être justement parce que le texte ne peut plus être connu autrement que par le *medium* incarné dans le prédicateur.[56]
>
> ([Paris, Bibliothèque de l'Arsenal,] MS 5057 of Guyart des Moulins's *Bible historiale* bears at the opening of its text an image representing the priest in his pulpit and a group of believers listening to him. But we know that the atmosphere in churches was not silent; that the faithful participate and that sermons, in the vernacular, more often work to stir up the imagination than to teach some doctrinal truth, perhaps precisely because the text cannot be known except through the embodied *medium* of preachers.)

Guyart-as-narrator stands in for a priest or private chaplain who might normally be charged with an aristocrat's religious education. He activates this role through shared reading and dialogue, asking and answering questions, and examining unresolved silences and discordances in biblical narratives. The silhouette created in the text by his name and the *je* through which he speaks, act as a representative of church doctrine, but one that creates at least the illusion of a responsive, interactive human presence. Salvador, noting the unique quality of Guyart's doubled voice as opposed to the more generalized case of a first-person narrator divided between narrative and discourse time, remarks:

> Cependant, si cette écriture schizoïde représente finalement la scission qui existe toujours entre l'auteur présent et le moi qu'il met en scène à l'intérieur de son ouvrage, ce qui est une forme de dédoublement diachronique, le dédoublement qui est opéré par nos auteurs dans la traduction biblique est

synchronique, constitutif de l'écriture puisqu'il doit en même temps *faire* l'événement et en *témoigner*.[57]

(However, if this schizoid writing ultimately represents the schism that always exists between the present author and the self that he stages inside his work, which is a form of diachronic doubling, the doubling utilized by our authors in translating the Bible is synchronous, constitutive of writing because it must at the same time *create* the event and *bear witness* to it.)

This mode of translation as narration, defined by its double consciousness of the narrative and the ever-present moment of its performance, both reproduces a familiar relationship between parishioners and clergy and conforms to familiar literary norms of narration. The *Bible historiale* thus responds to a medieval literary consciousness growing out of oral performance, dependent on a narrating *jongleur*'s presence. The repeated interventions of the translator's thoughts and actions (multiplied, in some copies, by scribes' first-person accounts of their own alterations) are not merely the result of a naive author transcribing a stream of consciousness. Rather, this style of narration follows norms common to verse and prose narrative of the Middle Ages, both fictional and historical. The translator takes on a voice as a particular kind of narrator: an implied author who overtly and self-consciously exercises the power to manipulate the text, direct the implied audience's perspective within it, and pre-empt anticipated questions, misinterpretations, and objections.[58] Even as late medieval prose narrative and illustrated books seem to lend themselves to an intimate, visual model of reading, the ubiquitous first-person narrator, a double for the author, continues to frame and interpret much literary narrative and to simulate dialogue with the reader (or a character doubling the reader), creating a fictional space for readers to inhabit and interact with the text in productive ways.

Guyart's recurring *je* who narrates the text therefore fulfils multiple functions for his readers that less overtly mediated translations do not. By emulating narrative norms of other French genres, he establishes a fictional rapport with the reader and makes the biblical text more accessible and interactive according to vernacular audiences' horizons of expectations. By rendering translation practices and choices visible to both end readers and intermediary readers (such as scribes who may modify the text in new copies or priests who might use it as an aid to vernacular preaching or chaplaincy), he gives the translation an aura of authenticity and lays the groundwork for further revision, expansion, and adaptation. Finally, this overt mediation directs the reader through a program of religious education, as it sets the terms of the dialogue by pre-emptively proposing questions for readers to ask, providing orthodox answers to those anticipated questions, and steering readers away from unwanted questions and interpretations, so as to allay concerns about the risks of untrained lay readers interpreting the Bible on their own. In some cases, his interventions to achieve these goals are countered by alternative strategies used in the manuscript tradition, but his approach to translating and framing biblical narrative sets in motion a dynamic balance between feeding readers' curiosity and delimiting the boundaries of their inquiries.

From *Bible historiale* to *Bible en françoiz*: Manuscript Transformations and the Making of a French Biblical Canon

Even as the *Bible historiale* dominated the medieval market for French-language Bibles, the questions of what a French Bible should look like and what it should do were continually in flux, subject to reinterpretation by compilers, *remanieurs*, and patrons of individualized copies. In fact, while Guyart's prologue and other manuscript clues have allowed scholars to reconstruct what his work looked like, no surviving manuscript contains his translation by itself and in its entirety; all documented surviving copies include additions, omissions, or both.[59] Within Guyart's own lifetime, learned copyists and enterprising bookmakers had already begun applying the "file of their minds" to reshape *Bible historiale* manuscripts according to wide-ranging notions of what a layperson's Bible should be.[60]

Some of the earliest surviving copies of the *Bible historiale*, such as BnF fr. 155, dating from 1310 to 1315, modify Guyart's work in small ways, adding Apocalypse or Psalms or both, from various sources, while excluding Guyart des Moulins's collection of apocryphal narratives. In a breakthrough stage of supplementation, seen as early as 1312 in London, British Library, MS Royal 1 A 20, it became common for copies of the *Bible historiale* to include, in addition to Psalms and Apocalypse, other biblical books starting with the New Testament from a separate thirteenth-century translation.[61] Samuel Berger, in his 1884 *La Bible française au Moyen Âge*, termed these expanded editions of Guyart's work the *Bible historiale complétée* and identified the main source of supplementations as a separate, lesser-known French translation of the Paris Bible (a late twelfth-century glossed recension of the Latin Vulgate in use at the University of Paris). Berger called this slightly earlier French translation the *Bible du XIIIe siècle* (alternatively known as the *Old French Bible*).[62] Glossed inconsistently from the *Glossa Ordinaria* (a compilation of glosses that was commonly added to Latin Bibles beginning in the twelfth century and whose "standard" contents expanded over time), the *Historia scholastica*, and other sources, it was most likely executed in the mid-thirteenth century by Dominicans at the University of Paris.[63] The composite or *complétée* manuscripts of the *Bible historiale* range in complexity from a first volume of Guyart's translation (Genesis to Esther) paired with a second volume (Proverbs to Apocalypse) of the university translation, to personalized compilations that choose texts, glosses, and prologues for each biblical book individually. This could mean, for example, pairing the *Bible du XIIIe siècle* version of the books of Maccabees and Luke with Guyart des Moulins's glosses of the biblical text, as some manuscripts did, or adding extra glossing programs to certain books of the Bible from additional sources such as the *Moralia in Job* or the *Bible moralisée*.[64] Some copies add new French translations of Jerome's prologues as well as litanies of saints and prayers for devotional use.[65] Berger's grouping of manuscripts ("petites," "moyennes," "grandes," "grandes avec prologues" according to the degree and types of supplementation) oversimplifies at times, but his classifications, as later given more nuance by Clive Sneddon, do at least offer a rough outline of the patterns and stages by which sets of books were commonly added.

Over several stages, a canonically complete *Bible historiale* came to include all the books of Jerome's Latin Vulgate translation, retaining Guyart's translations and *histoires* for most of the sections he translated, and adding the other books from the *Bible du XIIIe siècle* and other sources, many of which books included glosses of their own. A standard of comprehensiveness in conformity with the Vulgate gradually replaced Guyart's almost exclusively historical program, to the extent that a 1415 inscription on the flyleaf of London, British Library, Royal MS 19 D 2 (Royal 19 D 2) boasts "le Bible entier, oue tixt et glose, le Mestre de Histoires et incident, tout en memes le volym" ("The whole Bible, with text and gloss, the Master of Histories and *incidents*, all in the same volume"). One owner even took an older *Bible historiale* manuscript to a workshop to have it rebound with the "missing" books added after the English siege of Calais during the Hundred Years War in 1347 and commemorated that event in some marginal notes.[66] The replacement of Guyart's Gospel harmony with a full translation of the four canonical Gospels exemplifies this shift from a preference for historical and narrative continuity towards a standard of canonical completeness based on the Latin Vulgate. Guyart's version harmonizes extracts of the four Gospels into a single combined narrative, interspersed with commentary from Comestor's *Historia evangelica* and (where he has found Comestor lacking) Josephus's *Antiquities of the Jews*. However, most later copies replace Guyart's version with all four Gospels translated separately, lightly glossed, borrowed directly from the *Bible du XIIIe siècle*. Conformity with the Latin canon does not entirely replace the narrative unity prioritized by the *Bible historiale*, however; rather, both impulses coexist. With very few exceptions, the manuscript copies that combine the two translations – no matter in what proportions – retain Guyart's title *Bible historiale* and begin with Guyart's and Comestor's prologues explaining their historical approach. The manuscripts centre Guyart and his *Bible historiale* even where Guyart's text represents less than half of the manuscripts' contents.

The large number of manuscripts containing the *Bible historiale* as a base text suggests a widespread preference for Guyart's translation program despite the availability of an earlier complete French translation of the Latin Vulgate and, later, Raoul de Presles's 1375 translation, neither of which circulated as freestanding translations in numbers approaching the *Bible historiale*'s.[67] Meanwhile, the large degree of variation in the contents of manuscript copies demonstrates a process of canon formation that was agile and customizable, responsive to individual readers' needs and individual scribes' editorial choices, as well as broader cultural changes in how French vernacular readers perceived and used biblical texts. In this respect, French Bibles resembled other medieval French miscellanies, romance cycles, and continuations. Like these works, the French Bibles followed patterns in their modular composition (that is, clusters of stories tended to circulate together, but other parts could be added, removed, or rearranged), but they ultimately thrived in a constant state of revision, recontextualization, and expansion in each new manuscript copy.

In the case of the French Bible compilations, these expansions speak to a constant re-evaluation of the translator's vision for how his text should be used. Even as later manuscript compilers chose to retain most of Guyart's version rather than simply mass-produce the earlier, less overtly mediated *Bible du XIIIe siècle* translation of the complete Vulgate, Guyart's narrow, almost exclusive focus on the historical (i.e., narrative) books of the Bible was soon undone in most copies, which may reflect (at least in part) a shift in the political exigencies of the French monarchy. Over the course of the fourteenth century, an interest in reading biblical history through the lens of crusading ideologies and a desire to legitimize French Christian hegemony in those terms gradually shifts towards a more expansive and versatile Bible.[68] This shift is facilitated by the addition of the Psalter, the sapiential and prophetic books, and parascriptural material such as litanies of saints, prayers, catechisms, and moral treatises, all of which lent the Bible to a wider range of uses including private or communal prayer, moral and spiritual self-improvement, and various aspects of religious formation and practice. Two royal copies, Philippe VI's (partial) *Bible historiale* and one of King Charles V's several *Bible historiale complétée* manuscripts, offer an especially clear case study in this shift away from promoting crusade to a more holistic view of the education of a Christian monarch through study and prayer, moral discipline, and conscientious rule.[69]

Philippe VI, the first known French king to own a copy of the *Bible historiale*, was given a crusading miscellany in the 1330s, now London, British Library, MS Royal 19 D 1 (Royal 19 D 1). Alongside the heroic *Roman d'Alexandre*, fantastic travel narratives such as Marco Polo's *Devisement du monde* and the *Merveilles de la terre d'outremer*, and several crusading texts translated by Jean de Vignay, we find, at the end of the manuscript, Guyart des Moulins's translation of parts of the four Books of Kings pertaining mostly to King David. The colophon at the end of the *Bible historiale* extracts pointedly names them by their bellicose subject matter: "Ci finent pluseurs batailles des roys d'israel en contre les philistiens et assyriens" ("Here end several battles of the kings of Israel against the Philistines and Assyrians," fol. 267v).[70] Read in the context of a collection of texts promoting conquest and crusade, these biblical narratives encourage identification with David and other Hebrew kings, to share in their sense of a birthright to Jerusalem and the will to fight for it.

By contrast, one of Charles V's most decadent copies of the *Bible historiale*, now Paris, Bibliothèque nationale de France, MS fr. 5707, received in his youth in 1362 or 1363, ends with an acrostic prayer, written just for him, that spells out his name and titles in its initials. Above the poem is a large illumination that depicts Charles, then dauphin, praying to the Virgin Mary and infant Christ, with his *Bible historiale* open in front of him, in his private chambers. The portrait both invokes what would become his public persona as a studious and pious king and illustrates how he might in fact use the book itself.[71] This portrait recalls Philippe de Mézières's later praise for the late king's purported habit of reading the Bible "as a way of praying" ("par maniere d'oroison") as well as to attain practical wisdom, both of which the author cites as models for Charles V's son, the new king, Charles VI.[72] Whether accurate or apocryphal, these visual and verbal portraits of Charles V using the Bible point to a changing ideal of how the Bible should inform leadership, shifting (at least somewhat) away from the model of the warrior king David towards that of the wise Solomon, and from a French Bible that emphasizes historic claims to Jerusalem to one that could also be part of daily prayer and a manual for ethical governance.

Changing trends over time in manuscript copies, as well as a high level of personalized variation among manuscripts, reflected the diverse and changing self-images of its intended readers (who were not only kings, as we will see in examples discussed in later chapters), or at least how bookmakers perceived them. In turn, changes to the contents and presentation of French Bible manuscripts, including which biblical narratives and lessons they emphasized, would have affected readers' experience of the text and their reasons for reading it as well. In addition to individualized variations and changing trends over time, the textual contents, illumination programs, and cultural significance of the manuscripts also varied geographically, between the patterns in manuscript expansion that arose in Paris workshops and the more eclectic composite versions made in Flanders, the Netherlands, northern Italy, and the provincial margins of France.

As manuscript copies of the *Bible historiale* reached higher degrees of individual variation in their contents, print would, if only for a few decades, fix one expanded (or *complétée*) version of the text as the first complete printed Bible in the French language. Anthoine Vérard printed its first edition in 1498, and it was subsequently printed in twenty-six re-editions in Paris and Lyon, of which the last is dated 1545.[73] These editions vary in their formats, illustrations and prologues, but their contents generally reflect those of a group of similar manuscripts made for the royal family. The 1498 and subsequent editions were probably based on one of several manuscripts that had been passed down to King Charles VIII, who commissioned Jean de Rély (d. 1498), bishop of Évreux and Angers and the king's own chaplain, to edit it for print. The royal *Bible historiale* – or as Samuel Berger calls that group of manuscripts, the *Groupe des Bibles du duc de Berry*, a subgroup of his category *Grandes Bibles historiales complétées* – had become, in title and in fact, the *Bible en francoiz*.

Starting in 1510, several editions of the *Bible historiale* that were sold under the title *Bible en francoiz* and made in the Vérard family workshop in Paris open with a new set of editorial prologues (one for each volume) that partly mirror Guyart's, but that remove all references to his name and biographical details as well as most of his commentary about his translation and compilation choices. The new prologues turn their focus away from the translator and his work to make a more direct appeal to potential readers or buyers, making a case for who should read this Bible and why. They address their target audience with more precision than Guyart's brief references to "laies gens." The laity are still counted first among the printed French Bible's target readership, but it also recommends itself to Latin-illiterate religious as well as the clergy charged with the instruction of both of those groups.

The author of the prologues (possibly Anthoine Vérard or his son Bartholomé, who took over the press at his father's death in 1512) compares the *Bible en françoiz* favourably to other kinds of reading material popular among its target demographic. Specifically, a prologue to the second volume proposes the Bible as a worthier substitute for the chivalric romances that might also appeal to French-language readers: "[i]l vous vault mieulx occuper en divine escripture qu'il ne fait es rommans parlans d'amours et de batailles qui sont plains de menteries" ("it is better to occupy yourselves with Holy Scripture than with romances that speak of love affairs and battles and that are full of lies," Washington, DC, Library of Congress, Rosenwald 967 [Rosenwald 967], vol. 2, fol. 5v).[74] It is striking to find knightly adventures singled out as the French Bible's main competitor for readers' time, attention, and purchasing power. The comparison draws on familiar tropes about the frivolity and deceptiveness of fiction and the vanity of worldly intrigues that often fail to exemplify Christian moral codes. At the same time, the juxtaposition implies an enticing parallel with romances: the Bible also tells many tales of love affairs and battles; its redeeming virtue is that it is ostensibly not full of lies but of salutary truths. More than a mere denunciation of secular romances, the prologues strategically leverage their popularity to sell the Bible as a similarly entertaining but more commendable read.

The Vérard prologues assert not just the right, but the necessity of "all good Christians" to "read and ruminate" upon the Bible. Those who could not read are encouraged to listen to it being read, and all are urged to study and interiorize the text to find "food and pasture" for their souls. In short, according to the prologue of the second volume, serious study of the Bible was no longer just the province of the clergy or the privileged few laypeople who could read and afford luxury manuscripts. It was a moral obligation for all Christians with access to this French Bible, whose printing left no excuse for those of sufficient means to remain ignorant in their faith. Indeed, failing to redress that ignorance posed a risk to their eternal souls:

> Vous ne povez pas donc estre excusez de l'ygnorance de nostre foy, car vous avez des livres plusieurs qui vous monstrent la maniere de bien vivre en ce monde qui est le vray chemin et droicte sente pour aller au royaulme devantdit, c'est assavoir en la gloire de paradis. (Rosenwald 967, vol. 2, fol. 5v)
>
> (Therefore you cannot be excused for ignorance of our faith, for you have the numerous books that show you the way to live well in this world, which is the true path and the right way to go to the aforementioned kingdom, that is, into the glory of heaven.)

These are, of course, the words of an editor intent on selling books, not an official statement of church doctrine.[75] However, they are noteworthy in making no concession to any dissent over whether the laity should even be allowed to read the Bible on their own. There is no assurance that readers *may* read the Bible in translation, only arguments for why they *must: may* is taken for granted. As of 1510, and still in 1517, reading the Bible in French, at least in this particular version based on Jerome's Vulgate, was wholly uncontroversial. It would not be long before the Protestant Reformation and new translations based on the newly edited Greek New Testament would be met with controversy after centuries of relative openness to vernacular translation and lay readership of the Bible in France. Indeed, by the 1520s, the evangelist movement led by Bishop of Meaux Guillaume Briçonnet, Bible translator and commentator Jacques Lefèvre d'Étaples, and the rest of the so-called "Circle of Meaux" faced considerable scrutiny for producing and promoting unauthorized humanist, Greek-based translations.[76]

The fact that, on the eve of the Reformation, the *Bible historiale* had become, in title and in fact, the *Bible en françoiz* reflects the status it had achieved among readers and church authorities alike as the default canonical French Bible.[77] The only complete French translation printed before 1530, it had essentially become to French what the Vulgate was to Latin: the most authorized and authoritative Catholic Bible for the public it served. It was authorized insofar as its glossing apparatus reinforced institutionally condoned scriptural interpretations and church teachings and thus mitigated potential concerns about the independent use of translations by anticlerical, heretical, or Protestant movements.[78] It was authoritative in that, by the early sixteenth century, the *Bible historiale* had remained the uncontested favourite French translation (in terms of the number of copies produced) for over two hundred years, having adapted over that time to changing ideas about the French Bible's canon and purpose. Whereas the Reformation would give rise to new controversies and debates surrounding the textual criticism and translation of the Bible, early printed editions of the *Bible historiale (complétée)* briefly represented a default French biblical canon for just a few decades before becoming obsolete, as new translations based on the Greek New Testament would spur a series of feuding translations based on competing source texts. However, in keeping with medieval textualities, the *Bible historiale*'s translated text and internal commentary were never meant to represent the kind of fixed, stable, or universal text that would later become encoded into a print-era ideal of exact reproducibility as a guarantor of reliability in translation and textual transmission. Instead, the medieval *Bible historiale*'s internal dialogues and tensions depended on an agile, pliable manuscript culture that could remake the Bible to fit the perceived needs of new readers.

The chapters that follow examine the various ways in which Guyart's translation and its successive manuscript reiterations imagine and reimagine their target readers' relationship to the biblical text they translate. One important cultural lens through which that happens is that of French-language literary norms of narration. In the late thirteenth century, Latin-French translation was instrumental in the emergence of French as a literate and literary language, and as a language that would gradually take over some of the "high" cultural and institutional functions of Latin.[79] The effect of translation, and specifically of Bible translation, on French did not go unnoticed by medieval observers. No less a witness than Dante Alighieri, writing his *De vulgari eloquentia* less than a decade after Guyart's *Bible historiale*, praises French as a language into which the Bible had been translated.[80] Conversely, other influential French-language texts such as romances and histories had already begun to shape reader expectations and thus readers' receptivity to translated texts whose norms of narrative, style, and characterization were decidedly foreign to late medieval French literary culture. Some verse translations of the Bible fully embraced French literary expression to tell Bible stories in the style of French epic or romance, while others like the *Bible du XIIIe siècle* opted for a more "literal" and less explicitly mediated approach. I would argue that Guyart's *Bible historiale* is unique in its attempt to forge a middle path that, without fully "domesticating" the biblical text to conform to dominant French literary tastes of the time, directly acknowledges and negotiates the gaps between source and target norms. In the next chapter, I show how the translator's mediating voice ("je qui translatay") strategically interjects to resolve potential points of reader resistance to bring the Bible closer to what readers could understand, imagine, and believe based on their previous readings and lived experience.

2 Telling It Right: Confronting Reader Resistance

And these words seemed to them as idle tales;
and they did not believe them.

Luke 24:11

In his *histoires, gloses,* and rubrics that serve as translator's notes, Guyart des Moulins addresses head-on readers' potential resistance towards canonical episodes from the biblical text. These interventions most often concern material that his most sceptical readers may find jarring, incomprehensible, or even difficult to believe because it does not conform to their experiences and expectations about how people should act or how stories should unfold. Such episodes are plentiful in the Bible. In addition to accounts of prophecies and miracles that stand apart from ordinary experience, the narrative styles, idioms, and cultural references of the Hebrew Bible, even as translated in the Vulgate Old Testament, are quite foreign to medieval French literary norms and cultural frames of reference. The implied reader's anticipated questions, doubts, and moments of resistance create space for the translator-narrator to construct a dialogue between his own narrative voice – "je qui translatay" – and his reading or listening public about the text they are reading. Guyart's mediating interventions work to bring biblical stories and characters into harmony with reader expectations without dismantling the integrity of the translated biblical text.

One striking example of this mediation arises at the moment when Eve and Adam eat the forbidden fruit. Emblematic of human fallibility, ambition, and the consequences of sin, this episode is among the most represented Bible scenes in medieval art, literature, and popular imagination. In contrast to the effusive psychological and interpersonal drama typical of its popular retellings, the story's biblical source is the single verse Genesis 3:6, which is spare, paratactic, and decidedly undramatic.[1] The verse, as rendered in the Vulgate, the *Bible historiale*, and my modern English translation of both (with some minor differences indicated in brackets), reads simply:

> Vulgate: Vidit igitur mulier quod bonum esset lignum advescendum, et pulchrum oculis, aspectuque delectabile: et tulit de fructu illius, et comedit: deditque viro suo, qui comedit.
>
> *Bible historiale*: Donc vit la fame que li fruiz estoit bon a menger et biaus a regarder et delitabes, s'en prist et en menja et en donna a son mari et il en menja. (BnF fr. 155, fol. 5r)
>
> English translation: And the woman saw that the fruit was good to eat, beautiful [Vul.: to the eyes/BH: to look at] and delicious-looking, and she took some [Vul: of that fruit] and ate [BH: some of it], and gave some to her husband and he ate [BH: some of it].

In both the Vulgate and the *Bible historiale*, the description of eating of the forbidden fruit encapsulates in economical yet vivid terms Eve's compulsion to satisfy her senses and to share the experience with her husband. They do not elaborate, however, on either her or Adam's words, thoughts, motives, or emotions, and they do not interpret or pass judgment on their apparently abrupt decision. This spare, direct narration of characters' actions, uninflected by either the interiority of characters or by narrator commentary, is an example of what Robert Alter has described as the Hebrew Bible's characteristic "indeterminacy of meaning, especially in regard to motive, moral character, and psychology."[2] Jerome's Latin Vulgate translation, for the most part, preserves this aspect of the narrative in translation: while Jerome privileges translation choices that lend themselves to a Christological reading of the Old Testament, he does not embellish the text with characters' thoughts and dialogue not found in his source. In the Latin scholastic tradition, questions about the psychology behind and moral implications of biblical characters' actions are considered in historical commentaries such as Peter Comestor's *Historia scholastica*. Guyart's translation, supplemented by the *Historia*, not only supplies conventional answers to these questions (Comestor's and sometimes others'), but more explicitly acknowledges and attempts to resolve the cultural and narrative gaps between the biblical text and reader expectations that generated these questions in the first place.

The indeterminacy of the Adam and Eve story as rendered in the Vulgate contrasts with late medieval French literary norms of narrative and characterization, which frequently dwell on characters' inner monologues and provide more or less explicit moral judgments about their actions and motivations. In Guyart's estimation, the short, direct account of Adam and Eve in the Vulgate may leave readers unsatisfied, wondering what both characters were thinking, and surprised not to encounter some kind of conflict and resolution around such a consequential decision. In an *histoire* following his translation of the episode, Guyart, following the *Historia scholastica*, blames this disparity between how the story is told and how one imagines it playing out on "Moses's" hurried narrative style. Then, he attempts to alleviate that disparity with his own additional explanations and reflections about what is left unstated. As if anticipating his readers' expectation of a story arc more similar to that represented, for example, in the mid-twelfth-century Anglo-Norman *Jeu d'Adam* (in which the Devil wins over Eve by inflating her pride, then she provokes Adam by injuring his), Guyart calls to mind the "many words" lacking from this scene that, if included, might lend some subjective interiority and interpersonal drama to the universal, yet strangely silent, couple:[3]

> Donc s'en orgueilli la fame et voult resembler Dieu et vit que li fruiz estoit biaus a veoir et douz a mengier, si en donna son mari a mengier, et l'amonnesta a mengier en par moult de paroles ennortants a moult d'ennortemens, les quiex Moyses trespasse en la Bible pour plus briement passer, et ses mariz la crut de legier. Car quant il vit que sa fame en avoit mengie et si n'estoit mie morte et si leur avoit Diex dit qu'il morroient quant il en mengeroient, il cuida que Diex leur eust dit por ans espoenter. (BnF fr. 155, fol. 5r)

> (And then the woman became proud and wanted to be like God. And she saw that the fruit was beautiful to look at and sweet to eat and gave some to her husband to eat and admonished him to eat some of it, with many pleading words and exhortations, which Moses skips over in the Bible in order to speak more briefly and go on more quickly, and her husband carelessly believed her. For when he saw that his wife had eaten some of it and had not died, and yet God had told them that they would die when they ate of it, he believed that God had told them this in order to scare them.)

The missing words (Eve's "many pleading words and exhortations") call attention to their omission – not the translator's or even Adam's or Eve's, but the biblical author's. This element of Guyart's *histoire* is translated from the *Historia scholastica*, which notes in chapter 22 on Genesis, "De esu pomi, et statu post peccatum," that Adam's and Eve's decision to eat the fruit was made after "forte praemonens verbis persuasibilibus, quae transit legislator brevitatis causa" ("sternly admonishing words of persuasion, which the Lawmaker passes over for brevity").[4]

However, Guyart's version of the *histoire* expands upon Comestor's brief mention of a hypothetical dialogue to speculate about the contents of that conversation and its effects. It emphasizes Eve's state of mind, the persuasive effect of her words, and Adam's possible thought process as he weighed her words against God's, even as it also judges how easily he believes her. This short, speculative reconstruction meets the reader's imagination halfway to evoke an idea, if not the specific words, of the characters' dialogue and their internal motives and thoughts; it is up to the reader to complete the scene, perhaps with the help of memories of dramatic performances, paintings, and other stories about Adam and Eve. Vivid, humorous, and believable because their characters conformed to medieval audiences' stereotypes about men and women, the embellished or fictionalized medieval versions of Adam's and Eve's eating of the fruit become as much a psychic reality (to borrow Jung's term) as the bare-bones account of Genesis 3.[5] Whether or not readers recollect a specific, previously encountered dramatization of the scene, they are invited to imagine it on their own with the help of expressive miniatures in some manuscripts and especially this *histoire*, which also elaborates upon such details as how the serpent was able to speak and how the juice from the couple's fig leaf "petites braies" (underwear) had a "cooling" effect on their flesh.[6]

The supposed "missing words" of Adam's and Eve's argument call attention to how the narrative style of the first chapters of Genesis differs from the literary aesthetics of medieval, especially French, vernacular audiences. Guyart's invitation to readers to imagine the characters' dialogue for themselves represents one of the tactics the translator uses when confronted with textual elements whose divergence from readers' expectations and experience may impede their comprehension, raise scepticism, or even cast doubt on the translator's reliability. This chapter examines some of the editorial, narrative, and metanarrative strategies by which the *Bible historiale* – including Guyart's translation and its manuscript tradition – brings the Bible into the physical and textual world its readers inhabit and know or are at least prepared to imagine. First, I examine how the *Bible historiale*, while sharing common features of both prose and verse translations of the Bible, is unique in its approach to negotiating the competing goals of producing a translation that is "faithful" to its authoritative Latin sources and exegetical traditions but also "literary" in its vernacular legibility and appeal. Then, I examine Guyart's strategies for confronting reader resistance, such as editorial selection and rearrangement of texts and paratexts (glosses, diagrams, illustrations), and the addition of extratextual allusions to real-world places and shared cultural references. Through these dialogic asides to the implied reader, Guyart makes the Bible more "true-seeming" and facilitates its integration into readers' existing memories and mental structures of knowledge, experience, and belief. Finally, I reflect on how these approaches to mediating biblical narrative, amplified in some cases by their manuscript presentation, anchor the *Bible historiale* to medieval French literary traditions.

Bible and/as Romance: The *Bible historiale* and Its Verse Counterparts

Medieval vernacular translators of the Bible had to account for the reading habits, preferences, and competencies of their target-language audiences and bring biblical narrative close enough to that audience's experience and expectations to make the text accessible, attractive, and believable. Most medieval French Bible translations fall into two main camps in their approach to this task, divided along formal lines and probably envisaging different modes of reception and performance.[7] Verse biblical translations, such as Jehan Malkaraume's Bible, Herman de Valenciennes's *Romanz de Dieu et de sa mere*, the *Hystore Job*, and the *Chevalerie de Judas Macabé* make biblical narrative conform to the conventional versification of romance or epic, and these translations also tend to adopt more generally the narrative conventions of these genres.[8] They employ techniques of dialogic and descriptive embellishment similar to those found in medieval verse translations of classical pagan literature (especially epics such as the *Roman de Troie*), with the purpose of bringing biblical texts closer to medieval French literary norms and the larger set of knowledge, beliefs, and experiences of their target audiences.

In contrast, most prose Bible translations of the period seem less inclined to bend the source text to target-language norms of prosody, style, or narration. Interventions meant to guide interpretation instead come in paratextual form: glosses, prologues, rubrics, illustrations. For example, the prose *Bible du XIIIe siècle* (the translation frequently used to supplement the *Bible historiale*) contains exegetical glosses from the *Glossa Ordinaria* and other sources, as do fourteenth- and fifteenth-century prose translations by Jean de Sy and Raoul de Presles.[9] These prose translations vary in terms of the biblical and parascriptural contents they include as well as in some details of their translation style, but the editorial manipulation of their source texts is minimal. Notably, they do not modify, augment, or comment on narratives for literary effect, nor do they explicitly voice concerns about the way the Bible is written (in general or specifically in Jerome's Latin translation) or how its vernacular readers might receive and judge it and find it lacking as a literary text.

Guyart des Moulins's *Bible historiale* resembles other medieval prose biblical translations in its use of Latin-sourced gloss and commentary; like them, his translation also stays relatively close to its Vulgate source in the main translated text, labeled "*selon la Bible*" or "*texte*" to set it apart from the Comestor-sourced *histoires* and other layers of commentary whose translation Guyart more freely amplifies and adapts. However, the *Bible historiale* differs from other prose translations of the period in its explicit attention to the aesthetics and persuasiveness of biblical narrative, as judged according-ing to contemporary medieval French vernacular norms of storytelling.

This explicit engagement with French medieval literary norms aligns the *Bible historiale* with verse translation in some respects, but it also dif-fers starkly from them in its contents, structure, and translation style. A brief comparative analysis of some extracts from the *Bible historiale*, the French verse *Chevalerie de Judas Macabé*, and the Bible of Jehan Mal-karaume will elucidate the different relationships these texts have with their implied readers, their shared Latin source (the Vulgate), and French literary norms, even as they share some notable commonalities.

One set of elements that the *Bible historiale* shares with many other translations, prose and verse, is a common emphasis on the authority of their sources and on the trustworthiness of their translators, all under the shared umbrella of truth. We saw this in quotations from Guyart's prologue in chapter 1, and chapter 3 discusses in more detail his use of *vrai* or *verité* in defining and justifying his translation and editorial choices. We see similar language, for example, in the *Chevalerie de Judas Macabé*, a late thirteenth-century work that translates the biblical books of Maccabees into French chivalric romance. Like Guyart's proem, the first part of the *Chevalerie de Judas Macabé* insists upon the historical and church-sanctioned truth that the narrator is transmitting:

> Voirs fu, si com conte l'istoire
> De la bible, qui si est voire
> Com sainte eglise le tiesmogne,
> Que jadis ot, n'est pas mençoigne,
> En Gresce, un mott res poissant roi … (ll. 75–9)[10]
>> (It was true, just as the history of the Bible tells it, which is also
>> true, as witnessed by the Holy Church, that at that time – it's
>> no lie – there was in Greece a very powerful king …)

As a whole, the *Chevalerie* follows conventions of French romance, from its octosyllabic verse, familiar oral formulae ("Or m'entendés" ["Now hear me"], l. 22), and standard heroic epithets ("Matatias li preus" ["Matthias the valiant"], l. 69), to its narration style and liberal addition of invented dialogue. Its form, connoting fictional entertainment, jars with its biblical truth content. The cognitive dissonance of telling biblical truth in verse romance form, as well as the practical obstacles of translating not only from Latin to French but also from the Vulgate's prose to metred verse, spur the narrator to repeatedly emphasize the truth of the content to follow while excusing the quality of its verse, as if compromising the latter constitutes proof of the former:

> Veil ci encomencier la flor
> Des materes et metre en rime.
> Pour çou se ne faç lionime
> En pluisors lius, n'est pas mierveille,
> Car la matere s'apareille
> A verité, por coi li sens
> Ara mestier que ne mete ens
> Mençoigne por la rime aquerre. (ll. 4–11)
>> (I want to begin now the flower of subjects and put it into rhyme.
>> It is no wonder that the rhyme is not made leonine in
>> some places, for the subject matter is joined to truth, for which
>> reason the meaning necessitates that no lie be introduced
>> just to get the rhyme.)

The *Chevalerie* offers a foil against which to contrast the *Bible historiale*'s approach to managing the points of discord or unintelligibility among ancient Hebrew cultural and textual norms, scholastic Latin modes of knowledge, and a vernacular audience's literary horizons of expectations.[11] We have seen, in the example of Eve's imagined words convincing Adam to eat the fruit, how the *Bible historiale*, in the space of its secondary *histoires* and glosses, invites the reader to fill in gaps in the narrative with imagined, even fictionalized detail that finds some parallel in the way verse translations simply insert their own imagined dialogues. But whereas biblically inspired romances like the *Chevalerie* assert their truth claims as oral testimony in spite of their format, the *Bible historiale*'s scholastically glossed format paired with a purportedly "*mot a mot*" prose translation of the Latin Vulgate Bible projects authoritative truth in a way that verse romance does not. Its aura of truthfulness is not necessarily threatened by its fictionalization or appeals to imagination, especially insofar as any material that interrupts and departs from direct translation of the Vulgate is clearly marked as such (e.g., *histoire*, *glose*) and cannot be confused with the authoritative biblical *texte*.

In terms of the chapter-by-chapter, sentence-by-sentence translation choices vis-à-vis the Latin Vulgate Bible, the *Bible historiale* resembles other prose translations of the period far more than it does verse translations, and not only in the obvious ways that verse differs from prose (that is, the inevitable syntactic and lexical manipulation demanded by the constraints of metre and rhyme that risk semantic loss). Following the conventions of the epic or romance genres they emulate, the verse translations tend to shorten narration and description, while packing more information into dialogue. They interpret character motives and meanings more than the Vulgate and its anterior source texts do, but in direct and textually economical terms. A side-by-side comparison of the Latin Vulgate, *Bible historiale*, and Jehan Malkaraume versions (with English translations of each) of the episode of the binding of Isaac will help illustrate how generic conventions affect Malkaraume's translation differently than Guyart's (see Figure 2.1).

As the side-by-side presentation of the three texts illustrates, the Latin text's semantic translation units pass virtually intact into the *Bible historiale*. The translation differs slightly in meaning from its source only in a few details added to clarify or subtly interpret the events being described. Apparent departures vis-à-vis the Latin Vulgate are: "God had shown *them*" the place (instead of "him"), insinuating that Isaac also knew the plan beforehand; clarifying the sequence of events and the angel's interruption of the sacrifice by replacing two instances of "and" (et/-que) with "but" and "then" (mais, donc); switching the order of Abraham's actions to the more logical "*Then he took the sword and lifted his hand* to sacrifice his son"; specifying that "*The angel* said" to Abraham not to sacrifice Isaac rather than the ambiguous "he said to him"; and clarifying that the last lines are neither God's direct speech nor the angel speaking about himself, but the angel speaking on God's behalf, changing "for *my sake*" to "for *him*."[13]

These subtle interpretive translation choices of the *Bible historiale* contrast starkly with the degree and kind of textual manipulation seen in the roughly contemporary Malkaraume Bible.[14] Malkaraume's translation not only recasts narrative elements within the formal constraints of verse, but also adopts romance conventions of characterization and style. It is told in a unified narrative voice that does not distinguish the translator's voice from those of biblical authors or narrators, Latin source text translators, or commentators or eventual performers of the text.[15] Its anticipated mode of reception, namely oral performance, affects its form, style, and narrative pace, drawing out some episodes to build suspense and shortening others to prioritize dialogue or to mimic the rapid succession of events. It alternates freely between past tenses

Figure 2.1 Table comparing Vulgate with *Bible historiale* and Jehan Malkaraume translations of Genesis 22:9–12.

Vulgate Bible	*Bible historiale*	Jehan Malkaraume's Bible
Et venerunt ad locum quem ostenderat ei Deus, in quo aedificavit altare, et desuper ligna composuit; cumque alligasset Isaac filium suum, posuit eum in altare super struem ignorum. Extenditque manum, et arripuit gladium, ut immolaret filium suum. Et ecce angelus Domini de caelo clamavit, dicens: Abraham, Abraham. Qui respondit: Adsum. Dixitque ei: Non extendas manum tuam super puerum, neque facias illi quidquam: nunc cognovi quod times Deum, et non pepercisti unigenito filio tuo propter me. (Gn 22:9–12)	Si vindrent au lieu que Diex leur avoit moustré, si i fist Abraham .i. autel et mist la busche sus. Quant il ot lié Ysaac son filz, il le mist sus l'autel sus le moncel de busche. Donc prist il l'espee si leva la main por sacrefier son fil. Mais li ange Nostre Seigneur li cria du ciel et dist, "Abraham, Abraham." Il respondi. Je sui ci. Li ange li dist, "N'esten mie ta main sus l'enfant ne ne li fai riens. Or sai je bien que tu crains Dieu et que tu n'eusses mie espergné ton enfant pour lui." (BnF fr. 155, fol. 11v, Gn 22:9–12)	Adonc print Habraham l'anfant, Les mains li loie, l'espee estant: Sacrefier la le vouloit Pour faire de Dieu le vouloir. .I. angers vint, l'espee tint: "Dieus ton vouloir voit, pran ton fil; Pran ce mouton en cel boujon Sou sacrefie pour ton fil bon; Dieus a veü que as plus chier Son mandement que ton fil chier."[12] (ll. 648–57)
Vulgate (Douay-Rheims)	*Bible historiale*	Jehan Malkaraume's Bible
And they came to the place which God had shewn him, where he built an altar, and laid the wood in order upon it: and when he had bound Isaac his son, he laid him on the altar upon the pile of wood. And he put forth his hand and took the sword, to sacrifice his son. And behold an angel of the Lord from heaven called to him, saying: Abraham, Abraham. And he answered: Here I am. And he said to him: Lay not thy hand upon the boy, neither do thou any thing to him: now I know that thou fearest God, and hast not spared thy only begotten son for my sake.	And they came to the place that God had shown them, and Abraham made an altar there and put the log on top of it. When he had bound Isaac his son, he put him on the altar upon the woodpile. Then he took the sword and lifted his hand to sacrifice his son. But the angel of Our Lord shouted from heaven and said, "Abraham, Abraham." He responded, "Here I am." The angel said to him, "Don't bring down your hand on the child or do anything to him. Now I know for sure that you fear God and that you did not spare your child for him."	Now Abraham takes the child, binds his hands and holds up the sword; he intended to sacrifice him right there to carry out God's will. An angel came, held the sword: "God sees your intention, take your child; take this lamb with this arrow to sacrifice instead of your good son; God has seen that you hold his commandment dearer than your dear son."

("Sacrefier la le vouloit" ["he intended to sacrifice him right there"]; ".I. angers vint" ["An angel came"]) and historic present tense ("Les mains li loie, l'espee estant" ["binds his hands and holds up the sword"]), which adds a sense of presence and urgency to its most vivid moments, as if slowing time to pause on the image of the sword suspended over Isaac's head. It depicts characters' emotional states, character traits, and motivations (in its narration and dialogue, not in separate glosses or *histoires,* as Guyart does) where its source does not. For example, we are told that Abraham wanted to please God, and the angel adds that this intention was the reason for God's ultimate decision to spare Isaac. The simple adjectives "bon" ("good") and "chier" ("dear") suffice to convey that Isaac was innocent and that his father loved him, enhancing the emotional drama of the scene and denying any possibility that Abraham might have wanted to kill the boy for any other reason than to please God. The angel's and God's actions are more direct too: the angel does not merely yell at Abraham to stop but seizes his sword in mid-air. It is not simply suggested in the successive verses that the lamb that Abraham sacrifices was sent by God as a substitute; the angel says so. The densely narrated text is self-sufficient, easy to visualize and to interpret without added commentary.

Despite their clear differences, both the verse translations of the Bible and the *Bible historiale* are marked by a symbiotic relationship with secular literary conventions, coaxing readers' belief by playing to their expectations and their anticipated moral-aesthetic desire for a "good," "beautiful," and verisimilar or "true-seeming" story. However, where the verse translations bend biblical narrative to formal and stylistic conventions that characterize romance and epic, the *Bible historiale* repurposes scholastic glossing conventions in order to frame the narrative within a running fictional dialogue between implied author and implied reader. This dialogue not only serves as an interpretive aid but also as a space to negotiate gaps between the translated biblical text and the preconceived expectations, beliefs, and world views of its medieval readers. Throughout the *Bible historiale,* the translator acknowledges and pre-emptively explains material that its readers may find jarring, both with respect to the immediate Latin source text as well as to the foreignness it retains of its anterior Hebrew, Greek, and other ancient sources. Unlike the verse translations, Guyart's is relatively "literal," that is, semantically very close to the Latin Vulgate, but rendered in fluent French syntax. It does not resort primarily to the kind of cultural, lexical, syntactic, and stylistic adaptation described in translation studies as "domestication" (translation choices or approaches that lean towards assimilating linguistically and culturally "foreign" elements of a source text to the norms of the target language and culture) or, in Eugene Nida's terms, dynamic equivalence.[16] When the need arises to clarify potentially unfamiliar calques or cultural references, or to compensate for semantic losses in the translation of multivalent words, Guyart either relies on minimal interventions such as lexical doubling or he adds explanations in glosses marked as separate from the biblical text, either by their placement or with rubrics.[17] Finally, rather than simply smoothing over prominent cultural differences in the text by replacing them with familiar target-culture alternatives, Guyart profits from moments of culture shock to pause and "talk through" them with his implied reader. This typically happens in the *histoires*, with or without an explicit notice of how he modifies or adds to Comestor's text in translation, or in his own original glosses and translator's notes.

Editing Moses and Jerome

The *Bible historiale* intervenes to address reader questions, misunderstandings, and doubts in ways that are small and large, explicit and implicit. Some such interventions translate directly from the *Historia scholastica*, which supplements the biblical text with other Christian, Jewish, and pagan stories and interpretive traditions. In other cases, the translator adds his own voice to Comestor's effort to "tell the whole story," confronting the empty spaces of uncertainty with speculative possibilities. The meaning-generating interplay between reader and text, in which missing information spurs the reader's imagination to form, destroy, and reform expectations, recalls the "gaps" and places of indeterminacy proposed by Wolfgang Iser as a model for the experience of reading literary fiction.[18] Here, however, the "reader" in question is not one, but a series of readers built into the text, each one reading through the lens of the last: the reader of a *Bible historiale* manuscript is reading (one scribe's reading of) Guyart reading Comestor, both of whom read Jerome's reading and translation of several anterior biblical source texts. Each *Bible historiale* manuscript inscribes, to an extent, each of these stages of mediated reading, and the process of identifying and negotiating gaps between the text and readers' expectations can be said to occur at every stage. It is most visible in Guyart's narration, which models the gap-filling process and brings attention to it. Within this layered textual environment, reading the *Bible historiale* is a recreative exploration in which readers are encouraged, within the boundaries of dogmatic correctness, to take an active role in aligning biblical narrative with their prior knowledge and experience (and, conversely, revisiting their prior knowledge and experiences through a biblical lens).

As Guyart directly engages with multiple layers of source text, he interrogates the authorial voices and styles of the texts he translates and mitigates their foreignness by calling attention to their differences from the literary and cultural norms of the receiving, or target-language, culture. Moses, widely thought in the Middle Ages to be the sole author of the Pentateuch, is repeatedly invoked as such: I count thirty-two instances in Genesis and its accompanying *histoires* of formulae such as "Moyse dit" ("Moses says") or "selon Moyse" ("according to Moses"). Along with the frequently occurring "cy dit le maistre en hystoires" ("here the Master of Histories [Comestor] says") and similar citations for Jerome and an assortment of other authorities, these authorial citations form one of several concentric layers of authorship and narration, all in dialogue with one another and orchestrated by the translator's (and, in rare cases, a scribe's) *je*. Many of the references to Moses originate with Comestor, who does not often directly quote the biblical text unless to comment on a phrase, as his intended scholastic reader would likely have the entire Vulgate biblical text to hand for reference. Between Comestor's comments and those added by Guyart, a subtle commentary emerges about the spare narrative style of the Hebrew Bible, filtered through Latin translation but still understood as originating with its Hebrew source via the authorial figure of Moses.

Of course, the understated, paratactic elegance of Genesis could also be said to enhance its literary potential. Its indeterminacy generated many volumes of interpretive gloss in Jewish as well as in Greek and Latin Christian traditions, from the numerous Hexameron-style commentaries and encyclopedically exegetical *De Genesi ad Litteram,* to pseudepigraphal continuations like the *Vita Adae et Evae* that use imaginative narrative to make sense of the prototypical humans' thoughts and motives and the transformation wrought by the Fall. In Comestor's and Guyart's characterizations, however, Moses may hold a special place as prophet, patriarch, and codifier of Jewish law, but as a storyteller or historian, he comes across as rushed, skipping over details and refusing answers to the reader's questions. In addition to the aforementioned lack of dialogue between Adam and Eve when they eat the fruit, the treatment of Adam and Eve's progeny raises other questions. While only Cain, Abel, and Seth are named as children of Adam and Eve, Cain and Seth marry women whose origin is not explained, leaving readers to hypothesize whether they were unnamed daughters of Adam and Eve or whether there were other humans inhabiting the earth at the time, in apparent contradiction to the Genesis 3 account of Adam and Eve as the only two humans. This unexplained detail elicits Guyart's comment on Moses's priorities and his uneven rate of narration: "Ci passe briement

Moyses les engendreures Adam et va en haste au tens Abraham le père des ebrieux et se test de moult des filz et des filles Adam" ("Here Moses passes quickly through the descendants of Adam and hastens to the time of Abraham, father of the Hebrews, and passes over many of Adam's sons and daughters in silence," BnF fr. 155, fol. 5v).[19] This "passe briement" echoes the language used to describe Moses's style of narration in omitting any dialogue between Adam and Eve ("trespasse en la Bible pour plus briement passer") and points to a perception that, due to its narrative style, the Bible leaves a lot unsaid and a lot of questions unanswered.

Asking those questions of the text in the *histoires, gloses,* and other paratextual layers of Guyart's translation serves not only to transmit information, but also to prepare the reader's mind for an ethical and empathetic reading that can direct religious beliefs towards moral action consonant with dominant cultural values. In order to accomplish these goals, the translation must first ensure that narrative events are believable: laws must have reasons, and human actions need relatable human motivations. Second, there must be an effort to adapt the discontinuities of the canonical Bible to norms of narration that readers recognize and that therefore preserve Guyart's narrative authority and the reader's will to believe. In this regard, the Latin translator Jerome's scholarly dissection of sources is no more above scrutiny than Moses's supposed haste, and no less inappropriate to the *Bible historiale*'s audience and aims, even if Guyart shares Jerome's meticulousness in documenting his use of sources and how he manipulates those sources in translation. Indeed, to follow Jerome's editorial and translation choices in every instance would, in some cases, undermine Guyart's authority, introduce doubt, and detract from the aesthetic enjoyment of the text that Guyart has expressed as critical to lay faith and spirituality. As a case in point, let us consider his editorial approach to the Book of Esther.

"S'en semble a la laie gent l'istoire miex ordenee"

The Book of Esther tells the story of the Hebrew woman Esther who marries King Ahasuerus (Xerxes I) of Persia and leverages her status as beloved queen to save her people from a genocidal plot hatched by the king's spiteful viceroy, Haman. A distinguishing feature of the story is the central role it accords to the circulation of documents: a series of edicts, letters, and prayers, accessories to the main text that simultaneously determine the course of the plot and serve as material proof of its authenticity. The canonical Hebrew text of the book only mentions these supporting texts without transcribing them. Comparing Hebrew and Greek source texts, however, the Latin translator Jerome found the contents of the documents and prayers written out in full in the Septuagint, intercalated into the narrative at the moments they are introduced. Because of this difference in content and structure, the Hebrew and Greek versions of Esther privilege different aspects of the story. Whereas the Hebrew version merely mentions at the end of the book that Esther's uncle Mordechai had a prophetic dream predicting the Jews' vindication, the Septuagint version recounts the dream in full as a prologue to the main story, framing the whole in such a way as to place the story that follows within the register of prophetic fulfilment and divine will. While most of the other letters, edicts, and prayers transcribed in the Septuagint add little new information, as they mostly retell what did or will happen in the main narration, their inclusion lends these documents an air of corroborating evidence. Both versions of Esther are oriented towards ritual performance in their retelling of the origin story of the Purim holy day; the Septuagint version, however, differs in emphasis, making more visible God's hand in the reversal of the Jews' misfortune.[20]

Jerome's Latin translation differs from both of his source versions in its goals and in its presentation of the text. His version is that of a scholar, one that seeks to compare and reconcile the Hebrew and Greek sources. His main translated text shows a preference for the Hebrew version. However, Jerome views the additional materials from the Septuagint as authentic, although omitted from the Hebrew, and he sees their inclusion in his translation as advantageous to his goal of supporting a unified Christian reading of Jewish history and holy texts. Rather than simply translating the Septuagint version as it was structured, he settles on a compromise: he translates the Hebrew text as is and attaches those portions found only in the Greek separately at the end of the translated Hebrew text, with brief notes explaining his procedure and where each extract appeared in the Septuagint text.[21]

Presented as appendices in the Vulgate, the added pieces from the Septuagint take on the appearance of documentary "proof" supporting the authenticity and divine purpose of the events recounted and of the historical observation of the holy day established in their honour. However, these appended documents no longer fully serve the narrative function they served in the Septuagint version of the story, in which the prophetic foreshadowing of the opening dream vision, as well as the circulation of letters, edicts, and prayers that both drive the action and reframe it through different characters' perspectives, all play an important role in structuring the story and interpreting its meaning. Reading all of those texts after the story instead of within it dampens their literary effect, destroying the neat *mise en abîme* of stories within stories and the carefully plotted device of texts exchanging hands, prompting actions, and foretelling events before or reacting to them after they occur in the main text. In the Septuagint, these additional oral and written internal texts retell, reinflect, and reinterpret narrated events in the heart of the story. Their words are called as testimony when Mordechai reveals a plot against the king. They enact law with the king's seal, as edicts ordering the killing of Jews are publicly displayed and exchanged, and as the king cancels them with another letter. Prayers to God prompt his intervention and entreaties to the king change his course of action. The texts are performative: letters on the earthly plane and prayers on the heavenly one precipitate, and reverse, genocides and wars and the fates of communities.

The detrimental, even disorienting effects of Jerome's choices on the structure of the story of Esther are not lost on Guyart. There is no evidence that the French translator was familiar with the Greek text, or had access to it, or even read Greek.[22] However, based on Jerome's notes and Guyart's own sense of how his implied reader would expect the story to incorporate its supporting documents, Guyart manages to reconstruct the approximate order of the narrative as it appears in the Septuagint, with the exception of the dream, which he places where it is mentioned at 10:4–5 rather than at the beginning of the book.[23] Reversing the notes wherein Jerome indicates where he found the materials in the Greek version and how he has collected them at the end, Guyart indicates in rubrics where in Jerome's translation he found those texts and why he has chosen to reinsert them within the main narrative. He explains, more than once, that he has departed from "la Bible" (i.e., his Latin source, Jerome's Vulgate) in order to write a better-constructed story that suits reader expectations: "*s'en semble a la laie gent l'histoire miex ordenee, car laie gent porroient cuidier qu'ele fust transposeë*" ("*The story will seem better structured to laypeople this way, for the laity might think that it was out of order,*" BnF fr. 155, fol. 115v).[24] Lay readers, he suggests, have expectations for how such a story, shaped like an epistolary romance, driven by letters and dreams and internal narratives, should proceed. To adopt Jerome's academic solution of separating the internal texts from the surrounding story would tarnish his own rapport with the reader as a reliable translator and storyteller. He explains this further in a later rubric:

> *Et si gisoit ceste letre en la Bible apres la fin du livre Hester. Mais je l'ai ci mis dedenz le livre Hester. S'en semblera a la laie gent l'istoire miex ordenee, car il peust sembler a la laie gent que je eusse mon livre et mon commans transposé. Et pour ce le mis je ci en ordre dedenz le cors du livre Hester.* (BnF fr. 155, fol. 117r)
>
> (*And in the [Vulgate] Bible, this letter fell after the end of the Book of Esther. But I put it here, inside the Book of Esther. Thus the story will seem better ordered to the laity,*

*for it might seem to the laity that I had transposed my book and my comments. And for
that reason, I put it here, in order, in the body of the Book of Esther.)*

Guyart's editorial rearrangement of the translated text – making such
simple yet compositionally necessary changes as putting a dream before
its interpretation – even claims to make Jerome's writing better: *"et en la
Bible est ainçois escrite l'exposicion du songe que li songes. Mais j'ai ci mis ançois
le songe que l'exposicion pour miex en rendre l'escripture"* (*"And in the [Vulgate]
Bible, the exposition is written before the dream. But here I have put the dream
before its exposition in order to improve its writing,"* BnF fr. 155, fol. 117v). If
Jerome compiles and translates his source texts from the point of view
of a scholar writing for scholars, Guyart compiles and translates his from
the perspective of a vernacular author writing for lay readers. Rendering
the text in a way that matches their literary expectations and tastes is
important not only for attracting readers and holding their interest, but
also for earning their trust in the translator and their faith in the content
of the text.

Seeing Is Believing

The *Historia scholastica* and, even more so, the *Bible historiale*, are satu-
rated with appeals to the reader's faith. When faced with material whose
truth is uncertain or that offends expectations of verisimilitude, in order
to demonstrate his honesty and the veracity of his translation, the translator Guyart offers tokens of proof. These corroborating proofs can be
linguistic, visual, scientific, or material. Bits of Latin source text are juxtaposed with the French for comparison, at once bolstering the translator's credibility and absolving him from responsibility, such as when an
embarrassed or perhaps sceptical Guyart transcribes Comestor's Latin
in a *glose* before translating into French Comestor's claim, concerning
Noah's Ark, that boards joined by bitumen "ne peuent estre desjoins
ne deffais par nul art ne par nulle force *glose* sine sanguine menstruoso
mulieris non potest materia bituminata dissolui *texte* sans naturel sanc
de fleurs de femmes" ("cannot be disconnected or undone by any skill
or force [gloss: bituminous material cannot be dissolved without wom-
en's menstrual blood] without natural blood from women's flowers,"
Baltimore, Walters Art Gallery, MS 125 [W 125], fol. 7v).[25] Meanwhile,
references to purportedly surviving material artefacts and present-day
phenomena reassure readers that, should they wish, they might view
for themselves the material signs of miracles and prophecies that might
explain or corroborate them, as well as monuments memorializing the
lives of biblical figures. Guyart suggests that readers can go to Armenia

to see the remains of Noah's Ark (just ask the locals to show it to you), to Rome to see Veronica's veil, or a street in Damascus named after Abraham. Actually going on pilgrimage (or biblical tourism) in search of these objects and landmarks is not necessary for their evocation to have its desired effect. Situating these material remains of biblical history in the world readers inhabit substantiates the stories and helps readers orient themselves in an immersive biblical world understood as continuous with their own.

In their manuscript context, medieval texts are not only verbal: they are visual. Visualizing and mapping biblical narrative also corroborates the truth of biblical narrative and aligns it with readers' experience and expectations. As examples in this section illustrate, the *Bible historiale* anticipates and takes advantage of its manuscript format to mediate the meaning of its text and to orient readers' engagement with it. Just as workshops in Paris and other bookmaking centres began expanding Guyart's text during his own lifetime independent of his input, they also complemented it with increasingly conventional miniature cycles depicting vivid narrative scenes: the days of Creation; the battles of the Old Testament; the Crucifixion and Resurrection; the fantastical visions of the Apocalypse.[26] Guyart had no direct involvement in how manuscript copies would illustrate his work, but he does seem to have envisioned a specific set of maps and diagrams as an integral part of his translation, and he discusses them in his *gloses* and *histoires*. His narration also draws connections between the biblical text and a repertoire of shared cultural references, experiences, and iconographical codes, such as those common to the readable cycles of Bible scenes represented in the wall paintings, statues, stained glass windows, and altarpieces of churches.[27] Guyart des Moulins, in his mediating roles as translator and priest, interjects at times to invite his readers to remember and visualize what they are used to seeing, hearing, and doing in church. He connects familiar church art (e.g., crucifixes and wall paintings of the Nativity), spaces (the layout of the church, its altar, and its symbolic objects), and rituals (the Lord's Prayer, the Eucharistic rite) to their biblical inspirations. Individual manuscripts sometimes enhance these textual descriptions by illustrating them in ways that bring attention to particular aspects of the text. In this way, the reader's memory and imagination work to bring the Bible closer to their lived experience and enhance a reading that is instructive, affective, and relevant.

As in some of the earlier examples, many of Guyart's interventions of this kind occur in his *histoires* derived, in part or in full, from Peter Comestor's *Historia scholastica.* Especially on the Pentateuch (Genesis, Exodus, Leviticus, Numbers, Deuteronomy), these *histoires* frequently explain the practical as well as the symbolic reasons for Jewish rituals, rules, and temple features. In many cases, Guyart adds his own observations to Comestor's to comment on the appropriation of Jewish symbols and practices by the contemporary Christian church. For example, after a long *histoire* on Deuteronomy enumerating the categories of people barred from entering temples, Guyart notes how the church has adapted one of these rules, namely restricting the participation of illegitimate children in religious orders: "maintenant sont ostez hors des ordres de sainte yglise bastarz de toutes manieres. Car nus bastarz ne puet recevoir ordres de sainte yglise s'il n'est legitimez du pape" ("nowadays, all kinds of bastards are barred from the orders of the Holy Church. For no bastards can receive orders from the Holy Church unless they are made legitimate by the pope," BnF fr. 155, fol. 52r).

Occasionally, such reflections present Guyart with an opportunity to criticize contemporary practices as not justified by the Bible. In the episode where Jesus chases merchants and moneylenders from the temple (Matthew 21), Guyart takes the opportunity to denounce, albeit non-committally, the sale of candles as church offerings:

> Et selon ce font bien ceulx qui ne laissent mye vendre chandelles de cire es eglises pour offrir. Mais par aventure fist Nostre Sire ceste chose par mistere, si la sueffre l'en pour ce. (London, British Library, MS Royal 19 D 3, fol. 499v [Royal 19 D 3])
>
> (And according to this, those who do not allow the sale of wax candles in churches for offerings are right. But maybe Our Lord did this as a mystery, and that's why some allow it.)

Other interventions by the translator make use of visualization, either anticipating a diagram intended to accompany the text or inviting readers to contemplate a mental image from memory. One striking example occurs in Guyart's combined Gospels, just after Luke's description of the Nativity, when the translator evokes its conventional representation on the walls of churches: "et es paintures des eglises, qui sont aussi come livre as laies gens, voit on souvent paint l'enfant Jhesum gisant en le crebe entre le buef et l'asne" ("and in the paintings of churches, which are like books for laypeople, one often sees the baby Jesus lying in the crib between the ox and the ass," Paris, Bibliothèque Mazarine, MS 532, fol. 189r).[28] Recalling Gregory the Great's defense of the pedagogical function of images for illiterate parishioners, this gloss cites the iconographical conventions of church wall paintings as a supplement to the text that is, in itself, readable "like books." Whether or not the scene is also painted in a given manuscript, Guyart can assume that his readers

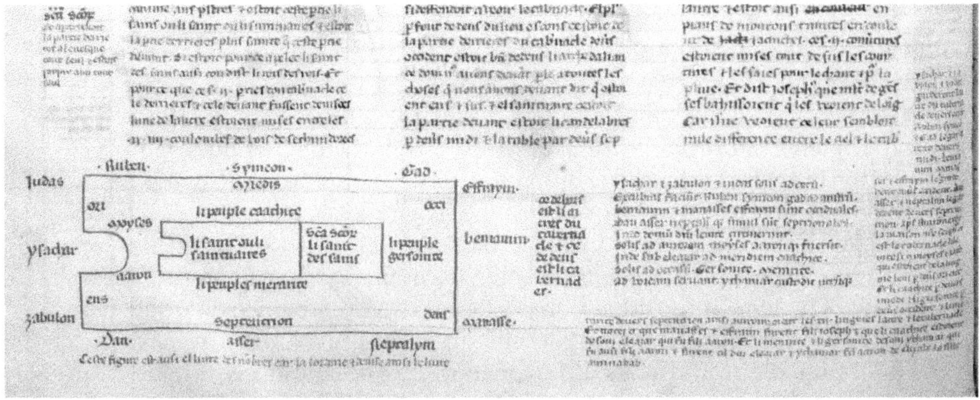

Figure 2.2 Map of the tabernacle and its accompanying explanations from Paris, Bibliothèque nationale de France, MS fr. 155, fol. 29v. Source: gallica.bnf.fr/BnF.

have seen a similar painting in their local church, cathedral, or chapel and that their mental image of the scene will resemble his enough to perform a reading of the absent image in conjunction with the text.

Finally, there are some occasions where a gloss or *histoire* makes explicit reference to a diagram or map that is intended to accompany it as a visual aid, not as extraneous decoration but as an integral part of the *Bible historiale*. The first of these, which appears in some form in most manuscripts, is a map of the tabernacle described in Numbers 2 but interpreted by Peter Comestor in his chapter on Exodus. Depending on the manuscript, the schema may appear in Exodus, Numbers, or both, usually accompanied by Latin instructions for the rubricator or illustrator, explaining how to arrange the names that appear inside it. In the form in which it appears in the oldest manuscripts (such as BnF fr. 155, dated to the first quarter of the fourteenth century), it is a simple line diagram of two concentric rectangles drawn in red ink (Figure 2.2). Its inner rectangle is divided in half, with doors on the left side of both rectangles marked "orient" to illustrate the custom of facing the tabernacle entrance towards the east. In a mix of French and Latin, the cardinal directions are written along the sides of the outer rectangle: "miedis" (south), "occidens" (west), "septentrion" (north), and the two rooms of the inner rectangle are labeled "Li saint ou li saintuaires" ("The Holy or the sanctuary") and "Sancta sanctorum, Li saint des sains" ("Holy of Holies"). Between the two rectangles – outside the sanctuary but inside the tabernacle – are the names "Moïse" and "Aaron" and the "caachite," "gersonite," and "merarite" peoples. The names of the twelve tribes of Israel appear around the outside of the outer rectangle. To the right of the map is a rubric that explains, "ce dehors est li aitres du tabernacle et ce dedens est li tabernacles" ("the area here outside is the parvis of the tabernacle, and inside is the tabernacle," BnF fr. 155, fol. 29v).[29]

The French text that accompanies the schema, a long *histoire* about Exodus translated from the *Historia scholastica*, explains the functional and symbolic reasons for the tabernacle layout as described in the text and visualized in the accompanying floor plan drawn into the manuscript. The altar is in the middle so that it can be properly guarded. The doors are positioned on the east side to let in the sunlight in the morning. Multicoloured drapes of Egyptian silk, cotton, and linen hang from columns that separate the Holy of Holies from the rest of the sanctuary to shelter it from public view. These curtains are interpreted as symbolizing the sky, which separates Earth from Heaven, and Guyart compares them to curtains hung in churches for Lent: "ausint c'on fait li dras c'on pent ores es yglises en quaresme" ("like we do with the curtains we hang now in churches during Lent," BnF fr. 155, fol. 29r.).[30] In addition to this explicit comparison to medieval Christian churches, the text and diagram share a vocabulary and a similar enough floor plan to suggest a material as well as a tropological relationship between ancient Levite practices and spaces and those of French Christian readers. In fact, some later manuscripts of the *Bible historiale* make this association more visible, transforming the red rectangles into a miniature representing a Gothic cathedral, or the Holy of Holies into a reliquary, with or without the rubric labels.[31] Reinscribing the tabernacle as a Christian church not only reinforces a link between Old and New Testaments, but also supports a dominant anti-Judaic and anti-Semitic trope of medieval Christianity that promotes Christians as the true heirs of the ancient Hebrews, on both secular and spiritual planes.

Such ideologies of Christian supremacy and exclusive Christian claims to biblical texts, objects, and territories surface frequently in the *Bible historiale* and find their most direct expression in its intertestamental book on John Hyrcanus. Translating from Peter Comestor's *Historia scholastica*, but adding emphasis to the holiness of this *translatio imperii*, Guyart writes: "Or fu li sainz regnes de Judee venus es mains d'un estrange et d'autre loi, encontre la venue Jhesucrist qui aprochoit" ("Then the holy reign of Judaea came into the hands of a foreigner, of another law, in preparation for the coming of Jesus Christ which was approaching," BnF fr. 155, fol. 136v).[32] An explanatory gloss on the same folio names Herod as the last Jewish king of Judaea and ends by further insisting that the prophecy – and perhaps also the transfer of power itself – proves Christianity right: "Et ainsi poons nous veoir et savoir apertement que li

Figure 2.3 Interpretation of the tabernacle described in Numbers 2, in a manuscript of the *Bible historiale* made in 1403–4 for Jean, Duc de Berry, in which some patriarchs wear blue fleur-de-lys robes. London, British Library, MS Harley 4381, fol. 71r. Source: http://www.bl.uk/catalogues/illuminatedmanuscripts/. © British Library Board

Juif sont deceu qui ne voelent croire la loi Jhesucrist, et nous crestiens rachaté qui le creons" ("And we can clearly see and know that the Jews who choose not to believe Jesus Christ's law are wrong, and we Christians who believe it are saved"). Among the purported Christian heirs of biblical texts, law, and lands, the French royal family saw themselves as occupying a place of honour. We can see this implied in one manuscript interpretation of the tabernacle map in a Bible made for the Duc de Berry, in which several of the patriarchs are represented wearing robes embroidered with blue fleur-de-lys (Figure 2.3).[33]

The other diagram described by Guyart des Moulins in his text, and included in almost all of the manuscripts that contain his version of the Gospels, illustrates two different forms of the cross: first in the shape of a "tau" (drawn as τ or T), and then in the shape of a patriarchal cross (✝), but with the vertical bar not extending above the top horizontal bar (Figure 2.4). Even when the drawings do not appear in the text,

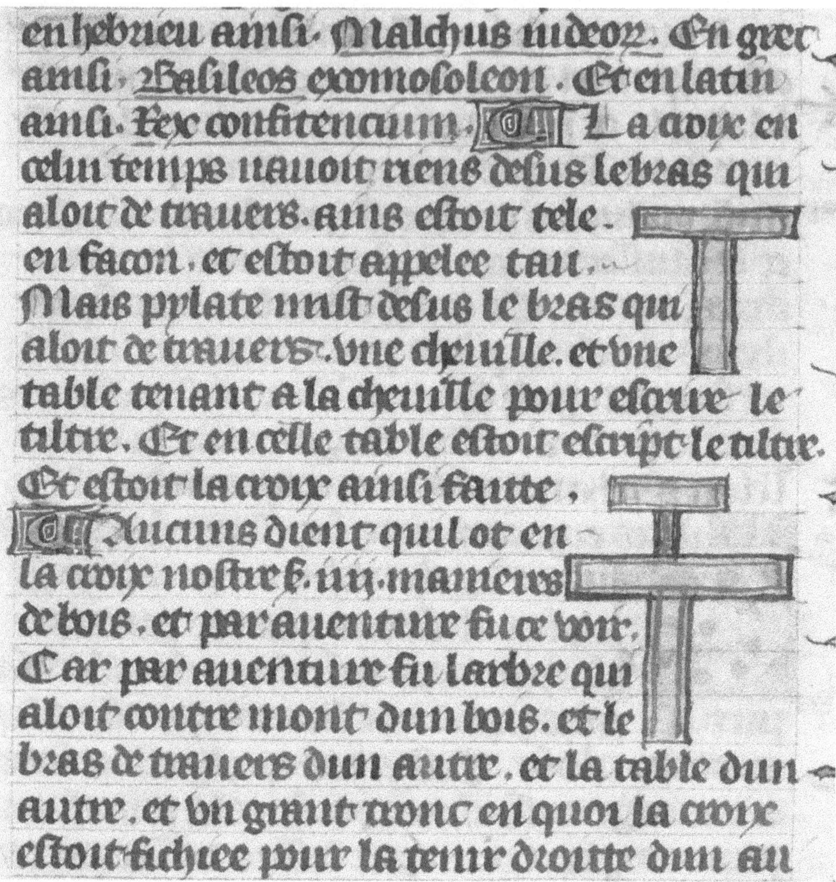

Figure 2.4 Detail of diagrams representing two forms of the cross in London, British Library, MS Royal 19 D 3, fol. 515v. Source: https://www.bl.uk /manuscripts/. © British Library Board

their presence is anticipated in the manuscript, such as in BnF fr. 155, fol. 107v, where a scribe has left two cross-shaped blank spaces inside the column of text, each one two lines of text in height. These drawings appear within the *histoire* appended to John 20 that explains the inscription on Jesus's cross and claims that Pilate updated the form of the cross previously used for crucifixions in order to add a plaque bearing the name or title of the crucified. Interrupting the story of the Crucifixion, the crosses drawn into the text slow down the narrative and invite the reader to pause, look at them, and reflect on the meaning of their form.

Guyart's narrative voice directs the reader's gaze and thoughts towards the contemplation of the details of the cross: its shape, its trilingual inscription, its history as an instrument of execution, the types of wood reportedly used to make it, and the symbolic or prophetic resonances of those trees throughout the Bible. A compassionate reading of Christ's Passion, through which one is supposed to suffer with him, is briefly suspended in order to observe and contemplate the material form of the cross that represents the focal point and climactic moment of the Christian Bible.

Reading *Bible historiale* Manuscripts with and through Literature

As we have seen, Guyart's interventions, including his reordering of biblical text, his imaginative embellishment and visualization of narrative, and his running commentary on the faith-affirming value of literary thinking, work together to align the French Bible with familiar texts, genres, and cultural references. The later *Bible historiale* manuscript tradition further reinforces a close relationship between the French Bible and other French texts. We find literary and functional texts added to complete *Bible historiale* manuscripts, such as the acrostic prayer and portrait at the end of Charles V's manuscript BnF fr. 5707 (mentioned in chapter 1) that reinforce Bible reading as a practice of piety befitting a king. Many more manuscripts add prayers, litanies, catechisms, poems, sermons, or moral treatises to full Bibles, supporting the manuscripts' use in conjunction with a systematic religious education and lifelong religious practice.

Moreover, parts of the *Bible historiale* and the *Bible du XIII*e *siècle*, with which it is frequently combined, appear in miscellanies alongside other kinds of literature including histories, romances, moral tales, and devotional poetry. These collections inflect the Bible with a variety of purposes, meanings, and approaches to reading by juxtaposing biblical texts with other kinds of literature as part of a sustained reading program. As discussed in chapter 1, King Phillip VI's crusader miscellany, Royal 19 D 1, presents the Books of Kings as a heroic epic alongside histories and romances in support of crusade. One privately owned manuscript made in the early fifteenth century situates the preface and Genesis from Guyart's *Bible historiale* alongside French and Latin saints' lives, a life of Christ, some apocryphal narratives, and the story of Griselda, suggesting a program of religious and moral education through storytelling.[34] Representing a slightly more learned program of religious reading, at least one mid-fourteenth-century manuscript (London, British Library, MS Royal 20 B 5) juxtaposes the New Testament with hymns and extracts – some in Latin, some translated into French – of a variety of religious narratives and treatises, including the Gospel of Nicodemus, treatises by Avicenna and Pseudo-Cyril, and *Barlaam and Josephat*, among others.[35] Yet another (Paris, Bibliothèque nationale de France, MS fr. 251) appends Genesis from the *Bible historiale* to the thirteenth-century *Histoire ancienne jusqu'à César*, which already tells the history of the world from the biblical Creation story to Julius Caesar's conquest of Gaul; the additions from the *Bible historiale* complete the universal history with a more detailed account of Genesis than the summary already included.[36]

Even within manuscripts primarily devoted to the Bible, rubric introductions sometimes signal how different biblical books or episodes might be read according to genre and purpose. Some rubricators introduce the Book of Job as "la vie du grant Job" ("the life of the great Job") as if it were a saint's life to be read for its moral example, and some title the war story told in 2 Maccabees 11, "Du blanc chevalier" ("On the white knight") as if it were an episode from chivalric romance. Some early print editions even describe Exodus as "la vie de Moyse et ses faitz" ("the life and deeds of Moses") as if were an epic of his heroic deeds.[37] Perhaps as a result of being assembled in the same workshops by the same scribes and artists as other popular medieval French works such as the *Roman de la Rose* and other romances, later *Bible historiale* manuscripts tend to move away from the marginally glossed format envisioned for them by Guyart. Rather, they more closely resemble other deluxe vernacular books, having two uniform columns of undifferentiated text with in-line glossing (i.e., glosses inserted into the column of text, introduced by the rubric *glose*).[38] The miniature cycles, painted by the same artists who were illustrating secular histories and romances as well as vernacular translations of classical works, visually draw the Bible into a parallel reading with those other texts through shared styles of formatting and iconography. The *Bible historiale*'s narrative and structural parallels to contemporary French literary norms are thus doubled by visual similarities imposed by the material conditions of large-scale manuscript production in Parisian manuscript workshops devoted to making deluxe copies of popular works in French.

Thus the *Bible historiale* and more secular works of French literature were connected in a two-way relationship where shared conventions of narrative and of manuscript layout facilitated readers' introduction to challenging biblical texts and highlighted connections between the Bible and other familiar stories. The Bible, paired with the scholastic programs of reading associated with it, that is, the tripartite exegesis – literal-historical, allegorical, and moral-tropological – proposed by church fathers such as Origen and Gregory the Great and elaborated by the twelfth century Augustinian scholastic theologian Hugh of Saint Victor, furnished interpretive lenses broadly applicable to all narrative.[39] Latin as well as vernacular commentators, authors, and translators applied biblical tropes and interpretive practices not only to canonical and non-canonical Hebrew and Christian texts, but also to the narratives of other religious and cultural traditions, histories, crusading propaganda, and even secular works of fiction. As the opening lines of the early fourteenth-century *Ovide moralisé* put it, everything written could be instructive with the application of a Christianizing interpretive key.[40] Translated across languages, cultures, and religions, everything from Greco-Roman myths to the Life of the Buddha (as in *Barlaam and Josaphat*) could be appropriated in translation for medieval Christian audiences, made to bear the fruits of Christian lessons through assimilation with biblical history and allegory.[41]

The *Bible historiale,* via Peter Comestor's *Historia scholastica,* already participates in such an assimilative, universalizing program as it applies historical gloss to situate biblical Hebrew and early Christian history in relation to ancient and classical African, Greek, and Roman histories and euhemerized myths (that is, with their deities reduced to mere humans). It hypothesizes intersecting origin stories, timelines, and genealogies, suggesting for example that Prometheus was an inventor and educator who lived in Isaac's time and that Hercules married a granddaughter of Abraham and his second wife Keturah after helping the girl's father establish tabernacles in Libya.[42] It also rewrites classical tales to replace their heroes with biblical characters: the legend of how Pythagoras invented music becomes how one of Cain's descendants, Tubal-Cain, invented music, and the legend of Oedipus growing up to inadvertently kill his father and marry his mother in fulfilment of a prophecy is repurposed as an episode in Judas Iscariot's life.[43] These practices of reading the Bible in parallel with other textual traditions and of harmonizing or appropriating texts of non-biblical origin under a Christianizing interpretive framework were not limited to ancient sources. In time, this trend would also extend to later medieval works of predominantly secular fiction or pseudo-myth composed in French. These could accrue Christian allegorizing or moralizing glosses as part of their original composition (as in Christine de Pizan's *Epistre Othéa*) to elevate basic stories to a more authoritative register and inscribe them in larger ethical frameworks. Alternatively, a later translator or editor could use glosses to rehabilitate or recontextualize a work, such as the "moralized" (i.e., expanded with moral glosses) versions of the *Roman de la Rose.* These moralized versions sought to steer readers away from a too-literal, unironic reading of Jean de Meun's text – controversial for its expressions of misogyny, anticlericalism, and licentiousness, all couched in disorienting layers of satire – that could yield lessons at odds with church-sanctioned beliefs, values, and acceptable behaviour. As exegetes had done for centuries with some disconcerting material from the Bible, such as the eroticism of the Song of Songs and the anger and defiance expressed by Job (to be discussed in chapter 4), applying allegory and moral typology allowed for readings that at least nominally extracted beneficial lessons from literature in spite of objectionable content. While these glossed works of French literature were mostly composed later than the *Bible historiale*, and there is no clear evidence of direct influence, the content and structure of their glossing programs reflect a shared interest in applying biblical, scholastic-inspired hermeneutic frameworks to all kinds of textual traditions.

Just as medieval methods of biblical exegesis and glossing influenced late medieval approaches to reading secular vernacular literature, medieval poetics also influenced the tastes, expectations, and reading habits that its target readers would apply to a Bible translated for them. For medieval experts on reading as well as for vernacular translators such as Guyart, the aesthetic pleasure of reading the Bible was considered secondary to its religious importance, but not in conflict with it. Hugh of Saint Victor shows some disdain for the reader who would treat the Bible as mere entertainment, "turning the divine announcements into tales"; he nevertheless affirms the seductive art of its composition, whose enjoyment is barren only when divorced from the pursuit of higher knowledge about God.[44] Medieval theologians such as Thomas Aquinas also helped pave the way for reading the Bible with sensitivity to its literary qualities by studying its language as the product of human art, which mediated the biblical authors' experience of the divine through the same kinds of figurative language, imagery, and stylistic flourishes used in secular poetry and narrative prose.[45] The relative flexibility of vernacular expression compared to that of Latin, the multiplicity of options in translation, and the less-formal, lower-stakes contexts in which lay readers would read a vernacular Bible (for personal education rather than to lead Mass or to engage in theological debate) all afforded translators some licence to apply their own artistic techniques in translation to produce desired effects. In packaging biblical knowledge for a vernacular, predominantly lay audience, a translator such as Guyart could freely embellish upon the sparse narrative style of the Pentateuch or rearrange parts of the biblical text to conform to the imagined reader's expectations, literary reading habits, and aesthetic tastes, provided that he truthfully represents his process and the relationship between the target and source texts. Later scribes and artists could expand and comment upon the version handed down to them as well, all without breaching the injunction of

Deuteronomy 4:2: "You shall not add to the word that I speak to you, neither shall you take away from it."

Narrative, iconographic, and manuscript-making conventions are not the only ways in which the *Bible historiale* works in dialogue with a larger corpus of French medieval literature. As the next chapter demonstrates, it also engages with fiction: specifically, a collection of stories that survives in only one known manuscript copy of the *Bible historiale* stands out for its careful renegotiation of what it means to read biblical "truth" through other kinds of narrative frameworks, especially those best described as fiction. The material in question includes a set of apocryphal legends that Guyart acknowledges may not be true, and yet he justifies their inclusion in a Bible translation that he defends as true or, more precisely, as adding "nothing but pure truth" to the authoritative Latin Vulgate Bible. In the next chapter, I examine how these fictionalized Bible-inspired stories leverage the imaginative habits of fiction in the service of faith, according to Guyart's stated principles of how truth operates in translation.

3 Soothing Listeners' Ears: Narrative Aesthetics and Poetic Faith

Alfred, Lord Tennyson, *In Memoriam*, Canto 36

Medieval Christian literature is full of narratives based on biblical characters and events. These stories, which circulated in Latin as well as in vernacular languages, adapted and expanded upon biblical episodes, characters, and motifs, recast in popular genres of the time, to speak to the aesthetics and politics, biases and values, anxieties and debates of their own cultural moment, in much the same way as modern films based on the Bible do.[1] These stories take a variety of forms, from theatrical dramatizations of biblical stories to localized versions of biblical apocrypha to a wide variety of overtly fictional narratives that infuse pagan or secular stories with Christian tropes, plot devices, archetypes, and lessons. While Guyart's work is, in large part, a translation of the Bible in the strict sense, it also engages in both "text-oriented" and "plot-oriented" modes of biblical "retelling," as defined by Tamás Visi.[2] As seen in the previous chapter, Guyart utilizes storytelling, often based on the *Historia scholastica*, to visualize and reconstruct biblical events, draw connections between them, fill in missing details, and resolve apparent contradictions, all with close attention to the language and structure of the Bible itself.[3] At the same time, he translates into his Bible some New Testament apocrypha, stories that reimagine biblical characters and plotlines to construct new meanings, establish new hermeneutic intertextual relationships between Old and New Testaments, and inflect the stories with new ideological subtexts. Notably, he acknowledges that these latter are not part of the canonical Bible and probably not true, but that readers may believe them if they so choose.

Specifically, Guyart des Moulins follows his Book of Acts with a set of biblically inspired apocryphal stories, extracted and compiled from several medieval Latin sources including Holy Rood legends and Jacobus de Voragine's *Legenda aurea* or *Golden Legend*. He introduces the tales as "apocryphal," which he explains in terms of the stories' inauthenticity, their uncertain truth value, and their position outside of the accepted biblical canon. Paradoxically, however, he adds that there is no harm in believing them, and he defends their inclusion as good, pleasing, useful stories. These qualities he attributes to the stories imply their multiple narrative purposes and intended effects. The stories and their discursive framing draw upon norms of preaching as well as those of vernacular literary fiction to offer memorable, easy to understand moral and theological lessons in pleasing form. They bring to life characters and events on the margins of the Bible with the aim of imposing narrative continuity on the canonical Bible around the Crucifixion, reinforcing its lessons for Christians, and recasting its meaning through the lens of contemporary crusading ideology.[4] Their narration engages readers' active co-creation of meaning by putting the imaginative habits of fiction in the service of faith. Emphasizing the tension between "truth" and "belief," Guyart coaxes readers' will to believe through the poetico-rhetorical principle of verisimilitude. All the while, Guyart's first-person interventions insist upon the boundaries of canonicity and biblical authority.

This chapter explores how Guyart's understanding of the relationship between "Bible" and "apocrypha" and between "truth" and (what we would today call) "fiction" inform his use of the stories and his advice to readers concerning how to approach them. First, I introduce the apocryphal narratives, their manuscript context, and their relationship to source texts and traditions. Then I interrogate the stated and implied purpose of their presence in the *Bible historiale* as understood both through Guyart's own words and in relation to broader medieval discourses about the value, uses, and risks of apocrypha. Based on Guyart's caveats to his readers as well as on analysis of literary narrative techniques in the apocryphal stories themselves, I show how their fictionalization of biblical narrative implicates the reader in an active dynamic of scepticism and wilful belief.

The fantastical narratives at the end of Guyart's *Bible historiale*, which recount the millennia-long journey of the wood of the True Cross and the lives of Julian the Apostate, the Evil Pilate, and the Very Evil Judas, mark an apparent departure from Guyart's stated purpose to add nothing "but pure truth" ("*fors pure verité*") to the Bible and its authoritative historical interpretation. In a Bible translation as invested as Guyart's is in proving and defending its truthfulness, the translator's statements demand a re-evaluation of how these extracanonical and more or less explicitly fictional tales relate to the putative biblical truth that defines the *Bible historiale* as a whole.

The *Histoires apocrifes* in Their Manuscript Context

Although mentioned in several manuscripts, the set of apocryphal legends attributed to Guyart des Moulins appears in full in only one copy of the *Bible historiale,* and the particularities of that manuscript raise some questions about the stories' authorship and original context.[5] Meant to follow the Book of Acts, they would have fallen at the very end of Guyart's translation, which did not include the Epistles or Apocalypse. Whether by accident or based on a scribe's conscious decision to omit the spurious tales (despite, in some cases, listing them in the table of contents), their absence from an early source manuscript affected most lines of transmission. The surviving manuscript that includes them is Royal 19 D 3, completed in 1411 and signed by the scribe Thomas du Val. The fact that other manuscripts retain at least references to the apocryphal legends in their tables of contents or in cross references found in glosses, including some of the earliest copies such as BnF fr. 155 (ca. 1310–15), suggests their inclusion in some earlier, now lost, copies and Guyart as their most likely author.[6] Even if we accept Guyart as the original translator and compiler of this material, however, some difficulties remain in terms of separating his words from those of Thomas du Val, a scribe whose editorial interventions refashion Guyart's work in other significant ways.[7] In comparison to the way the stories are ordered in the tables of contents in other manuscripts, Thomas's version in Royal 19 D 3 does transpose the stories of Judas and Pilate, and we cannot rule out the possibility that this scribe may have made additional changes or even inserted text or rubrics not attributable to Guyart.[8]

The five legends occupy six and a half folios (fols. 552v–558v) in Royal 19 D 3, nestled between the end of (Guyart's) Acts and the Pauline Epistles (from the *Bible du XIIIe siècle*). A page heading in the upper margin labels them "Hystoires apocrifes." Unlike each canonical book of the Bible in this manuscript, they do not begin with a table of contents, nor are they illustrated with miniatures, but their two-column text format is otherwise visually indistinguishable from any other part of this copy. Each story is introduced by a rubric, with a few glosses incorporated into the text block, bracketed by a rubricated pair "*glose ... texte.*" Latin citations are set apart by underlining. The rubric titles of the five stories, in order, are:

1. *La vie Julian l'Apostat, le mauvais empereur, renyé chrestian, et comment le signe de la croix a grant vertu* (fols. 552v–553r);
2. *Comment Adam envoya Seth son filz en paradys terrestre a l'ange* (fols. 553r–555r);
3. *Une autre oppinion de la vraie croix que je trouvai en autres anciens livres* (fol. 555r);
4. *la vie du mauvais Pylate qui crucifia Nostre Sire Jhesucrist* (fols. 555r–558r); and
5. *la vie du tres mauvais Judas qui trahi Nostre Sire Jhesucrist* (fols. 558r–558v).[9]

The stories fall into two groups according to their genres, content, and sources: lives of unsaintly characters and the metonymic "life" of the True Cross. Both types of stories share a common thread, however, as signaled by the references to the sign of the cross in the first title and the Crucifixion in that of the Life of Pilate. Together, the five stories centre the Crucifixion as the climactic, unifying moment of the Bible and the True Cross as its instrument, symbol, and relic. The two True Cross or Holy Rood legends (numbers 2 and 3) retell all of biblical history through the travels of the wood that would become the Cross of the Crucifixion, emphasizing through its miracles the uninterrupted presence of Christ in the world from its very beginning. Where the Bible establishes symbolic and prophetic resonances between the Tree of Life, the "tree" upon which Christ died (cf. Acts 5:30, 10:39, and 13:29), and Christ himself, the apocryphal stories transfer that symbolism to a material and historical continuity, using imaginative narrative to confirm a spiritual reality.[10] Similarly, the lives of Julian, Pilate, and Judas reassert the unity of holy signifier (cross) and signified (Christ), as they demonstrate the life-giving power Christ confers not only to the True Cross, but also to the crucifixes and gestures with which the faithful perform the sign of the cross for protection, and conversely, the defeat and death of those who reject the cross in all its forms. In their tales of anti-Christian villains, the apocryphal "lives" also offer an antithetical postscript to the martyrology of the Acts of the Apostles.

"Anti-Saints' Lives": Julian the Apostate, the Evil Pilate, and the Very Evil Judas

Three stories in the series (numbers 1, 4, and 5: the Lives of Julian the Apostate, Pontius Pilate, and Judas) are best described as "anti-saints' lives," in that they share common tropes and plot patterns with many saints' lives, but with the opposite aim: to offer moral counterexamples. Rather than showing extraordinary selflessness or courage to devote themselves to Christ or to good works in his name, the main characters' unchecked greed, cowardice, and malice lead them to reject Christianity and to harm those who stand in the way of their corrupt ambitions. Each villain's story arc reverses the common Christian tale of fall, redemption through penitence, and ultimate reward, as seen in the lives of many saints and in medieval schemas of salvation history. Instead, they tell of a rise to power followed by an accelerating descent into depravity, for which the wicked protagonists are punished in the end. Guyart's main direct source for the three "lives" is Jacobus de Voragine's *Legenda aurea* or *Golden Legend*, composed in the 1260s, no more than about thirty years before Guyart translated extracts from them in the 1290s. The *Golden Legend*, in turn, draws from earlier Latin versions of the stories or elements thereof.[11] The *Golden Legend*, however, is focused on saints, not inveterate sinners; its scattered references to the latter appear, rather, in chapters about Christ, his apostles, and saints so as to throw their martyrdom and their moral examples into greater relief. Guyart's interest – or his expectation of his readers' interest – in these villains entails some editorial intervention to make them the anti-heroic protagonists of their own stories. To tell the story of Julian the Apostate, he cobbles together extracts of the *Golden Legend*'s chapters on Saint Julian (30) and the Invention of the Cross (68), and his biographies of Pilate and Judas are culled mainly from its chapters on Saint Matthias (45), the Passion (53), and Saint James the Lesser (67). He also consults other written and possibly oral sources to furnish additional details and offer alternative versions of events.

The Life of Julian the Apostate begins with Helena's discovery of the True Cross. A prophecy foretells the death of Judas Quiriacus, a witness and participant in the discovery, at the hands of Julian the Apostate, thus setting up a contrast between the miraculous discovery of the True Cross and Julian's rejection of what it stands for and his violence against its followers. The tale then launches into a series of episodes encapsulating Julian the Apostate's descent into iniquity as he progresses from a corrupt but still Christian monk to a student of sorcery to a cruel emperor bent on destroying crucifixes and persecuting Christians. Guyart's version departs from the *Legenda aurea* by having Emperor Julian brought down by the same Quiriacus, who temporarily rises from the grave, in imitation of Christ, to put an end to Julian's reign. At the end of Julian's story in the *Bible historiale* is the story of Cyprian, whose life is presented as a mirror image of Julian's, beginning in depravity and ending in Cyprian's conversion. Cyprian attempts to seduce (or coerce) Saint Justine with the help of demons, which she overcomes by crossing herself. Cyprian, impressed, repents and converts to Christianity.[12] The moral of the paired lives is laid out in the rubric title introducing the story, "*comment le signe de la croix a grant vertu*" or "how the sign of the cross has great power," namely as an agent of divine justice: after rejecting the cross, the Apostate and Cyprian are foiled by it; in Cyprian's case, it motivates his conversion and rehabilitation as he recognizes a power greater than his own.

As with Julian and Cyprian, the lives of Judas and Pilate parallel one another, each conforming to a similar narrative formula. The titles of the stories reinforce this parallelism with the epithet *mauvais* attached to each man's name, signalling their essentially evil nature, particularly with reference to their misdeeds against Christ.[13] The plot similarities are striking. Their births are both presaged with signs of their infamy, and their unnatural childhoods marked by frightened parents, fratricides, and patricides. Their cowardly, self-interested, and treacherous adult lives end by their own hands, imagined not just once but in multiple grisly, shameful ways. Their lives even fatefully intersect when, in the Life of Judas, Judas takes up employment under Pilate, at which point the narrator highlights their affinity for one another based on their shared depravity:

> et puis s'en fouit en Jherusalem et se mist a servir en la court Pylate qui lors estoit prevost de Judee. Et servi si bien de mauvaistié comme celui qui estoit mauvais aussicomme Pylate que Pylate l'aima ma [sic] moult et le fist souverain de son hostel. (fol. 558v)
>
> (And then he fled to Jerusalem, where he entered the service of Pilate, Procurator of Judaea, as part of his court. And he served Pilate so well in his depravity – as he was just as evil as Pilate – that Pilate liked him a lot and put him in charge of his household.)

As portrayed in these accounts, the three *mauvais*, all instruments either in Christ's death (Judas and Pilate) or in the death of Christians (Julian), embody the antithesis of the saints and prophets in the *Legenda aurea* who make their lives mirror Christ's. As exaggerated types of evil treachery, their stories resemble not only one another, but also those of other figures known for their acts of betrayal. Echoing Cain's fratricide, both Judas and Pilate kill their brothers out of jealousy and spite. The same feelings later drive the young Pilate to murder one of his rivals in Julius Caesar's court; the rival happens to be the son of the King of France, setting up the French monarchy in parallel to Christ as the righteous and undeserving target of Pilate's ego-driven persecution. Similarly, in a Christian retelling of Sophocles's *Oedipus Rex*, Judas unknowingly kills his father and marries his mother in fulfilment of a prophecy, and it is the revelation of this fact that causes him to repent and become a disciple of Jesus. The stories are, in part, compelling for their moral exempla by negative example (as Brandon Hawk has argued), as well as for their examination of the psychology of evil, as case studies animating a debate about free will and the role of one's life events and childhood environment in shaping moral character and behaviour (as Gary Lim has argued).[14] Perhaps more importantly for Guyart, however, the three "lives" counter the almost interchangeably evil protagonists' rejection of Christ with examples of the power his signs and relics confer to those who place their faith in them. Christ himself is mostly absent from the stories, at least in the flesh; in his absence, his signs and objects serve as catalysts for conversion and justice. Just as Justine's sign of the cross protects her and converts Cyprian, Veronica's veil converts the emperor Vespasian in Pilate's story, and when Pilate puts on Christ's tunic in an effort to protect himself, he quickly loses that protection when the newly converted Vespasian simply takes the tunic from him.[15] This thread in the stories connects them with the True Cross legends placed alongside them.

From Sign to Relic: True(ish) Stories of the True Cross

The second and third apocryphal texts in Royal 19 D 3 offer fantastical origin stories for the wood used to make the Cross of the Crucifixion. They translate relatively well-known versions of the stories that circulated in Latin and, later, numerous vernacular translations, with episodes drawn from very early Hebrew pseudepigrapha and Christian apocrypha like Enoch, *The Apocalypse of Moses*, and the *Vita Adae et Evae*.[16] Guyart's main sources are two Latin texts that Wilhelm Meyer has edited in his collection of cross legends: the first ("*Comment Adam ...* ") translates what Meyer calls the *Legende* (VI), and the second ("*Une autre opinion ...* ") is based on what Meyer calls the *Historia* (I), alternately titled "de ligno crucis."[17] While Jacobus de Voragine's *Golden Legend* also includes a brief collection of such stories in chapter 68 (part of which Guyart uses to introduce the Life of Julian the Apostate), Guyart does not include those, preferring the other two versions except to take inspiration from Jacobus's way of signalling distinctions between biblical and apocryphal elements of the story (a point to which I return later in this chapter).[18] Holy Rood legends of this sort, often connected in some way with the Helena legend, grew in number and popularity during the Crusades, especially after Saint Louis's acquisition of a True Cross relic and his construction of the Sainte Chapelle (consecrated in 1248) to house it. Elements of these stories found their way into histories, romances, and miscellanies, from the *Estoire d'Eracles* to Grail legends to vernacular Bibles, all motivated at least in part by an ideological nostalgia for crusade that persisted long after the fall of Acre in 1291 – an event that Guyart laments as an apocalyptic failure for Christians of his time.[19]

Like the lives of Judas, Pilate, and especially Julian the Apostate, the True Cross legends emphasize the power of the cross as sign and avatar of Christ. They invest the wood that would furnish the material for Christ's cross with supernatural power long before it fulfils its destiny at the Crucifixion. The first of the two stories, whose Latin source dates to between 1260 and 1295, traces the wood's origin all the way to Adam, who sends his son Seth to Eden in search of the Oil of Mercy, instructing him that to enter, he must sign himself "du signe tau. C'est tel signe: .T." ("with the sign *tau*. Like this: T," fol. 553v).[20] An angel appears to Seth and shows him three scenes, culminating with a vision of the Christ child who will be the Oil of Mercy, then gives him three seeds to plant in Adam's mouth when he dies in three days. The three saplings that spring forth merge into one tree, and over several thousand years, the intertwined trees become Moses's rods; the inspiration for several of David's psalms; a bench in Solomon's Temple; the secret to the healing powers of the pond known as the *probatica piscina* or Pool of Bethesda, described in John 5; and a footbridge. The trees and their wood perform miracles and work as a medium of prophecy for the men and women who recognize their holy purpose.

The second True Cross legend that Guyart translates ("*Une autre oppinion de la vraie croix*"), whose Latin source Meyer dates to about 1050, is a much shorter account of a single prophecy of the same type. In it, David finds a tree with three kinds of leaves and worships it, and Solomon, in keeping with his father's reverence for it, has it gilded. It is the Queen of Sheba who reveals to him that on this tree will hang a man who will bring down the Jewish people.[21] Upset, Solomon throws it into the same *probatica piscina* mentioned in John 5 and in the previous story, which dries up at the right moment to offer up the wood for the Crucifixion.

Revealing to Old Testament figures from Adam to the Queen of Sheba at once the nature of the Trinity (by the three kinds of tree that grew together to make it) and its own holy destiny, the wood becomes in these stories a sign embodied. Linking Old and New Testaments and all of salvation history on a "worldly," literal-historical plane as well as a spiritual one, the myths come together as a stylized, fictionalized summary of the entire Bible, imposing on it a unified narrative direction, pointing towards Christ. At the same time, the stories' focus on the power of the relic and their hostile representation of Jews as enemies of Christ promote a crusading ideology invested in defending Latin Christians' claims to rightfully possess biblical texts, objects, and territories. While the 1204 sack of Constantinople during the Fourth Crusade was swiftly met with criticism for its questionable motivations and excessive violence against fellow Christians, the relics acquired (by pillage or purchase) as a result of the conquest were widely celebrated. The popularity of legends about fictional Passion relics in the decades following French King Louis IX's acquisition of purported True Cross and Crown of Thorns relics in 1238 might owe something to a phenomenon Beth C. Spacey observes in crusading narratives. In the aftermath of the controversial Fourth Crusade, Spacey argues, stories about the relics sought to authenticate the relics and justify the crusaders' actions by demonstrating (through the signs and miracles of relics) that God was ultimately on the side of the Latin crusaders.[22] In a similar way, the *Bible historiale's* "lives" of the True Cross offer a vindicating narrative for French Christians, even – or especially – after the crusaders' recent (as of Guyart's translation) defeat and expulsion from the Kingdom of Jerusalem.

The two accounts of the True Cross end Guyart's Bible with condensed, fanciful tableaux of biblical history, reinforcing its narrative continuity from the Old Testament through the New on both historical and prophetic-allegorical planes.[23] Together with some elements of the "anti-saints' lives," they translate abstract moral and allegorical interpretations of the Crucifixion into concrete, material relics and miracles intended to validate Christian faith in general as well as the particular claims to biblical texts and lands made by persistent crusading ideologies (which translator Guyart des Moulins, by and large, embraces). In that sense, the stories purport to convey a general truth about the Bible, while at the same time offending other standards of biblical truth: their historical veracity (whether they "really happened") is questionable at best, and they do not belong to the "true" (authentic, authoritative, canonical) Bible.

Truth in Translation

Guyart's caveats introducing the stories exhibit some ambivalence about their place in a Bible translation that, above all, lays claim to truth. A rubric introducing the second of the legends in Royal 19 D 3 emphasizes that the stories that follow are "apocrifes," which he adds, means that "l'en ne sceit pas se elles sont vraies ou non" ("it is not known whether they are true or not," Royal 19 D 3, fol. 553r).[24] The uncertain truth of these stories contrasts with his statement, in his prologue, that he has added "nothing but pure truth" ("fors pure verité") and seems at first glance to diverge from his approach to constructing his authority as a translator whose "truthfulness" resides in the weight of his testimony as a trusted priest and reliable teacher of the text. As Xavier-Laurent Salvador puts it in his *Vérité et écriture(s)*:

> Le premier postulat fondamental sur lequel repose cet ouvrage est donc que la traduction "dit vrai," ou plutôt, que le traducteur "veut dire vrai" ou, plus exactement, que le traducteur "*veut* que son lecteur *sache* qu'il dit vrai" et c'est là l'objet de son action argumentative. Le projet d'écriture du traducteur français doit donc être l'écriture d'un *ouvrage didactique* où il consigne les recueils d'une science donnée et qui les consigne avec fidélité.[25]
>
> (The first fundamental postulate on which my argument rests is therefore that translation "tells the truth," or rather, that the translator "means to tell the truth" or, to be more precise, that the translator "*wants* his reader *to know* that he is telling the truth," and that that is the goal of his argumentative action. The French translator's writing project must therefore be the writing of a *didactic work* that records a collected body of knowledge and records it with fidelity.)

If Salvador asks what it means for the medieval Bible translator to "tell the truth," we might equally ask what it means for that same translator to tell stories marked as "not true" or only "potentially true"; how he justifies their telling even while acknowledging that uncertain truth; and how their inclusion affects the translator's reliable, authoritative, "truth-telling" voice. To better understand the role of the apocrypha in the *Bible historiale* in light of Guyart's project, it is helpful to, first, take a closer look at his definition of "truth" as a standard of translation and then to contextualize the language he uses to categorize the stories and to instruct his readers about how to read them productively.

Guyart's repeated use of *vrai* (true, real, authentic) and *verité* (truth, truthfulness) to describe his own work participates in a pre-existing discourse concerned with the preservation of truth in Bible translation and transmission. In or near 1266, Roger Bacon complained of the increasing unreliability of the Latin text of the Paris Bible due to errors accrued through repeated copying by scribes and correctors who, he claimed, were "non scientes de veritate textus sacri," or "ignorant about the truth of the sacred text."[26] For Bacon, the "veritas" or "truth" that is vulnerable to the accidents of manuscript transmission is not the absolute truth content of the Bible (as opposed to lies or fictions) but rather the reliability and authenticity of a text whose transmission depended on the human mediation of scribes, any one of whom may misread a word, skip a line, or introduce new ambiguities.

It is in such a climate of doubt about losses in transmission that proving "truth" – in terms very similar to Bacon's – surfaces as a visible, explicit preoccupation of the *Bible historiale*. Compared to the scribal reproduction of Latin Bible manuscripts, vernacular translations such as Guyart's involved an additional layer of active mediation that depended not only on the translator's accurate understanding of the source text, but also on the translator's own agency in choosing how to communicate it in the target language. Medieval vernacular translators held an important responsibility as gatekeepers of Latin learning both for their immediate Latin-illiterate readers and for the broader, second-degree vernacular reception of the translated text and its interpretation. In promising a truthful translation, Guyart's prologue and other interventions justifying his choices as editor and translator therefore simultaneously address two audiences whose trust he must earn: fellow clergy who can verify the accuracy of his translation and lay reading audiences who, for the most part, cannot.

It is in this intellectual context that we must interpret both Guyart's statements about the truthfulness of his translation and his caveats about the contested "truth" of the apocryphal stories. Set against our translator's copious use of the words *vrai* and *verité* to defend the reliability of his translation vis-à-vis his Latin sources, is Guyart's use of the same terminology to classify (in negative terms) those stories whose authenticity and referential truth he explicitly questions. This apparent exception to the translator's emphasis on the truthfulness of his translation marks a conscious and purposeful exercise of the translator's agency if we understand Guyart's "truth" as a multivalent term encompassing a hierarchical set of principles governing his translation choices. After all, Guyart has not claimed to have added nothing at all to the words of the Bible and Comestor's commentary, but to have added nothing "*fors pure verité*" – *but pure truth.* In other words, he *has* added something: truth. We might even go so far as to say that truth in this translation resides precisely in what is added, insofar as the Latin Bible requires the translator's mediation and compensation to make the Bible intelligible, accessible, and believable for a medieval lay audience reading it in French. Following his own stated criteria, the "truthful" translator is one who does not stray from the truth ("*de la verité ne sui je de riens issuz*"); he may augment the text, but only in ways that are consistent with that truth ("*je n'i ai riens mis ne ajousté fors pure verité*"). The truth in question is to be found in the Latin of the source texts ("*verité si com je l'ai trouvé el latin*"). Qualified clerics may verify that truth by way of comparison (*"et qui les voudroit regarder on y pourroit certainement prouver la pure verité de toutes ces translacions"*) and are invited to correct any errors they may find.[27]

Taken together as a promise to not falsify the text, we may infer from Guyart's statements in the prologue and throughout his translation at least three conditions for "truth" in translation.[28] First is the degree to which the content of a passage or narrated event is understood to represent a phenomenal, historical reality, as witnessed by the Bible or authenticated by another trusted authority. An important corollary of this standard of truth is canonical authority or authenticity; the "true" Bible approved by the church as opposed to its implied "counterfeits" (such as apocrypha) whose marginal, inauthentic status opened them to scrutiny. It is in both of these senses, historical accuracy and canonical authenticity, that Guyart acknowledges that the stories of the True Cross and the lives of Judas and Pilate may not be entirely true; church authorities did not accept them as part of the canonical Bible, and even their immediate Latin sources expressed doubts about whether many of the episodes they recounted really happened. If the apocryphal legends are of dubious historical accuracy and excluded from the biblical canon and its exegetical traditions as inauthentic, then their inclusion in a new, vernacular French Bible canon must be justified by other, compensatory measures of *verité*.

On a second, extradiegetic level, Guyart's *verité* includes the translator's honesty, as it were, or the requirement that he "tell the truth" to his readers. This truthfulness includes, first of all, the accurate rendering of Latin semantic units into the target language, and second, transparency as to the translator's choices and actions upon the text. Guyart performs this standard of truthfulness by signalling his additions, omissions, and modifications to the text. He distinguishes between what is from the Bible and what is from other sources; how reliable those other sources are; which interpretations provided are credible and which are not; what should be believed literally and historically, allegorically or figuratively, conditionally, or not at all. The mention of a false belief or spurious legend acknowledged as such does not negate the truthfulness of the whole because the reader has been provided with the necessary information to reject it or to suspend their judgment. This applies to pagan, idolatrous, or heretical beliefs mentioned and dispelled in the *histoires* of the Old Testament as well as to the apocryphal legends that Guyart labels as non-biblical and unverified, presented for enjoyment rather than as authoritative doctrine.[29]

Third, we might posit an overarching truthfulness of purpose. This truth is a moral and aesthetic principle of composition governed by a desire to instruct laypeople in biblical history while also providing what Janet Coleman has identified as a mainstay of late scholastic ideals of historical veracity, namely "an intelligible, imageable coherence of edifying and exemplary behaviour."[30] The "true" translation's main purpose is to reproduce "truth" in the minds of its readers, bringing their beliefs and actions into consonance with accepted church teachings. As a corollary to this goal of doctrinal truth, orthodox interpretation of biblical narrative shaped and constituted the reality of biblical events as they were integrated into the reader's knowledge and set of beliefs. In other words, some passages of the Bible, such as the figurative language of biblical poetry, proverbs, prophetic visions, and parables, might only express truth through exegesis.[31] And yet, their figurative and even fictional language promised access to truths. It was evidently important, in Guyart's view, that the layperson's Bible should capture the imagination with good and credible stories capable of transforming its readers, remaking them in the image of the Text.

In sum, the words *vrai* and *verité*, as they appear in the *Bible historiale*, may evoke any or all of these criteria. Anticipated doubt and tensions between conflicting criteria for truth press the mediative *je* of the translator figure to the surface of the text to confront them. Not all that is reported in the Bible or the *Historia scholastica* is consistent with the French translation's overall project, and thus is not translated "as is." Some biblical narratives, such as the morally dubious actions of Lot and other Hebrew patriarchs, only become "true" in every sense with the help of the commentator's discretionary censure or rationalization. Conversely, unverified narrative, even fiction, has a place in biblical history so long as its status and purpose are clearly defined. The value of Christian apocrypha or fictions was not unanimously agreed upon among medieval clergy and scholars, nor among copyists of the *Bible historiale*. Both Guyart's apparent (if ambivalent) endorsement of their aesthetic and moral didactic value for lay audiences and some later scribes' apparent rejection of the material as not meriting inclusion in a self-proclaimed Bible find support in medieval discourse on the subject.

Apocryphal Scriptures: Lies, Potential Truths, or Useful Fictions?

Rubrics and page headings in Royal 19 D 3 refer to the narratives, somewhat paradoxically, as *histoires apocrifes* (apocryphal histories or stories) and as *escriptures apocrifes* (apocryphal scriptures or writings). In both of these genre designations, the dominant meanings of the nouns – *histoires, escriptures* – identify the narratives as belonging to the same general categories as the rest of the *Bible historiale*: history and scripture, categories of narrative that most often connote truth. The appended adjective, *apocrife(s)*, along with its definition in the rubric ("*l'en ne sceit pas se elles sont vraies ou non*"), calls that truth status and authority into question. Guyart's apparently simple definition of "*apocrifes*" as denoting material of uncertain truth or authenticity belies a more complex subtext about the accrued connotations of the concepts "apocryphal" and "*vrai*" (true, real, authentic) in the history of discourse about the Bible and its associated extracanonical literature. In sum, the oxymoronic formulae *histoires apocrifes* and *escriptures apocrifes* define the stories by the tension they generate between "true" history and its counterfeit. Ultimately, however, Guyart defends the inclusion of the stories as an integral part of his Bible translation, and both the terms of his endorsement and certain features of the stories themselves valorize fiction in the service of "true" faith.

In a biblical context, apocrypha are texts or traditions based on biblical characters and events but excluded from one or more biblical canons.[32] From the Greek word for "hidden," the word did not always connote "untrue," "fictive," or even "inauthentic." In his history of the term and its applications, Péter Tóth traces the steps by which the term obtains these connotations. At first, "apocrypha" referred to an obscure, esoteric, or arcane corpus of oral or written religious texts, ideas, or "mysteries" intended for a limited audience. Tóth attributes the shift in meaning to church fathers' efforts to exclude Gnostic apocrypha (a term Gnostics used for their own texts) from authorized biblical canons. To justify the exclusion of the Gnostic texts, the church fathers applied techniques of pagan literary criticism to compare them to the canonical Gospels, looking for evidence that these texts, already deemed heretical, were "fakes" or "forgeries" not written by real apostles but invented for fraudulent purposes.[33] Representative of this process is a passage in Augustine's *City of God* 15.23, in reference to the Book of Enoch, in which he defines apocrypha by their unknown origins and their rejection by church fathers, then remarks that they mix "truth" (*ueritas*) with "fables" (*fabulas*) and "falsehoods" (*falsa*), and concludes that those untruths decided their exclusion from the authoritative, "true" canon.[34] However, in the Middle Ages, despite remaining suspicions inherited from the church fathers, a subcanon of apocryphal concepts, stories, and traditions survived and flourished in less official contexts. If their "apocryphal" label cast doubt on their veracity, it also lent more freedom to imaginative retellings of the stories that made them better fit dominant medieval ideologies and religious doctrines while downplaying any of the stories' heterodox implications. Apocryphal touchstones such as Veronica's veil, the Harrowing of Hell, tales of Jesus's childhood, and the lives of Judas and Pilate pervaded medieval Christian cultures; they were transmitted outside the formal biblical canon through art, literature, and sermons, endlessly readapted and recontextualized.

Brandon Hawk has shown that New Testament apocrypha including Holy Rood (or True Cross) legends and the lives of Judas and Pilate, as well as pseudo-Gospels, martyr stories, and Apocalypses, played a significant role in preaching. Based on evidence from the seventh to thirteenth centuries from homiliaries and other preaching-related manuscript collections containing such apocryphal stories, as well as references to elements of those stories in early English vernacular sermons, he illustrates how these narratives fulfilled a variety of pastoral purposes. Apocryphal stories provided moral exempla in the tradition of saints' lives (if, in Judas's and Pilate's cases, in reverse); concrete, simplified demonstrations of complex theologies (such as the Trinity or theodicy); exercises in *imitatio Christi*; and ways to resolve gaps and contradictions in the canonical Bible.[35] As Hawk argues, even some religious authorities who cautioned against taking apocrypha at face value, such as Aelfric of Eynsham, valued some such narratives for their didactic value and included them in sermons, with judicious commentary about their relative authority (as some stories' acceptance in previous authoritative sources lent them greater credibility) and the specific lessons to be taken from them.[36]

In Hawk's examples, apocrypha are at times treated as potentially or even de facto true touchstones of Christian doctrine supplementing spare biblical narratives, and at other times as useful fictions beneficial to the cultivation of Christian faith and morality. Guyart's direct source for his "lives," Jacobus de Voragine's *Golden Legend*, seems to take a similar approach in its collation of canonical and apocryphal sources for its collected lives of biblical figures, saints, and martyrs. As Suzanne Hevelone has argued, the *Golden Legend* itself appears to be written with a primary goal of furnishing material for preachers, as illustrated by Jacobus's own use of its stories in his separate compilations of model sermons.[37] He exhibits some ambivalence about the episodes he labels "apocryphal," and he signals to his clerical readers that they should proceed with caution in preaching them to the laity, either warning them of the stories' uncertain veracity or skipping them altogether. I discuss his caveats and Guyart's modifications to them in more detail in a later section; suffice it to say for now that, despite these caveats, Jacobus's inclusion of New Testament apocrypha in the *Golden Legend* suggests a recognition of their value as a tool for preaching akin to saints' lives.

In the same rubric that introduces the added stories in the *Bible historiale* as "apocryphal" and thus of uncertain truth, Guyart goes on to explain that he has chosen to include them because "*moult de gens lisent voulentiers escriptures apocrifes pource qu'elles sont moult plaisans et agreables et assoagens les oreilles des escoutans*" ("*many people gladly read apocryphal scriptures [writings] because they are very pleasant and agreeable and soothing to listeners' ears*," fol. 553r). This justification suggests prior knowledge of the stories' popularity as well as familiarity with a scenario in which they would have been read aloud (or paraphrased in translation). He was therefore likely aware of the use of these episodes from the *Golden Legend* and Holy Rood legends in oral vernacular preaching and may have even used them that way himself. In chapter 1, I discussed how Guyart's mediating first-person voice in the translation takes on roles akin to those of a priest and a storyteller as well as those of translator and editor. In his efforts to both preach the Bible and tell it in an engaging way that follows literary norms and expectations, Guyart's adoption of the apocryphal stories as a final coda to his Bible is consistent with contemporary ideas about how to use apocryphal stories in preaching and with his own purpose in translating the Bible for lay readers. The apocryphal narratives interrogate the details of their more authoritative counterparts, applying imaginative speculation to generate alternative explanations, exaggerations, and spinoffs that propose solutions to questions left unanswered in the official account. At the intersection of biblical truth and fiction, the resulting narratives employ the techniques of fiction while promising potential truths.

Fictionalizing Biblical (Hi)stories

In defining the stories at least partially in opposition to "truth," and moreover, as having a primary purpose of aesthetic pleasure, Guyart aligns his apocrypha with what we might call "fiction" today. Some modern definitions of fiction exclude or only provisionally allow for medieval fictions; these definitions are based on the premise of an exclusively modern capacity for self-conscious scepticism that allows readers to entertain fictions while being fully conscious of their conceits (that is, as opposed to either believing them at face value or rejecting them as lies). However, recent scholarship on medieval fiction has challenged the assumption that medieval readers and authors could only think of narratives in terms of a truth/falsehood binary and were thus incapable of understanding fiction as it is understood today. Notably, Julie Orlemanski's "Who Has Fiction? Modernity, Fictionality, and the Middle Ages" shows that even though medieval theories and practices of fiction differ from those of the modern realist novel, presumptions of a uniquely modern consciousness of fictionality break down under a hermeneutic comparison of medieval and modern fiction techniques.[38] Neither Guyart nor his medieval audiences would have understood the *Bible historiale,* on the whole, as fiction. However, its apocryphal stories offer an interesting case study in medieval understandings of the relationship between fiction and faith, given their mix of purportedly true events and more fanciful episodes of dubious veracity as well as their framing discourse that explicitly asks readers to entertain the stories as potential truths before ultimately deciding whether to believe them. Before speculating about what the example of Guyart's apocryphal stories adds to ongoing critical discussions of medieval fiction, let us consider medieval discourse (including Guyart's) about the relationship among fiction, truth, and faith on their own terms.

Fiction, in the Middle Ages, could be the enemy of truth or its ally, and the diversity of opinions about the value of fiction for Christian audiences is apparent in the words used to define it. Rather than using a single, all-encompassing term for imaginative fiction, Latin and medieval European vernaculars employed a rich vocabulary and discourse to describe various modes of storytelling and to theorize the power of imaginative narrative. Religious fictions could fill the same functions (social, didactic, aesthetic) as more secular counterfactual imaginative literature, but could also achieve exegetical and devotional aims. Salutary fictions, such as Christ's parables, appear in the Bible itself: lessons presented in an agreeable form that, with the help of an interpretive key, could be more easily visualized, comprehended, and retained than abstract moral codes.[39] Though religious fictions could be well regarded, some patristic and medieval Christian authors cast suspicion on stories based on non-Christian understandings of the world. Medieval Latin and Romance discourse about the types and purposes of fictional narrative was largely inherited from classical Greek and Roman as well as biblical Hebrew and patristic traditions. All of these traditions hold up pagan myths as their primary point of reference for what they understand as fiction, which inflects the connotations of the vocabulary used to describe it. Cognates of modern English "fiction," *fictio* and *res ficta* (Old French *ficcion*), denote "fabrication," both as in creation (by divine or, more often, human art) and as in lies. Augustine uses *fictus/ficti* and the related *fingere* in the *City of God* (9.7) to express Apuleius's view that "the poets' fictions," both falsehoods and false idols, consisted of fashioning demons into gods. In Latin translation, Saint Paul praises *fide non ficta* (1 and 2 Tm 1:5): faith that is "not man-made," and thereby authentic because it is God-made. In this view, pagan poetry is about gods made in man's image; biblical history is about man made in God's image. Especially in early Christian contexts, *fictio* and related words connote artifice, deception, and idolatry, and are often used with the intent of dismissing the stories of the Greco-Roman pantheon as pure products of human imagination, neither true nor worthy of faith, in contrast with Christian scriptures.[40]

The more ambivalent *fabula* or *fable* does not fully escape this truth/ lie dichotomy but allows for useful fictions that guide the imagination towards moral, cosmological, or theological truths not immediately available through the senses. Macrobius, in his influential *Commentary on the Dream of Scipio*, argues that fables "serve two purposes: either merely to gratify the ear or to encourage the reader to good works" (1.1.7).[41] In Macrobius's taxonomy of fictional narrative genres (expanding upon Cicero's), only what he calls the *narratio fabulosa* is justifiable as a serious philosophical pursuit, because, unlike purely fantastic stories, the *narratio fabulosa* "rests on a solid foundation of truth, which is treated in a fictitious style" (1.1.9). The worthiest stories, he argues, are those in which "the argument is real but it is presented in the form of a fable" (1.1.10), or in which "a decent and dignified conception of holy truths, with respectable events and characters, is presented beneath a modest veil of allegory" (1.1.11). The *fabula* worthy of the philosopher's attention – and in later works citing Macrobius, the Christian exegete's – conceals its meaning by way of its form.[42] Recalling early uses of the word "apocrypha," the *fabula* is invested with an esoteric density of meaning, "untrue" on the surface, but enveloping truths inaccessible through the senses and unavailable to the uninitiated except through layers of gloss.

Outside of theology and Christian philosophy, the vocabulary for narrative styles and genres moves further away from true/false, good/bad binaries to emphasize instead the act of storytelling. Old French words for fictional genres like "dit" and "conte" both derive from verbs meaning, respectively, "to say" and "to tell," emphasizing oral performance of the stories rather than the truth value of their content.[43] Despite presenting itself as history rather than fiction, the *Historia scholastica* – the source of Guyart's historical commentary or *histoires* – makes frequent use of the verb *fabulor*, which denotes storytelling, particularly in the recurring "Hebraei/Judaei ... fabulantur" ("The Jews tell the story"), a formula Comestor uses to cite Jewish oral tradition and pseudepigrapha not attributed to a named author. Despite *fabulor*'s obvious shared etymology with *fabula*, Comestor does not treat these accounts as allegories to be decoded as Macrobius does, nor necessarily as fictional inventions or even apocrypha. His use of the verb *fabulantur* accentuates not the stories' questionable veracity, but rather their belonging to an oral tradition and practice, a nuance Guyart seems to have appreciated in translating Comestor's phrase as simply "Les Hebrieux dient que ... "

("The Hebrews say that ... ").[44] Such language emphasizes the predominantly oral composition, transmission, and reception of stories, with greater focus on the narrative act of (re)telling than on the referential truth value of the stories' content.

The *Bible historiale* does not claim to treat *fables* or *ficcions, dits* or *contes*; it translates and (re)tells (*conte, raconte*) *histoires,* even in the "histoires apocrifes." It is common enough in critical parlance to equate *historia* and *fabula* in the Middle Ages to an implied opposition between "history" and "fiction," categories of narrative defined by whether the events they recount were or were not believed to have actually happened, even if it is also widely recognized that those categories sometimes commingled in individual texts.[45] Indeed, the intermingling of imaginative embellishments, hearsay, speculations, apocrypha, and fiction with authoritative history is common in saints' lives as well as other types of purportedly historical narrative of the period, Latin and vernacular alike. However, this is not to say that the *Bible historiale* and its Latin sources for the apocryphal stories fail to distinguish between canonically accepted truth and spurious legends, or that they present them in the same way without comment.[46] On the contrary, each text is framed by a discourse concerned with questions of truth and belief, about whether discrete episodes "really happened," whether their sources are reliable, and whether the reader will (or should) believe them or not.

The word *histoire* itself is multivalent in Guyart's French, and it would be misleading to translate it in every case as "history" without further explanation. Guyart frequently uses the term *histoire(s)* specifically to refer to the *Historia scholastica* or to the individual chapters thereof that he translates between chapters of the Bible. He also uses the term more generally to denote "history" and its exposition (historical exegesis). However, *histoire* can also simply mean "story," whether it purports to relate historical facts or not, or even the act of narration, such as when Guyart's narrating *je* signals its movement in the text and across narrative time: "j'iray avant à l'ystoire" ("I will skip ahead in the story").[47] This occurs, for example, when Guyart finds the generations of Esau (Gn 36) an unwelcome interruption in the story of Joseph and skips ahead, and again (as we will see in chapter 4) when he skips a large part of the Book of Job.[48] When he writes in his prologue that his work aims to teach laypeople about "les histoires des escriptures anciennes," he could mean any or all of these things: the focus of his translation is on the historical (narrative, plot-driven) books of the Bible; he is using the *Historia scholastica* to perform historical exegesis on the text to clarify its literal meaning through historical context; and his translation and commentary emphasize the power of satisfying stories to explain the world and influence actions and beliefs. His use of *histoire* signals a relationship to canonical biblical history and its truth claims but does not imply a strict boundary separating the Bible from other, less authoritative, or even fictional narrative modes.

The apparent dichotomy between "true" or "real" history and "imagined" fiction breaks down even further in the verb form of *histoire, historier.* There is some evidence (as observed by Peter Ainsworth) that late medieval French writers understood *histoire* and *historier* as distinct from *chronique(r)*, a generic term for the narration of historical events.[49] *Historier* implied a particular historiographic approach that embellished and illustrated the narrative, giving it form and meaning and colourful detail, as in "historiated" initials; it is a way of glossing the narration of events by way of deliberate arrangement, vivid description, and filling in missing details to complete the story as it might be dramatized in the reader's or listener's imagination.[50] Ainsworth's main point of reference is Jean Froissart, but the use of the verb "historier" to refer to both narrative and visual embellishments predates Froissart, as do historiographical methods relying on imagined details to make events more vivid, more realistic, more believable.[51]

As we saw in the previous chapter, Guyart's narration and extradiegetic interventions throughout the Bible and *histoires* reflect a fictionalizing impulse similar to Froissart's to illustrate and embellish narrative with imagined dialogues (e.g., Adam and Eve's in the canonical Bible, or more explicitly, King Solomon and the Queen of Sheba's in the apocryphal stories of the Cross) and sensory details (e.g., picturing the infant Jesus between the ox and the ass). Such narrative practices engage readers' cognitive processes of memory and imagination to make the *vrai vraisemblable*, the truth *appear* to be true. The stories' mode of verisimilitude is not exactly that of modern realism; rather, with their basis in a biblical narrative world where miracles signified God's power and justice, the stories should conform to readers' desires and culturally contingent expectations about what *should* be true or what they *want* to be true within that world. In this respect, they might be said to resemble fan fiction in the sense that the reality or truth to which they must conform to be persuasive (as fictions) is not primarily that of readers' everyday experience but that of the canonical textual world on which the stories are based.[52]

The *histoires apocrifes* resemble some portions of the *Historia scholastica*-based *histoires* of Guyart's Bible in that they help explain underexposed details in biblical stories, add complexity and interiority to their characters, and provide satisfying structure to their narrative arc.

Where the other *histoires* achieve this through commentary and framing dialogue with the implied reader, the apocryphal narratives employ the narrative techniques of fiction to do so within the story itself. For example, Judas is an underdeveloped character in the Gospels, and the evangelists disagree somewhat in their accounts of his actions and their assessment of his motives and moral responsibility. In the apocryphal Life of the Very Evil Judas, Judas's decision to become a disciple of Jesus and then his subsequent betrayal of his teacher are cast within a cycle of rejection, redemption, and betrayal in which each of Judas's missteps prefigures and precipitates the next. The apocryphal stories in the *Bible historiale* also invite the reader's active agency in co-creating the story: readers imagine for themselves what kind of torture Vespasian may have had in mind for Pilate, and readers can ultimately decide which of the multiple accounts of his death they prefer for him to suffer.

This interactive function of medieval storytelling, occurring at the intersection of "true (hi)stories" of the Bible and "other-than-true" imaginative fiction, bears some resemblance to what Wolfgang Iser calls *fictionalizing acts*. In Iser's model, "fiction" is not opposed to "non-fiction" as "false" versus "true" or "real" content. In Iser's formulation, to engage in fiction (writing, reading, reconstructing) is to engage in a kind of organized negotiation, or play, between the given world and an imaginative projection of the self into a fictive world, a kind of "boundary crossing" through which the reading or writing subject, doubled by its simultaneous occupation of its own and an alternative world, becomes present to itself.[53] Iser's model of fictionalization takes as its primary object the modern novel. However, we find parallels to this way of thinking about the self-doubling or self-reflexive function of fictionalizing acts in both Aristotelian thought about the cognitive processes of imagination and its application in certain strands of classical, patristic, and medieval modes of historiography.[54] For example, in reference to Quintillian's advocacy of imaginative or fantastic embellishment in narrative discourse (a process continued in the mind of the reader or listener) as the essence of representation, Eugene Vance remarks that

> In a sense, then, fantasms translate the soul even to itself. Once moved by a *phantasia* (or in Latin, *imago, visio*), the soul elaborates upon it, inventing details that are "true" to the extent that they are probable, and thereby making the original image both more intense and more clear; the result is *enargeia*. Quintilian gives an example: the report that a town has been sacked (VIII.iii.68). In itself, a mere report is not moving.[55]

In the example Vance cites, Quintillian emphasizes that embellishing the account with vivid and emotionally charged details about burning houses, collapsing roofs, and "wailing women and children" – fictional though they may be – gives the "impression of truth." The purpose of such embellishment is not to fool readers nor merely to entertain them, but to engage their active memory and visualization to reconstruct events based on their lived experience, to elicit empathy and self-reflection, to "move" them and, by so doing, to "translate the soul even to itself."

In a move that echoes some medieval preachers' embrace of biblical apocrypha, later medieval authors would embrace imaginative contemplation of the events surrounding the Crucifixion. They did this in terms similar to Quintillian's justification for imagined detail that prompts self-reflection and empathy. For example, Jean Gerson asserts in his 1403 sermon *Ad Deum vadit* that realistic, true seeming (*vraisemblable*) fictions or "conjectures" did not falsify religious truth, but strengthened its hold on the contemplative soul:

> J'esleve a present les yeulx de ma pensee et regarde maintenant a la lumiere de vraye foi et ou livre des evangiles, maintenant en l'ombrage de conjecture probable et devote estimation [...] Je puis religieusement penser [...] une religieuse pensee et consideration, en remembrant ce qui vraisemblablement pouvoit estre fait out dit sans peril quelconque d'erreur ou de folle assertion.
>
> (At present, I raise the eyes of my thought and look now with the light of true faith in the Book of the Gospels, and now in the shadow of probable conjecture and devout estimations [...] I can think religiously [...] a religious thought and consideration, remembering what was likely to have been done or said, without any danger whatever of error, or of foolish assertion.)[56]

While what Gerson describes is his own self-generated contemplation, he (as well as some of his contemporaries, such as Christine de Pizan) also wrote vernacular French texts meant to guide readers in visualizing the events surrounding the Crucifixion, projecting themselves into the scenes and prompting them to imagine and evaluate their own emotional and moral responses to what they "see."[57] While much later than Guyart's work (but near contemporary to Royal 19 D 3), such works reflect in some ways the kind of interactive fictionalization Guyart encourages in his version of the *histoires apocrifes,* in which he invites readers to choose what to believe, to take enjoyment from seeing the story conform to how they might want it to unfold, and even to participate in driving the course of the narrative itself.

"Au jugement du liseur"

The apocryphal and fictionalized details of the *histoires apocrifes*, combined with the translator's direct invitations to the reader to imagine and complete the stories and to decide what to believe, engage the reader's subjective self-awareness as an imaginative co-creator of narrative truth. However, the stories offend the most basic standards of historical truth and canonical authenticity, and their presence in a Bible nevertheless demands explanation. Responding to anticipated critics, a learned tradition that discouraged biblical fictions, and even the hesitations of his sources, the translator is compelled to defend, repeatedly, the legends as truth *in potentia* and as viable conduits to true belief.

With the exception of the story of Julian the Apostate, which is not based directly on biblical events or characters and thus may not fit Guyart's understanding of "apocrypha," each of the stories is introduced by a rubric indicating that the story to follow is apocryphal. In Royal 19 D 3, the first and most elaborate of these caveats falls between the first apocryphal text (Julian the Apostate) and the second (the first True Cross narrative).[58] I have discussed parts of that rubric in separate contexts above; the entire rubric reads as follows:

> *Cy apres ensuivent aucunes hystoires apocrifes de la Sainte Croix. Et sont dittes apocrifes pource que l'en ne sceit pas se elles sont vraies ou non. Si ne la doit on mye affermer pour vraie. Mais je l'ai cy mise pource que moult de gens lisent voulentiers escriptures apocrifes pource qu'elles sont moult plaisans et agreables et assoagens les oreilles des escoutans.* (fol. 553r)
>
> *(Hereafter follow some apocryphal histories of the Holy Cross. And they are called 'apocryphal' because it is not known whether they are true or not. So they must not be confirmed as true. But I have put it here because many people gladly read apocryphal scriptures because they are very pleasant and agreeable and soothing to listeners' ears.)*

Three of the apocryphal texts also include internal rubrics or notes that clarify which events narrated in the stories match those recounted in the Bible, which ones are corroborated by Comestor or another historical authority such as Bede or Josephus, and which ones are derived from unknown or less trustworthy sources. For example, in the Seth legend, following a short recital of Adam's first 930 years, an added note, underlined in red, explains that

> Tout ce qui est cy devant dit est escript en la Bible ou livre de Genesis et est vrai, mais ce qui s'ensuit est apocrife. Si le croie qui veult, toutesvoies ne

le doit on mye affermer pour verité. Mais c'est moult plaisant hystoire et
doulce a ouyr. (fol. 553r)

   (Everything that was just said is written in the Bible in the Book of Genesis
   and is true, but what follows is apocryphal. Whoever wants to believe it may
   do so; however, it must not be confirmed as true. But it is a very pleasant
   story and sweet to hear.)

After recounting Pilate's suicide and his corpse's tumultuous journey to
its final resting place, but before offering Comestor's, Bede's, and Eusebius's more authentic but less satisfying possibilities as to Pilate's end, the
translator interjects, in this case paraphrasing his source:

   jusques cy avons nous dit de Pylate chose que l'en ne sceit pas vraiement
   se elle est a croire ou non, si la laissons au jugement du liseur. (fol. 557v) [59]

   (Up to this point, what we have said about Pilate, no one really knows
   whether it is to be believed or not, so we will leave it to the reader's
   judgment.)

Likewise, once Judas meets Jesus, which is where the apocryphal account
coincides with what the Gospels say about Judas, a similar disclaimer
reads,

   Jusques cy est ceste hystoire apocrife, et se elle a croire et a recorder ou
   non, nous le laissons au jugement du liseur. Si le lise et croie qui vouldra,
   et qui ne veult, si ne le croie mye. Et toutesvoies vault il mieux que on ne la
   lise mye que ce que on vueille affermer pour vraie. (fol. 558v)

   (So far, this story is apocryphal, and whether it is to be believed and
   remembered or not, we leave it up to the reader. So whoever wishes to read
   and believe it may do so, and whoever does not want to may not. However, it
   would be better if one only read what one were willing to confirm as true.)

This last statement, viewed alongside the earlier justifications for including the apocryphal tales, has curious implications for the concept of fiction as a medium for religious truth. In this instance (as in the previous
quotation about Pilate), Guyart's comments closely echo those of Jacobus de Voragine in this episode of the *Golden Legend,* but with a significant shift of perspective. The notion that one should only read what one
is willing to believe differs markedly from the *Legenda aurea*'s "whether it
should be *retold* is left to the reader's judgment, though probably it is *better left aside than repeated.*"[60] This latter admonition, consistent with other
instances of direct address in the *Legenda,* distinguishes between Jacobus

de Voragine's implied Latin reader and a broader secondary audience to whom that clerical reader or preacher might read, recite, or translate the text. The judgment (*arbitrio*) in Jacobus de Voragine's case is that of Latin-literate clergy to whom he transfers the responsibility to decide whether and how to relate fictionalized or unverified elements to others, expressing some caution about the propagation of at least some apocryphal material (despite the fact that he is "repeating" the stories himself).

In his role as translator, Guyart is both (source text) reader and (target text) author, and he performs both of these functions in fulfilment of his promise to his own implied reader to translate truthfully. As is often made evident in the self-conscious commentary liberally interwoven into his biblical translations, what we are reading in the *hystoires apocrifes* is Guyart reading the *Legenda aurea*. He does so surrounded, as it were, by open books, as he is often represented in author portraits, comparing what he encounters in the *Golden Legend* to the Bible, the *Historia scholastica*, and other readings, and reacting to moments of contradiction, difference, and doubt. Taking inspiration from Jacobus de Voragine's disclaimers to his target audience (which would include priests and translators like Guyart) to address his own lay public, Guyart defers to the vernacular readers' judgment in deciding first, whether to read the stories, and second, whether to believe them. Somewhat cryptically, he enjoins them only to never claim unequivocally that the stories are true, and he asserts that it is better for them to read only what they *want* to claim as true ("vueille affermer pour vraie").[61] The stories' truth value is deliberately suspended: truish but unprovable, they are as true as one wishes them to be.

If the purpose of Guyart's disclaimers, that is, to read only what one is willing to believe, is to discourage his readers from reading the stories, the placement of this warning in only the last of the stories would seem counterproductive, especially after some earlier rubrics introducing the other stories praise them. Alternatively, we might view the warning less as an injunction against reading biblical fictions and more as an invitation to read or listen to them with an open, receptive mind. Guyart may be hinting that the transformative power of fiction is the source of his strongly implied justification for the stories' appearance even in a Bible that he otherwise asserts to be true. The *will* to believe, something like a positive affirmation of the suspension of disbelief, or Coleridge's poetic faith, predisposes the reader's imagination to fictionalized truth-making.[62] Without necessarily believing the stories to be accurate representations of real events, assenting readers are asked to entertain them as tentative, morally and aesthetically satisfying answers to the Bible's unanswered questions.

Jacobus emphasizes the indeterminate truth of the apocryphal episodes to inform his clerical readers' use of the stories and Guyart emphasizes that same indeterminacy to inform his readers' attitude towards them. Based on similar cases of medieval authors' treatment of marvels in medieval travel literature, Michelle Karnes argues that these episodes "represent possibilities neither true nor false, offered to readers who did not need to label all textual content either one or the other. Marvels instead appeal to imagination precisely because of their resolute indeterminacy."[63] Among her examples, Karnes quotes Jacques de Vitry, who, in response to a claim about Alexander the Great's encounter with birds with healing powers, expresses an attitude similar to Guyart's in concluding that "whether it is true or possible, we leave to the judgment of the prudent reader."[64] In a more explicitly religious context, Guyart's overt separation of belief from certain truth, coupled with his invitation to readers to believe what they will, lends support to Steven Justice's answer to the question he poses in the title of his article "Did the Middle Ages Believe in Their Miracles?"[65] Noting the unsatisfactory attempts of scholars to answer with a definitive "yes" or "no" and thereby to explain away or dismiss the miracles found in medieval historical narratives in ways that reduce their authors to either cynics or dupes, Justice challenges the idea of belief as a question of knowing or rejecting facts, or the credulous "reflex of an enchanted world."[66] Instead, recalling Augustine and Aquinas, he reframes belief in the domains of faith and, importantly, of the will, as not a passive credulity but an active, deliberate, and self-aware response to doubt, scepticism, and cognitive dissonance. Tales of marvels and miracles provoke a back and forth in the reader's mind between a sceptical attitude towards supernatural elements in the narrative and the active negation of that scepticism as a wilful act of faith: as Justice puts it, "in belief, thinking always accompanies the assent, remains continually vocal within it: the self is always potentially talking to itself, confronting assertion with doubt and doubt with assertion."[67] Guyart's apocryphal narratives neither demand nor enforce belief. At the same time, they are not pure fantasy, inventions whose impossibility the author and reader accept. Instead, they use fictionalization, and especially its self-doubling potential as described by Iser, to spark the cognitive processes of negotiating belief, where the open-ended will to believe is the operative condition for their intended effect. If readers are not meant to confirm the stories as definitely true, they are meant to identify with their alternative reality, to feel invested in choosing which version of a story they wish to believe, and to learn about themselves in the process.

Curiously enough, Guyart echoes the formula Macrobius uses to dismiss idle, unworthy fictions – those that merely "gratify the ear" – to make a case for the ostensibly morally edifying stories he wishes to tell. No longer opposed to Macrobius's nobler goal to "encourage the reader to good works," Guyart's primarily aesthetic justification for the stories ("because they are very pleasant and agreeable and soothing to listeners' ears") comes to imply the moral one as a secondary effect of aesthetic perfection and even presents the more compelling argument for fiction. Like David's well-tuned instrument (or Pythagoras's, or Orpheus's), whose beautiful melody placates and heals the disordered soul at the same time it soothes the ear (1 Kgs 16:23, "David took his harp, and played with his hand, and Saul was refreshed, and was better"), the well-crafted verisimilar narrative opens the ears and attunes the mind with its pleasing form, helping to awaken a latent memory of divine truth, as theorized by Augustine and others.[68] This effect is advantageous to correct belief even if the story itself cannot be confirmed as literally and historically true, as a brief analysis of these stories' treatment of fantastic and uncertain elements will show.

Possible Truths, Alternate Realities

The *Bible historiale* admits the possibility of fictions that are not lies but potential truths, and its apocryphal legends put these forth as legitimate paths to true belief. In some cases, the coexistence of several competing potential truths does not force a choice on the reader, nor does it imply that the different versions of the story are mutually exclusive, one true and the others false. Rather, the presentation of branching narrative paths contributes to a multidimensional imaginary space in which each possible trajectory complements the other(s) in symbolic significance, their conjunction more completely "true" than any one of its parts. It is up to the reader to negotiate options and choose which among them (or all of them together) resonate with what they wish to believe. In this final section of this chapter, I present by way of example some episodes from the Life of the Evil Pilate that set in motion the implied reader's active negotiation of narrative truth, or the will to believe within a controlled fictionalized space.

Whereas Jacobus de Voragine only mentions discrepancies between the apocryphal and more authoritative histories, Guyart rationalizes them, inventing scenarios that allow both to be simultaneously true, or at least possible and believable. In one example, Guyart insists that Pilate's fear-driven suicide in Vespasian's prison as seen in the *Vie du mauvais Pylate* need not contradict Comestor's claim that Pilate was sent to Lyon to finish out his life in exile, nor Eusebius's and Bede's spare account of an unspecified miserable end:

Ceste chose pot bien estre vraie, et pot bien estre que l'empereur le remanda querre de cel exil pour le faire mourir de plus grant martire quant il ouy dire qu'il avoit occis Jhesucrist. (fol. 558r)[69]

(This thing [the exile] may well be true. And maybe the emperor sent for him to come back from this exile in order to have him die in a crueler manner when he heard that he had killed Jesus Christ.)

Without authoritative proof of how Pilate died, his imagined suicide is offered as a morally and aesthetically appealing possibility. It reinforces parallels of Pilate with Judas that are already emphasized in the *Bible historiale* by the juxtaposition of their "lives," their similarly ambitious and vindictive personalities as depicted in the two stories, and their account of Judas's service in Pilate's court before leaving to follow Jesus. Second, to paraphrase Vespasian's own purported reaction upon hearing the news of Pilate's suicide, Pilate *had* to die thus ("tele mort devoit il avoir," fol. 557v) so that no one had to sully his own hands with Pilate's execution, and because suicide was the cruelest death one could suffer.

Above and beyond Jacobus de Voragine's text, Guyart's French translation encourages the reader to relish in killing the villain over and over again, imagining every possible gruesome and shameful end for him. First, Pilate is sentenced to exile *and* prison *and* death for his multiple crimes, then Vespasian (and the reader with him) contemplates unspecified cruel and creative methods of execution. Then, following Pilate's suicide, a gloss enumerates potential instruments that Pilate might have used. The French reader imagines him killing himself not once, but three times, by increasingly desperate means: Guyart reports that some say he was killed by a "coutel" (knife), others by a "fer" (iron file), and still others, by smashing his head against the prison wall (fol. 557v). The accumulation of Pilate's crimes, judgments, and imagined punishments, the repetition of his imagined deaths, and finally, the repeated rejection of his body by the natural world in the marvelous events that follow, emphasize by their multiplicity the singular importance of this death. Meanwhile, the insertion of exile into the story as an added episode rather than a spurious conflicting version draws attention to the fact that, whatever crimes or disputes may have prompted his exile, Pilate was destined to die for having Christ crucified, and of all the ways his death might have happened, it had to be by his own hand.

That Pilate's death might not have occurred that way is hardly relevant. The reader is meant to wish for such an end for this caricature of a cowardly megalomaniac, and indeed, the arc of the story demands it; it wraps up with delicious irony a string of escalating treacheries and assassinations Pilate performs to protect his own power, fatefully culminating with the killing of the incarnate God. His particular destiny is made in the reverse image of the life of Christ, from the astrological portent that allows his father to foretell the birth of a son whose name would never be forgotten to a series of natural disasters (anti-miracles) provoked by his itinerant corpse as it floats down the Rhône. He is a type of anti-Christ who dies by the same hand as Christ did, namely his own. Neither poetic justice nor the magnitude of his crime would allow anything less. Lacking evidence to the contrary, the readers' willingness to believe even the most outrageous details of Pilate's apocryphal life is not an offence to biblical truth. In a sense, its truth *in potentia* is all the more forceful as it represents "ce que on vueille affermer pour vraie" – "what one wants to confirm as true." There is little information about Pontius Pilate in the canonical Gospels, but his apocryphal biography fills in the missing details to tell a tale of depravity and fall proportional to Christ's perfection and redemption. The story's symmetry and its conformity to expectations about what a villain such as Pilate must have been like and how he should have been punished make it pleasing to the ears and resonant with a conditioned aesthetics of what *should be* true.

Not only the life and death of Pilate, but also the other events and characters surrounding the Crucifixion enjoyed a rich imaginative life in French literature well beyond Guyart's translation. The canonical Gospels as well as apocryphal texts such as the Gospel of Nicodemus (or *Acta Pilati*), an ultimate source for some episodes about Pilate, Vespasian, and Veronica in the *Legenda aurea* and in the *Bible historiale*, had for at least a century played a role in the development of a vast corpus of Grail romances.[70] Lives of saints and biblical figures, which often exhibit similar narrative patterns to those of Julian, Pilate, and Judas, even if they usually focus on more admirable characters, reach back to the very earliest vernacular poetry, long before the *Legenda aurea* organized and codified them. Similarly, Guyart's (or the scribe's) observation that many people enjoyed reading and listening to the apocryphal legends of the cross is confirmed by the ubiquity of similar material throughout vernacular literatures of the time. Imaginative engagement with the Passion, its aftermath, and its prophetic and material figurations allowed the medieval Christian to relive each scene through the perspectives of various characters and observers, which enabled forms of divine contemplation that did not require advanced training in theology or *lectio divina*. If Hugh of Saint Victor criticized as frivolous or "senseless" those whose undisciplined curiosity about the Bible would "[turn] the divine announcements into tales," in the same way we "turn to theatrical performances ... [so that] we may feed our ears, not our mind," Guyart and other vernacular authors were quicker to find benefit in the feeding of ears as a way to awaken the minds of a less scholarly audience.[71]

While Guyart frequently encourages his readers to ask questions of the biblical text and to fill in its gaps with speculative possibilities, he also expresses the common clerical opinion that lay audiences, eager to hear good stories but perhaps less well prepared to read as challenging a text as the Bible, would not all have come to the Bible with the same level of literacy and preparedness needed to read it productively. The Book of Job – the subject of the next chapter – offers an example of how one specific kind of internal tension in the *Bible historiale* generates a multiplicity of readings and responses within the manuscript tradition. Departing from his usual tendency to anticipate or simulate a dialogue with inquisitive readers, translator Guyart des Moulins responds to theologically fraught material in the Book of Job with a self-conscious act of self-censorship. His explicit reservations and omissions as well as his ambivalent representation of Job's suppressed speech indirectly call attention to the questions and debates his translation sought to quell by presenting the story as an easily digestible moral parable. By first considering the translator's ambivalence about the book's contents and reception against the backdrop of opposing exegetical traditions, and then examining manuscripts' individual and collective responses to these concerns, chapter 4 presents Job as a case study of the dynamics of medieval Bible translation, operating between generative questioning and its suppression.

4 *Les paroles dont je vous ay fait mention*: The *Bible historiale*'s Two Books of Job[1]

Who will grant me that my words may be written?
Who will grant me that they may be marked down in a book?
With an iron pen and in a plate of lead,
or else be graven with an instrument in flint stone.
For I know that my Redeemer liveth,
and in the last day I shall rise out of the earth.

Job 19:23–5

Chapters 2 and 3 have shown how translator Guyart des Moulins uses his mediating voice to encourage readers' imaginative engagement with biblical narrative in order to facilitate belief. However, the clerical translator's mediation can also constrain or control readers' access to and interpretation of the text. When encountering socially, morally, or theologically fraught topics, the translator's "je qui translatay" takes on the mantle of an institutionally sanctioned gatekeeper who not only offers interpretive guidance, but also decides for his lay readers what they should and should not read as part of their biblical education. Guyart's overt explanations of how and why he has modified or omitted source text, ostensibly for the benefit of his implied lay reader, open space for debate about the benefits and risks of Bible translation for lay readers, the translator's role in directing or even restricting their reading program, and readers' right to determine for themselves their access to fully and accurately translated texts. We catch a glimpse of these debates in manuscripts of the *Bible historiale* as compilers and scribes respond to or reject the editorial choices of their source manuscripts and as they explain their choices in terms of their own visions for how best to meet the needs of the manuscript's intended recipient or of lay readers in general. In many cases, they concede that different readers may have different needs and therefore different versions of the Bible whose contents may vary.

This chapter traces the contours of such medieval debates about Bible translation through the treatment of material Guyart refuses to translate, especially in the Book of Job. First, I analyze Guyart's treatment of the Book of Job and his stated and implied reasons for "abridging" or bowdlerizing it. Situating his reticence within the context of medieval debates and commentary traditions about Job, I make the case that his "silencing" of Job is an interpretive choice that skirts controversy by reducing the complexities of Job's story to a moral fable for lay readers. Then, looking at the book's varied treatment in manuscript, I examine a variety of different approaches to presenting the Book of Job, how they encourage different readings of the book, and how they reveal competing or changing attitudes towards their target readership and what lessons the Book of Job holds for them. I then link the dual tradition of telling the story of Job in the *Bible historiale* to a long history of reading it in one of two ways, not only in major exegetical traditions but also as replicated in medieval literary adaptations of the work. Finally, I connect Job's example to a broader tension that emerges in Guyart's translation and its manuscript recensions between a productive questioning of the text and enforced silence when faced with taboo topics and potentially subversive questions.

My Hand upon My Mouth: Censoring Job's Words

The Book of Job begins with Satan's challenge: would the pious and morally upright Job, accustomed to receiving the reward of his good works, remain loyal to God under hardship? God allows "the adversary" to test Job's faith by destroying his property, servants, and children, his good name, and good health. As one messenger after another arrives with bad news, Job at first submits to God's will without complaint. "If we have accepted good things from the hand of the Lord," he asks his wife, "why should we not accept evil things?" The reader is assured that "in all of these things, Job never sinned with his lips" (2:10).[2] As news spreads of his misfortune, Job's friends arrive to console him, and after seven days of silent mourning in their company, he speaks.

What follows is a poetic commentary on the opening story, taking the form of a debate or judicial trial. Speaking in turn, Job and his friends grapple with the breakdown of the expected grammar of providence, according to which actions should be rewarded or punished according to the logical mechanism of God's presupposed justice (good works → God's favour → prosperity). Faced with the aporia of undeserved suffering (good works → ? → calamity), the sick and grieving Job attempts to recover the middle term – the nature of God's intervention in human affairs – by re-evaluating the basis of his understanding. Under the strain of faith and reason tested, and faced with his own mortality, Job raises the problem of evil with questions not conceivable under his friends' formulaic moral theology that reads calamity as a sign of past misdeeds. Accused by his friends, Job pleads to God to vindicate his testimony of his blamelessness; God appears in response to Job's plea, briefly opening the potential for cross-examination between human and divine before confirming Job's innocence and granting his return to prosperity.

In Guyart des Moulins's version of the Book of Job, at verse 3:1, when Job first breaks his silence, Guyart des Moulins abruptly censors him. Citing "great mysteries that are in the words," he delivers a halting synopsis of the missing chapters (3 to 41 of 42), interrupted by expressions of his own qualms about translating them, before skipping ahead to the book's "happy ending" (italics added for emphasis):[3]

Apres ce ouvri Job sa bouche si maudi le jour qu'il fu nes et dist *moult de paroles que nus ne doit translater* et si parlerent moult longuement si ami a lui. Et ces paroles qu'il distrent li uns a l'autre sont *de si fort latin et plaines de si grant mistere* que nus n'en puet le mistere entendre s'il n'est trop granz clers de divinité. *Et pour ce les trespasserai je ci car nus ne les devroit oser translater car laie gent i porroient errer.* Si m'en irai avant a la fin du livre Job comment Nostre Sire regarda a sa penitance et li rendi .ii. tens d'avoir quil n'avoit oncques eu et li donna .vii. filz et .iii. filles com il avoit devant eu. Quant Job ot moult parlé a ses amis, Nostre Sire parla a lui et il a Nostre Seigneur en moult de manieres. Et ce ne fait mie aussi a translater *pour les granz misteres qui sont es paroles,* si les trespasserai ci aussi et irai avant a l'ystoire. Quant Nostre Sires ot parlé a Job les paroles dont je vous ai fait mention, il s'en ala a Eliphaz Themanicen … (BnF fr. 155, fol. 99v)

(Then Job opened his mouth and cursed the day he was born and said *many words that no one ought to translate,* and then his friends spoke to him for a very long time. And those words that they spoke to one another are *in such difficult Latin and full of such great mystery* that no one can understand the mystery unless he is a very great cleric of divinity. *And for this reason I will pass over them here because no one should dare to translate them, since laypeople might err here.* Therefore I will go ahead to the end of the Book of Job, how our Lord looked at his penitence and gave him back twice as much wealth as he had ever had and gave him seven sons and three daughters as he had had before. When Job had spoken at length to his friends, our Lord spoke to him, and he to our Lord, in many ways. And this also is not to be translated *for the great mysteries that are in the words,* so I will skip them here as well and

will go forward in the story. After our Lord had spoken to Job the words that
I have mentioned to you, he went to Eliphaz the Themanite ...)

Guyart's usual response to difficult passages throughout the Bible is to
offer interpretations by Comestor and other authorities (via Comestor
or directly), sometimes adding his own opinion, while warning against
unacceptable interpretations, and signalling areas of indeterminacy.
For example, the episode of Lot's incest with his daughters – a morally
dubious example and taboo topic – is not omitted or bowdlerized, but
translated in full and followed by an *histoire*, citing Jerome and Strabo,
that analyzes the characters' motivations and evaluates their levels of cul-
pability.[4] In other cases, Guyart's glosses and *histoires* dispute the interpretations or beliefs of pagans, Jews, and heretics, or simply those with
which he disagrees. Guyart even occasionally counters Comestor's interpretations with ones he finds more credible, responding, for example, to
Comestor's claim that "grans fornications" could have caused the Flood
with a simple "ceste opinion tient saint Augustin a fausse" ("Saint Augustine believes this opinion to be wrong," W 125, fol. 7r).[5] Although interpretive interventions are usually the default option to resolve textual
difficulties and incoherencies, caution against taking biblical characters'
less admirable actions as models, and dispute unwanted readings, in the
Book of Job, the impulse to interpret is abruptly cut off, both for the
characters in the book and for the reader. If, as a rule, canonical truth is
completed by the addition of expository glosses, in the exceptional Book
of Job, which questions the very possibility of reading God's intentions,
glossing is achieved through the *subtraction* of biblical text that obscures
and refracts that truth through its use of poetic language and debate.
Guyart's ambivalent gesture indicates both the existence of something
not translated and also the fact of repressing it, and this self-conscious
omission effects an overdetermined reticence that recalls Job's own performance of silence after God's speech at 39:34 ("I will lay my hand upon
my mouth"). It signals something that one might wish Job had not said,
at least not in a vulgar tongue, for a lay audience.

The Scholar's Job and the Layman's

By Guyart's own admission, we should not expect the Book of Job to
appear at all in his translation. As noted in previous chapters, the "*historiale*" in the title *Bible historiale* refers mainly to its dependence upon
Peter Comestor's major school text that combines literal-historical exposition of the Bible with universal history.[6] Guyart translates the historical
books of the Bible, interspersed with relevant chapters from the *Historia*

scholastica and supplemented by his own glosses and translator's notes.[7] The *Bible historiale*'s critical apparatus of *histoires, gloses,* and *incidents* ensures both intercultural and institutional mediation, contextualizing and familiarizing foreign elements of ancient Hebrew culture for a medieval aristocratic French-speaking audience.[8] Meanwhile, the first-person "je qui translatay" narrates Guyart's manipulation of source material and warns readers about what they should and should not believe about the text they read. The strong discursive presence of a narrating translator-priest between the reader and an inaccessible source text reinforces the translator figure's role as both a teacher who anticipates and answers questions and a gatekeeper of scriptural knowledge who at times discourages the reader from interrogating the text.

Given the translation's close adherence to the *Historia scholastica,* departures from its principles of organization are noteworthy. Despite their absence from Comestor's commentary, two non-historical books – Job and Proverbs – are singled out in the *Bible historiale*'s table of contents as deserving exceptional inclusion:[9]

> J'ensuis du tout et ensuivrai le Mestre en Histoire en toute s'ordenance sauve ce que les paraboles Salemon et li livres Job ne sont mie contenuz en Hystoires, mais je les ai mis en cest livre, mout abregies, pour la bonté d'aus. (BnF fr. 155, fol. 1r)[10]
>
> (I will follow the Master of Histories and his order in everything, except that the Proverbs of Solomon and the Book of Job are not included at all in the *Historia*, but I have put them in this book, much abridged, for their goodness.)

Both of these books Guyart considers "good" for their lay audience, but only if they are translated selectively, or "much abridged." Each of the two abridgements short-circuits its prescribed path to wisdom by minimizing the interpretive pursuits of study (in Proverbs) and debate (in Job).[11] What remains is the reserved, pious contemplation of Proverbs 9:10, "The fear of the Lord is the beginning of wisdom," echoed by Job 28:28, "Behold the fear of the Lord, that is wisdom, and to depart from evil is understanding." If the destination is the same, the layperson's (and hence, the layperson's Job's) road to understanding must yet be different, and necessarily less circuitous, than the learned cleric's.

Two Books of Job

Guyart's "abridged" Book of Job, which later scribes would title the "Petit Job," is not the only medieval vernacular retelling of Job's story to privilege the framing story. The verse *Hystore Job*, which, like the *Bible historiale*, dates from the late thirteenth century, similarly concentrates on the story told at the beginning and end of the book, noting that anyone curious about the internal debate (which is only briefly summarized) should read Gregory the Great's exposition of it. Later, William Caxton's Middle English adaptation of the *Golden Legend* would include a chapter on "Saint Job" that also, perhaps inspired by Guyart's "Petit Job," only summarizes the framing story. Painting cycles produced throughout the Middle Ages also focus on his misfortune and recovery, and mystery plays such as the fifteenth-century *Pacience de Job* embellish details about Job's life but tend to minimize or omit his own protracted interpretation of it. While it is unsurprising that a well told story should capture lay audiences' imagination more than complex philosophical debates, our translator's strong reaction hints at other reasons for this tendency to privilege parts of Job's tale that trace their roots to a divided exegetical tradition.

Katharine Julia Dell argues that the reception of Job has always split into two camps, mirroring the text's two-part composition. One privileges the narrative prose prologue and epilogue (in other words, the part Guyart translates), making the Book of Job primarily a moral parable about patience rewarded. The other gives greater attention to the internal debate and understands the work as a sceptical critique of conservative theologies.[12] The reformative, even subversive, politics that defines the periodic shifts between the two camps dominating Job commentary within a religious tradition and time period is reflected in the book's contents. After all, the effect of Job's misfortune is to shake him from his predictable world into a state of unknowing, from which standpoint he must confront inconsistencies in a belief system that is no longer viable for interpreting history.

If some modern scholars have explained away this tension between the framing story and the internal debate by pointing to complexities of the book's composition, patristic and medieval Christian readers, who took for granted the book's unity of authorship, had to reconcile the "patient" Job with the one who curses the day he was born:

> Let the day perish wherein I was born,
> and the night in which it was said: A man child is conceived.
> Let that day be turned into darkness,
> let not God regard it from above, and let not the light shine upon it.
> Let darkness, and the shadow of death cover it,
> let a mist overspread it,
> and let it be wrapped up in bitterness. (3:3–5)

A Job who brazenly demands answers from God for the injustice he experiences:

> I will speak, and will not fear him:
> for I cannot answer while I am in fear. (9:35)

> My soul is weary of my life,
> I will let go my speech against myself,
> I will speak in the bitterness of my soul.
> I will say to God: Do not condemn me:
> tell me why thou judgest me so. (10:1–2)

And whose theology even entertains the idea of a capricious or even cruel God:

> One thing there is that I have spoken,
> both the innocent and the wicked he consumeth.
> If he scourge, let him kill at once,
> and not laugh at the pains of the innocent. (9:22–3)

Job's "speech against himself" is both self-incriminating and self-negating. After renouncing his initial humbled resignation, Job later repudiates his own speech after God responds with questions answerable, in turn, only by silence:

> And the Lord went on, and said to Job: Shall he that contendeth with God be so easily silenced? Surely he that reproveth God, ought to answer him. Then Job answered the Lord, and said: What can I answer, who hath spoken inconsiderately? I will lay my hand upon my mouth. One thing I have spoken, which I wish I had not said: and another, to which I will add no more. (39:31–5)

There remains some ambiguity about what Job retracts and whether there is something in his speech he still defends.[13] Likewise, God's equivocal judgment that only Job has "spoken what is right" defers resolution.[14] Ultimately, it is Job's ambivalent *return* to silence, not his initial, unquestioning one, that occasions the end of his torments and his return to the life he formerly enjoyed, as if God found his first reaction (non-speech, or non-interpretation) insufficient.

Job the Saint, Job the Scholar

The Book of Job's poetic theodicy has always been a pivotal and much contested mainstay of Jewish and Christian thought. Hotly debated in medieval Jewish communities, its comparatively few important Christian commentaries cluster around tipping points in long cycles between opposing systems of biblical hermeneutics.[15] As Manlio Simonetti and Marco Conti have noted, Job tends to generate the most debate at moments of political uncertainty and religious conflict, and its major commentaries arise out of tension between Alexandrian (allegorical) and Antiochian (literal) modes of interpretation.[16] New developments in the church and university made the late thirteenth century a ripe time for interest in Job. At the same time that the church reckoned with the failure of the Crusades and perceived threats to its hegemony from heretical and anticlerical movements, an Aristotelian renewal in scholastic theology raised questions not previously conceivable. The work of Thomas Aquinas posed a serious challenge to both Alexandrian interpretation of scripture and its historical foundation, as exemplified by Comestor's work, and his *Expositio super Job ad litteram* unsettled a long-standing tradition of reading Job.[17]

Early Christian writers such as Chrysostom and Olympiodorus could extol Job's character, and Augustine could see in Job's final repentance a model of submission to mysteries beyond the grasp of fallen human understanding. It is only with Jerome's translation, however, that Job's more significant typological identity, and thus his uniquely Christian value, takes shape. One word in particular, which Jerome translates as *Redemptor* (otherwise understood as "avenger," "defending counsel," or "the favoured of God") in Job 19:25, would assign Job prophetic importance as affirming Christ's redemption as the answer to Job's central question and would pave the way for allegorical readings to come.[18] Foremost among these readings in Guyart's time was Gregory the Great's *Moralia in Job.*

Inspired in part by Jerome's translation, Gregory the Great's *Moralia in Job,* composed in the late sixth century, remained an important authority on the Book of Job in the Latin Christian Church in the thirteenth century. His "saint" or *beatus Job* spoke infallibly as both a prophet and figure of Christ, yet like Guyart, Gregory finds parts of Job's speech troubling: "See here, for instance, in that blessed Job is described as having cursed his day, and said, *Let the day perish wherein I was born, and the night in which it was said, There is a man child conceived*; [Jb 3:3] if we look no further than the surface, what can we find more reprehensible than these words?"[19] The *Moralia* grants literal-historical value only to the framing story, while chapters 3–41 attain their meaning only by looking "beneath the surface" to unveil Christological prophecies and understand Christ's Passion through a compassionate identification with Job's suffering. Applying allegorical and moral exegesis to that which he finds literally problematic, Gregory dissolves apparent contradictions and subordinates the central debate to Job's salutary example. "Whereas ye see our superficial form to be destructive to us," Gregory says of Job's words wherein he wishes to die, "look for what may be found within us that is in place and consistent with itself."[20] Among Gregory's three senses – historical, allegorical, moral – it is the middle term that looks "within" to negotiate points of discord and arrive at Job's typological value announcing Christ's suffering, the salvation of the Gentiles, and the resurrection of the dead.[21]

By redefining literal interpretation as a focus on human language, Thomas Aquinas's *Expositio super Job ad litteram* (written between 1261 and 1265) recovers a comprehensive reading of Job. Aquinas's is not the superficial literalism of Gregory's unsympathetic "readers of little experience" who, like Job's friends, judge him wrongly because of their lack of compassion. However, like Gregory's reading of Job, Aquinas's also requires empathy: one that asks the reader not to suffer with Job, but to think with him. Like Moses Maimonides before him (in the 1190 *Guide of the Perplexed*), Aquinas reads Job as a parable not only about providence, but about *debating* providence, or the student's progress in learning to examine and defend his faith. Here, a good but human Job is allowed to curse and to err in his judgment, while his willingness to question his and his friends' assumptions about God is to be commended as the mark of a good theologian. What God rebukes and Job recants are poorly chosen words that, in his zeal to prove his innocence "according to human reason," scandalize his friends and fall short of communicating Job's true beliefs.[22] Above all, Aquinas's Job regrets saying that he "wished to debate with God" and "that [he] put [his] justice first when it was a matter of divine judgments."[23] A double for the student of theology to whom the treatise is addressed, Aquinas's Job learns the necessity of moderating his arguments with humility, grounding them in scripture, and tempering them with sensitivity to his audience's horizons of expectations.[24] Whereas Gregory uses allegorical detours to *censor* Job's words, Aquinas *censures* him, parsing Job's "inconsiderate" speech to separate Job's good theology from the errors and excesses of his emotionally charged language, which are salutary as a counterexample so long as they are clearly marked and denounced.

The exegetical tradition from Gregory the Great to Thomas Aquinas reveals the Book of Job to be a book about its own reading and the potential misreadings (or heresies) that result from using incorrect assumptions to interpret the text-event of Job's misfortunes. Describing the book as "a parable intended to set forth the opinions of people concerning providence," the twelfth-century Jewish scholar Moses Maimonides, in his *Guide of the Perplexed,* identifies each of the debate's interlocutors with a contemporary belief system with the intention of dismantling each one's error.[25] For Gregory the Great, "the friends signify heretics" – "*Amici haereticos significant*" (as his argument is summarized in a marginal gloss to Job 2:1 in the *Glossa Ordinaria*) – and the assault of Job's mind by the deceptive arguments of his wife and friends constitutes part of his trial.[26] In Gregory's interpretation, what Job ultimately realizes and his "heretical" friends do not is that the aporia he faces in attempting to resolve the problem of evil according to human logic signifies the need for Christ's mediation, through that of the church and its sacraments.[27] The "heretic," by this definition, is the one who, refusing to acknowledge the insurmountable gap between human and divine (and thus the need for the church), "so preaches God as thereby to be fighting against him."[28]

While carefully guarded against heretical readings of the book (refuting, for example, Manichean or Cathar dualism at length in chapter 10), Aquinas's nuanced recuperation of Job's words opens the door to more radical interpretations and offers up a problematic model for the laity. The lack of clear signposts as to what Job has spoken "right" (Jb 42:7) presents a special danger. If the "granz clers de divinité" might, in Guyart's estimation, fruitfully ask Job's questions, the spectre of lay readers debating them with their peers must have conjured the church's worst fears about the abuse of translations. Indeed, Job and his friends are not unlike the suspected Waldensians, described in Innocent III's 1199 letters to the Bishop of Metz, who were said to meet in secret with vernacular Bibles to "belch out" ("eructare") their opinions as they preach to one another and make a mockery of church institutions, without the clergy's *discretio* to distinguish good from evil and right from wrong meanings.[29] It did not help that, as Christine Thouzellier has shown, Waldensians and Cathars took special interest in the Book of Job and met to debate it.[30] Cathars in particular cited the drama staged between God and Satan and Job's seeming ambivalence about God's role in both prosecuting and defending him as evidence of a second, malignant creator responsible for the material world and its evils.[31]

Guyart's conservative solution to guard against his readers' potential misinterpretation or misappropriation of the Book of Job accepts Gregory's premise, repeated among the Victorines, that Job's central poem had only "spiritual" value and could gravely mislead those who read too literally.[32] However, by pre-emptively removing the dialogue between Job and his "heretical" friends, circumventing the temptation of real and imagined heresies, Guyart's silence imposes another reading. It transforms a book foregrounding interpretation, questioning, and debate into one about resisting the impulse to translate as well as to interpret. It closes the gap between Job's first and second silence, removes the distinction between them, and recentres the text on Job's act of self-censorship. The effect is amplified by the translator's repeated justifications for his own, secondary self-censorship. In the space of a single folio, we are:

1. Reminded twice that "En toutes ces choses ne pecha riens Job de sa bouche" ("in all of these things, Job did not sin at all with his mouth");
2. Told that his wife, urging him to curse God and die, is speaking like a "femme fole" ("foolish woman");
3. Warned of three kinds of "paroles que nul ne doit translater" ("words that no one ought to translate"), i.e., Job's, his friends', and God's; and
4. Denied even Job's repentance speech, such that God's first words after "les paroles dont je vous ay fait mention" ("the words that I [Guyart] mentioned to you") are to cast down Eliphaz for having misspoken: "Je me suy moult courrouciez a toy et a tes amis. Car vous n'avez mie parlé droitture encontre moy aussi comme Job mon sergent a fait" ("I am very angry at you and your friends. For you have not spoken what is right concerning me as my servant Job has"). (W 125, fols. 232v–233v)

Dense in injunctions against speaking foolishly, the lesson is transparent: uninformed speech about God is dangerous. The only "droitture" or "right thing" – indeed the *only* thing – this layperson's version of Job speaks in direct discourse is his initial rebuke to his wife that they should graciously accept their fate. He models silence, or non-interpretation, as the correct reaction to both personal tragedy and the biblical text.

Two Jobs, Side by Side

It would not be long before readers, scribes, and stationers sought to rectify Job's enforced silence. As explained in chapter 1, it became common in bookshops to supplement Guyart's translation, adding biblical books he did not translate from a second translation known as th**e** *Bible du XIIIe siècle*. A complete translation of the Book of Job was among the first books added to Guyart's Old Testament, appearing as early as 1320 and becoming standard in most manuscripts produced after about 1340.[33] When the Job from the *Bible du XIIIe siècle* is included, the complete translation does not replace Guyart's "abridged" one, as happens with Proverbs; instead, a majority of copies include two Books of Job: the "Grand Job" and the "Petit Job."[34] Guyart does not call his translation "petit"; rather, the "Petit," or censored, Job only becomes "Petit" after the addition of the "Grand," a complete translation of the Vulgate's Book of Job with just a few glosses, most of a lexical nature.[35] Of the eighty manuscript copies and early editions of the *Bible historiale* that contain any version of the Book of Job and whose contents have been catalogued by Clive Sneddon (or that I have personally consulted), twenty-four include only the "Petit Job." A mere five – all of them exceptional for other reasons – contain only the "Grand."[36] The remaining fifty-one manuscripts, or about 64 per cent, contain both.

Among copies that share the same translation(s) of Job, certain patterns generally hold:

1. Most copies that include only the "Petit Job" fall under Berger's categories of *Bible historiale* (i.e., Guyart's Old and New Testaments, replacing apocryphal legends with Apocalypse) and "Petite Bible" (the first among the "complétée" stages, which merely replaces Proverbs to Apocalypse with a *Bible du XIII* siècle* volume 2 without touching volume 1, unless to add Psalms).[37] These manuscripts never refer to Guyart's version of the book as the "Petit Job," but only "Job," "abridged Job," or "the beginning and end of Job." The short text has no rubricated chapter titles, and textual variants that affect meaning are few. Among copies quoted regularly in this book, BnF fr. 155 belongs to this category.

2. The inclusion of the "Grand Job" first occurs in a 1320 manuscript and becomes common beginning in the mid-fourteenth century with the collection of contents Berger calls the "Bibles moyennes"; the "Grand Job" is usually retained in the "grandes Bibles" and other later expansions.[38] Where both the "Petit" and the "Grand" are included, they are labeled as such. Rubricated chapter headings are usually added to both versions of Job, seven short chapters for the "Petit" and forty-one or forty-two for the "Grand."[39] Representative of this group are W 125–6 and Paris, Bibliothèque de l'Arsenal, MS 5057–8 (Ars. 5057–8), both "grandes Bibles." In both of these two-volume sets, both books of Job appear in volume 1 (W 125 and Ars. 5057), as is typical.

3. More extensive textual revisions, including customized rubrics and glosses, become more common in later copies (of the fifteenth and sixteenth centuries), as well as in copies made outside the relatively standardized book manufacturing centre of Paris. It also becomes common to add Jerome's prologues in translation, including two to the Book of Job. For the purposes of this chapter, my primary examples from this group will be Royal 19 D 3 and Paris, Bibliothèque

nationale de France, MS fr. 15370–1 (BnF fr. 15370–1); in the latter, both books of Job are in the first volume, BnF fr. 15370.[40]

The "Grand Job" Answers the "Petit"

In the late fourteenth and fifteenth centuries, some of the more learned and attentive copyists sought to rationalize the choices – their own, Guyart's, and those of other copyists in between – that produced the *Bible historiale* in its present state. For example, in Royal 19 D 3 (the same manuscript discussed in chapter 3 for its inclusion of the apocryphal stories), Frère Thomas du Val (or his source) adds to the usual note justifying Guyart's inclusion of Job and Proverbs a list of other non-*Historia* books his copy adds to Guyart's translation. He also expands Guyart's rationale for including Job and Proverbs to a second justification for the inclusion of all of the non-historical books, namely that their addition makes the Bible complete (emphasis added to denote additions made to Guyart's note):

> Car j'ensui du tout et ensuivrai le Maistre es Hystoires et en toute son ordenance, sauve ce que les Paraboles et les livres de *Sapience,* de Job, *du Psaultier, de Paralipomenon, et des Epistres* ne sont mye es Hystoires, mais je les ai cy mis pour la bonté d'eulx *et pour l'acomplissement de la Bible.* (Royal 19 D 3, fol. 1v)
>
> (For I will follow the Master of Histories and his order in everything, except that the Proverbs and *the sapiential books,* Job, the Psalms, *the Paralipomenon, and the Epistles* are not included at all in the Historia, but I have put them here, for their goodness *and for the completion of the Bible.*)[41]

Scribal observations about the text's composition and transmission are not always accurate; Royal 19 D 3 and BnF fr. 15370, among others, conflate the Latin author and his translator and replace Comestor's biography in the second prologue with Guyart's. BnF fr. 15370 additionally makes the anachronistic claim, in the "Petit Job," that Charles V was responsible for having the "Grand Job," Esdras, Nehemiah, and the Paralipomenon (also known as 1 and 2 Chronicles) translated and henceforth added to copies of the *Bible historiale,* even though these additions had appeared in copies made before that king was born, and were sourced from a translation that predates both Charles V and the *Bible historiale* itself.[42] Despite such errors, attempts to recreate the textual history of the *Bible historiale* suggest an awareness of the need for a translation to adapt in response to changes in language, readership, and the church's obligations to the literate laity.

In the case of the two Jobs, scribes often acknowledge that the (Latin) Bible has only one Book of Job and nonetheless justify the inclusion of both.[43] Insufficiently glossed, the "Grand Job" alone is no more complete than its "abridged" counterpart, but together, the two are seen to complement one another or to cover the needs of different kinds or levels of readers. The "Grand Job" usually appears first, with the presence of the "Petit" sometimes explained in rubrics as a simpler alternative for the less educated, or as an epilogue to the "Grand Job" meant to clarify its meaning in the reader's mind:

> *Cy fenist le livre de Job. Et pour ce qu'il estoit trop fort a entendre aux gens laiz le nomment aucuns le Grant Job, combien que il ne fut nulx autre que celuy Job soulement. Maix il est appelles le Petit Job pour ce qu'il est abregier pour le mieulx faire entendre aux laiz et aux simples gens.* (BnF fr. 15370, fol. 130v)[44]
>
> *(Here ends the Book of Job. And since it used to be too hard for the laypeople to understand, some call it the "Grand Job," even though there was none other than this one Job. But it is called the "Petit Job" when it is abridged to make the laity and simple folk understand it better.)*

Unlike in most manuscripts, in Thomas du Val's Royal 19 D 3, the "Petit Job" comes first, which implies that it is the default version, with the addition of the "Grand Job" explained as a necessary supplement to satisfy more advanced readers' curiosity:

> *Cy fine le livre Job abbregié. Mais pource qu'il ne souffist mye a pluseurs de veoir l'abbregié, si veulent veoir tout le long, pource l'ai je cy apres mis tout au long ainsicomme il gist en la Bible.* (Royal 19 D 3, fol. 244v)
>
> *(Here ends the abridged Book of Job. But since it is not enough for some to see the abridged one, if they want to see all of it, I have put the whole thing hereafter, as it is in the Bible.)*

In either configuration, the "Petit Job" fulfils a dual purpose with respect to the "Grand." In retelling the same narrated events that frame the "Grand Job," it disguises itself as a simpler, supposedly equivalent alternative to be read in place of the full Book of Job. For the more ambitious reader, the "Petit" still complements and reinforces lessons to be privileged from the "Grand Job" while cautioning against unguided reflection and debate on the difficult central poem. The "Petit Job" poses as a kind of gloss to Job, or better yet, *histoire*. In fact, at least one scribe appears to have misunderstood Guyart's version of Job to be exactly that, labeling it the Book of Job "selonc Hystoires" ("according to the *Historia*"), mimicking Guyart's language for introducing some chapters in Comestor's *Historia* that "expose" a book or chapter of the Bible merely by way of summarizing those narrative episodes that deserve emphasis.[45]

Framing Silence, Silence Framed: Mirroring Job in Royal 19 D 3 and BnF fr. 15370

Designating Job's cries and arguments as "mysteries" beyond the lay reader's grasp while concealing their content recalls the image in Gregory the Great's *Moralia in Job* likening the saint's heart to a closed vessel: "For as we know nothing what vessels that are closed contain inside, but when the mouth of the vessels is opened, we discover what is contained within; so the hearts of the Saints, which so long as their mouth is closed are hidden, when their mouth is opened, are disclosed to view."[46] The "Petit Job" is like a reliquary sealed to all but the priests and clerics who hold its keys; it must suffice for the faithful to be reassured by expert testimony that it contains the blessed speech of a saint.

When the vessel is opened to curious eyes by the addition of the "Grand Job," its dense poetry and unresolved theological arguments complicate, and perhaps at times contradict, the polished, deceptively transparent lesson of patience rewarded in the "Petit Job." For some of the "clercs entendant escriptures" who continued to tailor the *Bible historiale* even against the opposite current towards standardization in the early years of print, the illusion of identity between the "Petit" and the "Grand Job" was a frail one. From the perspective of these *remanieurs*, what was once considered inappropriately complex for the laity (in BnF fr. 15370, the "Grand Job" "*estoit* trop fort a entendre aus gens laiz," i.e., "*was*" or "*used to be*" too difficult for laypeople) perhaps no longer eluded the more sophisticated among their readership. Still, some scribes of personalized manuscripts understood the Book of Job, as represented in the full translation, to be a dangerous one for lay readers to interpret on their own, however curious and well-read they might be, and wished to guide their reading towards acceptable lessons for moral behavior and for the practice of their faith, without giving them free reign to arrive at their own answers to the book's more piercing questions about God. Telling the whole story of Job meant bringing the "Grand Job" into harmony with the "Petit" and directing readers' attention to the salutary lessons of each.

Thomas du Val's revision in Royal 19 D 3 (1411) effects coherence by extending the usual rubric chapter headings of the "Grand Job" to summarize not only each chapter's content but also an important Christian lesson to be learned from it.[47] Thus it is that chapter 6, "*Comment Job requiert a Dieu que ses pechies soent mis en balance contre sa misere*" ("*How Job asks God to weigh his sins against his misery*," as it reads in W 125, fol. 221v) becomes "*Comment Job dit que sa paine est plus grant que ses pechiez, et si la sueffre paciemment*" ("*How Job says that his punishment is greater than his sins, and yet he bears it patiently*," Royal 19 D 3, fol. 247r). To Chapter 7's usual heading, "*Comment Job se complaint et dit que vie de homme est brieve*" ("*How Job complains and says that man's life is short*," W 125, fol. 221v), Thomas du Val adds, "*et requiert a Dieu qu'il lui pardonne*" ("*and asks God to forgive him*," Royal 19 D 3, fol. 247r).[48]

Directing the reader's attention away from theological conundrums raised in the book, the rubrics feature Job demonstrating his patience and humility and acknowledging God's power (ch. 12), condemning hypocrisy (ch. 13), denouncing the malice of heretics (ch. 30), and talking about the virtues (ch. 31). Like the common scholastic iconography in *Bible historiale* manuscripts that shows Moses, Saint Paul, and other biblical authors in the guise of masters lecturing to followers, these rubrics describe Job as a teacher instructing his friends (and the reader) in the virtues and Christian doctrine through his "sermon" and his active example. The limitations of these headings as a form of glossing become evident when they venture beyond emphatic summaries to allude to prophetic and allegorical revelations not easily deduced without further exposition. These include, for example, Job's prophecy of the Resurrection (ch. 14), and – a bigger leap of the imagination – the "grans merveilles" of the church (ch. 39), a heading that only begins to make sense when read alongside books 30–2 of the *Moralia* (evidently a direct or indirect source for the rubrics), where Gregory allegorizes each animal mentioned in the chapter (each of whose creation God touts as evidence of his power and wisdom) as a segment of the church or society. The total effect of the interpretive rubrics is to remake the "Grand Job" in the image of the "Petit," bringing out Job's imitable qualities of patience, humility, and penitence, while tracing the silhouette of a second, mystical content beyond the imagined lay reader's reach.

Another Bible manuscript, BnF fr. 15370–1, completed for Simon de Rye and Jeanne de la Baume at the turn of the sixteenth century, takes another approach. Perhaps a gift commemorating their marriage in 1497, the manuscript bears the imprint of its owners, whose names are inscribed on ribbons framing some miniatures and whose arms appear several times in the margins. Its textual contents are highly personalized as well, containing in addition to Guyart's work and books supplemented from the *Bible du XIIIe siècle*, texts from numerous other sources: catechisms, prayers, and a moral treatise as well as new glosses (of an

Augustinian bent) found in no other known copies.[49] It proposes flexible reading options, offering not only two versions of Job, but two ways to read the Gospels: where most manuscripts include either the four Gospels of the *Bible du XIII* *siècle* or Guyart's Gospel harmony (a combined narrative of the four Gospels, Comestor's *Historia evangelica,* and passages from Josephus), this manuscript contains both, with new glosses added. Samuel Berger imagines Simon de Rye as a *père de famille* lovingly assembling his own Bible for the religious education of their children, perhaps even hand-choosing its contents and glosses for that purpose.[50]

It is hard to know to what extent Simon or Jeanne directed the illustrations, textual contents, and glossing program of the manuscript, but what is clear is that it was made for them and that it was read attentively, with annotations bearing witness to what (probably several generations of) readers thought about and prioritized. If it was Simon and Jeanne who added the greater part of the *notae* that fill the margins, they paid special attention to the glosses, including this one on Apocalypse 16:4 privileging the mystical, or spiritual, senses and promising damnation for those who read too literally:[51]

> Per la fiole au tier ange qui est espandue signifie que ceulx seront dampnez qui ont corrompus lez Escriptures et ont torner la doulceur des esperituelx entendement en ordeure de charnez sens sicomme les heritez et ceulx qui preschent pour lez chosez temporellez et ceulx qui tornent l'Evangile en plaideriee. (fol. 355v)
>
> (By the third angel's poured-out vial is intended those who will be damned who have corrupted the scriptures and have turned the sweetness of the spiritual meaning into the filth of the carnal sense, such as heretics and those who preach for temporal things and those who turn the Gospel into legal arguments.)

Materialism, heresy, the pedantic excesses of scholastic argument – these are precisely the flaws for which Job's friends are rebuked, against which the *Moralia* and the *Expositio* warn (albeit differently), and which this Bible's owners fervently wished to avoid.

This expanded *Bible historiale* customized for Simon de Rye and Jeanne de la Baume, BnF fr. 15370–1, walks a fine line between following Guyart's historical program of commentary and confronting the insufficiencies of literal-historical exposition in elucidating doctrine and for attaining knowledge about God. Nowhere is this clearer than with Job, where Gregory the Great's *Moralia* is chosen to gloss the "Grand Job" so as to support the example of patience in the "Petit" while salvaging Christian lessons from Job's complaint. As another gloss – also marked with a marginal *nota* – in this copy emphasizes, such an approach is valid because, according to a gloss on John 10:1, "les prophetes creoient une meisme chose que nous creons, maiz ilx creoient les choses a advenir et nous, les venues" ("the prophets believed one and the same thing as we believe, but they believed in the things to come and we, those that have come to pass," fol. 306v).

Respecting the *Bible historiale*'s historical orientation, this glossing program favours the deceptively named "historical" chapters of the *Moralia,* which nonetheless are aimed at proving Job's sainthood by the resemblance of his historical life to Christ's and by reading his words as a real-time narration of a prophetic vision rather than as an emotional response to his own situation. In chapter 14, Job "regardait l'incarnation nostre Redempteur" ("saw the Incarnation of our Redeemer"). Following 19:23–5, "Who will grant me that my words may be written? Who will grant me that they may be marked down in a book? With an iron pen and in a plate of lead, or else be graven with an instrument in flint stone. For I know that my Redeemer liveth, and in the last day I shall rise out of the earth," the permanence Job desires for his words is explained as the vivid and irrefutable revelation of Christ and his Passion:

> … ainsy comme sy dit en prophetizant, "ung chascun mescreant coignoistra celuy: c'est mon Redempteur, batuz, moqués, feruz de palmes, coronnez de coronnes, despiné, soilliers de crachet, crucifier, et mors. Maiz je le croy par foys certainne vive apres lay mortz. Je le regehis de voix liberal que mon Redemptour, que morut entre les mains des felons, [vit] et que je resusciteray de la terre au tresdarniers jours. (fol. 127r)[52]
>
> (… as if he said, prophesying, "every unbeliever will know him: he is my Redeemer, beaten, mocked, nailed by his hands, crowned with a crown, pricked with thorns, spit upon, crucified, and dead. But I believe him, by certain faith, to live after death. I confess with an eager voice that my Redeemer, who died in the hands of evildoers, [lives] and that on the last day I shall rise from the earth.)

Despite laying claim to the "historical," these glosses negate Job's speech at the literal level. It is up to the glossator's hand to fix – engrave in stone, as it were – his meaning and prevent him from speaking against himself in contradiction. For example, an unannounced gloss promptly corrects Job when, at 16:23, he seems to deny the resurrection of the dead that, according to the gloss quoted above, he affirmed at 19:25:

> Nous alons ou sentier de la mort par lequel nous ne retornerons pas. Non mie que nous ne soyons ramenes en la general resurection a la vie de la

chars mais nous ne retornerons aux labours de ceste vie mortelle ne pour acquerir guierdon par labours. (fol. 126v)[53]

(We are going down the path of death by which we will not return. [Begin gloss:] Not that we will not be brought back to the life of the flesh at the universal resurrection, but we will not return to the labours of this mortal life, nor to earning wages by labour.)

When Job first begins his complaint at 3:1, another gloss summarizing vol. 1, book 4, chapters 5–7 of the *Moralia* interrupts to silence Job's cry in its own way, having him curse not the day of his birth but the false (day)light of Satan, who had promised divine knowledge but delivered instead a fallen state of darkness, sin, and of unknowing:

> Et pour ce quoy le saint homme desire par ce qu'il dit, "le jour perisse que je fuz neiz" et ung poc apres dit, "et soit enveloper de amertume," mais que par ce jour il ne veult autre chose entendre que le dyauble ... ainsy comme s'il dist, "Perisse l'esperance inferee du malvais ange que foingnait ly estre jour et resplandit par la promission de la diviniter. Perisse le anciens ennemis que nous ait promis lumiere et nous ait trabuchier en tenebre de pechier." (fol. 124r)

> (And as for what the holy man desires when he says, "Let the day perish wherein I was born" and a little later, "and let it be wrapped in bitterness" he means by this day none other than the Devil ... as if he said, "Let the infernal hope of the evil angel perish who feigned daylight and shone with the promise of divinity. Let the old enemy perish who promised us light and made us stumble in the shadows of sin.")

Much rides on the glosses' "ainsy comme s'il dist"; following Gregory the Great, they replace Job's more troublesome words with what he might have, should have said. Reinforcing Guyart's claim in the "Petit Job" that his real words are too full of mystery for the lay reader to understand, the *Moralia* glosses effectively rewrite his speech to offer a model of Job that, if not identical to the self-censored and self-censoring protagonist of the "Petit Job," complements him in his Christian exemplarity.

"Crabbed Eloquence": Job's Double Legacy

Saint Job, as he appears in the "Petit Job" and the *Moralia in Job*, became known in the Middle Ages as the patron saint of those suffering from leprosy and syphilis, had a feast day of 10 May, and even figured in the *Acta Sanctorum*.[54] Hugh of Saint Victor recommends the *Moralia* in his *Didascalicon* (5.7) not in the category of exegesis, but in that of saints' lives (*facta sanctorum*), a testament to Gregory's success in "canonizing" Job in the double sense of appropriating him as a Christian saint and of establishing that interpretation of his life narrative into Christian tradition. Rubrics in some copies of the *Bible historiale* introduce the Book of Job as "*la vie de Job*" or "*la vie du grant Job*" ("The life of Job" and "The life of the Great Job," as rendered in W 125, fol. 221v), orienting readers' expectations towards familiar saints' lives and alerting them that Job's life (if not his words) is an exemplary one. He was an aristocratic saint, "le plus grant sire de tous ceulx d'orient" ("The greatest lord among all those of the East," W 125, fols. 222r and 232v), holding up a mirror to the ruling class for the justice, charity, and humility with which he recalls having ruled over his household and territory.[55] The knight and the serf alike find their labours vindicated at 7:1: "Vie d'omme est comme chevalerie sur terre et ses jours comme jours des sers servans a loyers" ("The life of man upon earth is a warfare [or knighthood], and his days are like the days of a hireling [serf]," BnF fr. 15370, fol. 124v).[56] As the fifteenth-century play *La Pacience de Job* shows, his example might be leveraged to teach peasants, exemplified by comic characters Gason and Rusticus, two of Job's servants given prominent roles in the play, to be contented with their lot (perhaps no coincidence, following the late fourteenth-century rebellions). Possibly aided by his story's circulation in the *Bible historiale*, the unlikely saint permeated late medieval works of theatre, moral literature, and poetry, such as Pierre de Nesson's *Les vigiles des morts*, based on readings from Job in the Office of the Dead.[57]

The reinvention of Job as a literary type in the later Middle Ages would multiply opportunities for identification and perspectives from which to judge Job's story. During the same period as the scribes of Royal 19 D 3 and BnF fr. 15370 were working to unite the "Grand" and "Petit" versions of Job in a common message, the two grew apart in fictionalized adaptations, which were free to probe further (with Aquinas's work, for example) the logical ends of Job's questions. The quintessential undeserving sufferer, Job's story and words were assimilated into common tropes for trials and suffering: from the lovesick poet's unrequited love, to the *mal mariée*'s quiet fidelity to an abusive husband, to the prisoner's unheeded calls for justice. No longer a figure of Christ, but a dramatic interpreter of that figure, Job's literary avatars, protected by their secular masks, could express the anger and despair denied to a saintly Job, level criticism against the one "testing" them, and show defiance in the face of injustice, whether implicitly divine or purely human. The sacred and secular versions of Job mutually gloss one another as well: Job's story and words come to shed light on the secular social realities of grief, injustice, and abuse, and those familiar, human stories of suffering offer an emotionally accessible means to understand the spiritual meaning of suffering and compassion.

Chaucer's Clerk's Tale sets the contrasting Job-types in dialogue with one another by first presenting the reticent, submissive "Petit Job" in the person of Griselda, who bears her trials with perfect serenity, and then partially negating that model with an envoy that reads her unquestioning silence as a negative example, or at least one open to scrutiny.[58] Urging mistreated wives to "Lat noon humylitee youre tonge naile" (v. 1184), "Ne dreed hem nat, doth hem no reverence" (v. 1201), and "Beth nat bidaffed for youre innocence,/But sharply tak on yow the governaille" (vv. 1191–2) with "The arwes of thy crabbed eloquence" (v. 1203), the Clerk's envoy humorously evokes a fight worthy of "He that contendeth with God" (39:27) and "would set judgment before him, and would fill my mouth with complaints [or reproaches]" (23:4), and as Ann Astell has argued, offers a feminine corrective to Gregory the Great's stoic, hypermasculine reading of Job.[59] The potential for ironic play in pitting the silent Job against the indignant, plaintive one was not lost on François Villon, who compares his life to Job's in his *Testament* and concludes that God, "Combien que le pecheur soit ville,/Riens ne hayt que perseverance" ("However vile the sinner,/[God] hates nothing more than perseverance").[60] In his lyrical poetry, Charles d'Orléans alludes to Job's situation to convey a psychology of unrequited love (and vice versa), dramatizing tensions between patient devotion, experienced injustice, and prayer unanswered in lyrical laments that operate on both sacred and secular planes. Job's literary reinventions expose the dangerous limits of an otherwise desirable identification with Job, liberating questions that, as far as Guyart was concerned, should never be translated.

"Words That No One Ought to Translate"

Taboos put pressure on translation. Insofar as taboos differ from culture to culture and language to language, a translator's choices often become most visible when faced with a word, topic, or text that is felt to be more strongly tabooed in the target language than in the source language. Guyart is sensitive to the differences between Latin and French, and between clerical and courtly subcultures, when it came to norms governing language use and especially the discussion of sensitive topics. The Book of Job represents the most visible and most extreme example of the translator's refusal to translate based on a perceived difference between Latin and French readers, but it is not the only instance in which taboo language or subject matter prompts his self-conscious discomfort with rendering it in French. For example, after omitting some details about leprosy and reproductive disorders in Leviticus, he apologizes to his readers and casually remarks that such subject matter "is improper to speak of in French, but in Latin, everything is proper" ("n'est mie moult honeste chose en romans mes en latin est toute chose honeste," BnF fr. 155, fol. 36r.).[61]

The widely perceived social impropriety of speaking directly about sex and bodies in courtly French settings is well documented in texts that flaunt and poke fun at the false modesty of euphemisms and the hypocrisy or conceit of those who insist on them. Examples abound, such as Lady Reason's argument with the Lover in the *Roman de la Rose* over her use of the dysphemistic but direct word *couilles* (balls), and a fabliau mocking a young woman who looks down on the language habits of her father's hired labourers and "feels sick" upon hearing lewd sex talk ("La Damoisele qui n'öit parler de fotre qui n'aüst mal au cuer"), but enthusiastically has sex with one of them who knows how to employ "courtly" euphemisms that are arguably more graphic thanks to their vivid imagery.[62]

Many of the topics that sometimes, but not always, elicited a reflexive act of self-censorship in Guyart's translation map well onto Keith Allan's and Kate Burridge's taxonomy of "taboo words," which most often include "bodies and their effluvia; the organs and acts of sex, micturition and defecation; diseases, death and killing" as well as culture- or context-specific social and religious prohibitions.[63] When dealing with material that he finds unfitting for a lay readership or provocative according to the norms of aristocratic courtly politesse, the translator's strategies include obfuscation (euphemizing or mistranslating problematic content), excision (omitting words or passages), non-translation (leaving them in Latin), and the addition of mitigating commentary.[64] It is not uncommon for him to combine several strategies (e.g., excision or non-translation with commentary explaining the choice in euphemistic terms).

Beyond the social decorum of avoiding words and topics that might shock, offend, or disgust readers, a number of social, moral, and religious prohibitions gave Guyart pause when translating. He worried about the sanctity of the Latin Eucharistic rite being tainted or falsified merely by translating it fully into French:

Le maistre dit es hystoires aucunes choses sur ceste partie devant dicte de l'Euvangile saint Mathieu dont il n'appartient mye a parler en rommant pour les paroles du corps et du sang Nostre Sires dont il est sacrez en l'autel, lesqueles sont contenues en l'Euvangile. Mais ce qui en appartient a dire dirai je. Nous devons donc cy noter que par la force de ces paroles

> qui sont dictes ou canon de la messe, "C'est mon corps, c'est mon sang,"
> est faicte transubstanciation. Et est creable chose que quant Nostre Sires
> dist ces paroles qu'il mua le pain et le vin en char et en sang. (Royal 19 D
> 3, fol. 508v)[65]
>
> (The Master says in the *Historia* some things on this last part of the Gospel
> of Saint Matthew about which it is not appropriate to speak in French on
> account of the words, which are contained in the Gospel for the body and
> blood of our Lord, by which they are blessed on the altar. But I will say what
> it is fitting to say. We should note here that by the power of these words
> that are said in the canon of the Mass, "This is my body, this is my blood,"
> transubstantiation is performed. And it is believable that when our Lord
> said these words, he changed the bread and wine into flesh and blood.)

The language surrounding the preparation of the Eucharist was off limits both in terms of maintaining an abstract sense of sacred authority (under which Latin was a holy language appropriate for the rite, but French was not) and for more practical reasons. If the sacraments, and Christ's material presence, could pass into French, lay readers might attempt to perform the Eucharist in the absence of a priest, in which case translation threatens to undermine, rather than support, church institutions. For these reasons, the words priests would use to consecrate the host and wine are left untranslated in French missals as well, with justifications similar to Guyart's.[66] The theology surrounding transubstantiation had also become a contentious topic in the thirteenth century, since Innocent III's Fourth Lateran Council in 1215, requiring a cautious approach in a translation for lay readers.[67] Conscious of an important difference of readership, the translator emphasizes the doctrine of transubstantiation in relation to his readers' experience as parishioners attending Mass while declining to translate a section of Comestor's commentary directed at priests who would perform the ceremony in Latin.

There are other moments where Guyart hesitates over whether he should trust a lay readership with exposure to non-Christian or heretical religious beliefs or ambiguous moral examples. For instance, as Rosemarie Potz McGerr has noted, Guyart silently omits from Genesis some of Comestor's more in-depth commentary about Greco-Roman pagan ideas.[68] He also omits the parable of the unjust steward in Luke 16, noting that it is "not very profitable to laypeople," perhaps on account of the ambiguity of its moral lesson.[69] Most of these omissions are small and unintrusive, and they are few in number compared to Guyart's more frequent strategy of explicating material he found incongruent with medieval French social norms or prone to interpretations deemed heretical. However, his moments of discomfort in translating some portions of biblical text and of Comestor's commentary reveal the boundaries of Guyart's trust in his imagined readers even as he also asks for their trust that he will translate only what is beneficial to them and what will not cause them undue distress or put their souls at risk. Where Guyart takes the position that certain words are best left untranslated, some later scribes and compilers of manuscripts containing the *Bible historiale* disagreed, enacting a debate about who could and should read the whole Bible in French, and how best to prime them to read it with maximal benefit and minimal risk (to themselves, to church authority, to society).

As the next chapter demonstrates, different kinds of vernacular Bible formats envisaged different target audiences, with tailored contents and reading programs intended to deliver biblical lessons in a way that matched the perceived needs and competencies of their audience. As one fifteenth-century scribe put it, the *Bible historiale*, with its long text and expansive glossing program, required patience on the reader's part. As I argue, readerly patience is not only a prerequisite for reading the *Bible historiale*, but also one of its goals. Modeled on scholastic and devotional approaches to reading the Bible, as well as the kind of "patience" attributed to Job in his ultimate humility in deferring to God's will, Guyart's translation and its visual formatting work together to define a role for the reader as a student who will be trained in how to read the Bible with the patient, disciplined curiosity necessary to ask productive questions of the text.

5 The Patient Reader

Romans 8:25

The preceding chapters have explored several aspects of the relationship between the *Bible historiale* and its implied reader(s): how translator Guyart des Moulins imagines and defines his audience, how his translation and commentary frame biblical narrative to fit that audience's horizons of expectations and encourage belief, and how later scribes and artists involved in producing new manuscripts of his work expand and modify it to fit changing norms or to suit the needs of individual manuscript recipients. Some of the strategies Guyart and scribes employ to achieve these goals are primarily reactive: that is, they respond to the real or perceived wants, needs, and behaviours of target readers, whether aristocratic, French-language lay readers as a category, or a specific intended recipient of a manuscript. Other strategies are proactive, meant to actively shape the reception of the text as well as the receptiveness of the reader. By positioning the implied reader in the role of student, these strategies aim to move the real readers who willingly adopt that role from a position of (presumed) lay ignorance, resistance, and impatience towards one of institutionally validated knowledge, compliance, and patience. Reactive and proactive strategies are not mutually exclusive. Some choices, such as Guyart's self-censorship of the Book of Job, involve both.[1] By omitting Job's questions to and about God, Guyart not only reactively forestalls anticipated readings that could threaten church authority or run afoul of orthodoxy, but proactively refashions the story to foreground a model of "patience" – the quality for which Job is best known and most praised in his medieval manifestations – according to which readers should not ask the kind of probing questions Guyart censors from Job's speech, but should trust in and submit to divine (and ecclesiastical) authority.

It is partly in reference to this example of Job that I invoke the virtue of "patience" as being emblematic of the ideal reader of the *Bible historiale*. By ideal reader, I mean the compliant reader who accepts the narrator's (or here, translator's) point of view, obeys his directives about how to interpret and interact with the text and, on the whole, conforms to the reading program laid out by the implied reader position constructed by the text.[2] In fact, one learned medieval reader familiar with the *Bible historiale* evokes patience as a quality befitting its ideal reader, in contrast with the target readership of a different kind of biblical rewriting, the *Bible moralisée*.

This clerical reader, the scribe of the manuscript now called Ghent, Universiteitsbibliotheek 141 (Ghent UB 141), compares the two textual traditions in the preface of his manuscript, which is one of several fifteenth-century manuscripts that combine features of *Bible moralisée* and *Bible historiale* source texts and formatting conventions. For the most part, Ghent UB 141 is a sparsely illustrated *Bible moralisée*, but it draws some additional material from an expansive combined *Bible historiale* and *Bible moralisée* manuscript, Brussels, Bibliothèque royale de Belgique, MS 9001–2 (KBR 9001–2). This latter manuscript inserts moral commentary (*moralités*) from the *Bible moralisée* into the *Bible historiale* as a secondary layer of gloss.[3] Defining the genre of the *Bible moralisée* – and, in fact, coining the title *Bible moralisée*, a point to which I shall return – the scribe of Ghent UB 141 explains that his manuscript will proceed by matching brief *histoires* summarizing discrete biblical narratives with tropological *moralités* interpreting their moral application.[4]

Drawing upon his direct knowledge of both the *Bible moralisée* and the *Bible historiale* as separate, but complementary, French-language biblical traditions catering to lay readers, he compares them in order to define the audience he foresees for the *Bible moralisée* text he copies. Notably, he recommends its short, condensed format for readers or listeners who lack the patience required to read the more "prolix" *Bible historiale*.

Pource que pluseurs s'esjoissent d'oir briefves matieres car aucune foiz par la prolixité et longueur du langage ilz sont empeschiez en leur entendement, siques ilz ne peuent pas comprandre de ce qu'ilz oyent, et les autres se ennuient par impacience. Et autres sont qui demandent longues et extendues escriptures, et pour tant qui vouldra oir les histoires de la Bible plus a plain et plus prolixement, il pourra recourre a celle qui est exposee selon le Maistre es Histoires, ou les escriptures sont grandes et extendues en pluseurs volumes. (Ghent UB 141, fol. 1r)[5]

(Because many enjoy hearing short things, since sometimes, due to prolixity and length of language, they are prevented in their understanding such that they cannot comprehend what they hear, and others become bored out of impatience. And there are others who ask for long, extended scriptures, but whoever wants to hear the [hi]stories of the Bible more fully and more verbosely may have recourse to the Bible that is exposed according to the Master of Histories [i.e., the *Bible historiale*], where the scriptures are large and span several volumes.)

The scribe of Ghent UB 141 recognizes that different readers needed Bibles adapted to their literacies and their ways of engaging productively with texts, and that the predominant French version of the Bible at that time, the *Bible historiale*, was not equally suited to all readers' needs and abilities. The "impatient" readers in the above description are those who "se ennuient" or become bored or agitated, for whom reading or listening to complex texts for an extended period of time produces negative emotions that prevent them from fully understanding, remembering, or benefiting from the text. In contrast, the *Bible historiale* demands "patient" reading, by readers who willingly "ask for long, extended scriptures" and who will not give up easily but will apply the necessary effort to understand them. Based on this scribe's comparison of the two texts and their readers, we might read (im)patience as a shorthand for the nexus of attitudes, approaches, and reading practices the two Bible formats (and their combined versions) each exploit to their advantage and to the advantage of their readers.

Lessons for the Impatient: Ghent UB 141's Answer to the *Bible historiale*

When the scribe of Ghent UB 141 surmises that the lengthy text of the *Bible historiale* might be ill-suited to the readers he envisions for his manuscript, he is actively rejecting the *Bible historiale* and defining the *Bible moralisée* in opposition to it. Despite modern scholars' close association of the title *Bible moralisée* with its thirteenth-century versions dominated by full-page, eight-panel illustrations that visually represent the allegorical and typological relationships between Old and New Testament scenes and their moral interpretations, Ghent UB 141 (which lacks those eight-panel illustrations) is the earliest surviving manuscript to call itself a *Bible moralisée*.[6] We might even surmise that the scribe of Ghent UB 141 coined the title *Bible moralisée* in explicit opposition to the *Bible historiale*, the title

Guyart gave his own translation to emphasize its historical focus and program of exegesis based on Peter Comestor's *Historia scholastica.* The two titles suggest different ways of thinking about their approaches to teaching the biblical text to lay audiences: Guyart's adjectival *historiale* (historical) indicates that the Bible is already, at least in part, historical, whereas the past participle *moralisée* (moralized) suggests that the scribe of Ghent UB 141 has *made* it moral where it had not been. This grammatical difference is borne out by their compilation choices: Guyart teaches the historical lessons of the Bible by adding to the translated biblical text a scaffolding of historical commentary (to which later scribes of expanded copies such as KBR 9001–2 could add additional text and commentary without negating its historicity). In contrast, the *Bible moralisée* "moralizes" the biblical text by selectively editing its narrative down to include only brief references to episodes that lend themselves to moral lessons. Biblical history – in fact, most of the biblical text – recedes into the background, distilled into snapshots that serve mainly as mnemonic devices to retain the moral aphorisms with which they are paired.

The *Bible moralisée*'s governing force of "brevity" obscures the connective tissue of biblical narrative as well as the hermeneutic processes that produce its *moralités.* In addition to discouraging readers from pondering challenging questions that a complete telling of the stories might raise, these visible gaps in the chain of interpretation remind readers of their dependence upon clerical mediation and the role they are to inhabit as consumers, not producers, of meaning. This idea finds some parallels in the *Bible historiale,* such as in Guyart's "abridged" Job as well as in the more localized etymological shortcuts, or "biblismes," that Xavier-Laurent Salvador defines as moments in the *Bible historiale* where we can intuit from missing lexical information that "il 'se passe' quelque chose dans l'original" ("something 'is happening' in the original") whose interpretive steps are elided in translation.[7] Both the *Bible historiale* and the *Bible moralisée* traditions situate lay readers in a subordinate and dependent position in need of clerical mediation, and both Ghent UB 141 and its partial source manuscript, KBR 9001–2, represent unique fifteenth-century projects that combine features of the *Bible historiale* and *Bible moralisée* to enhance that mediation.[8]

Where these two related manuscripts disagree is on the form the mediated text should take for their respective readers. Ghent UB 141 uses selective editing to produce a truncated *Bible moralisée* with some additional pedagogical aids copied from a uniquely expanded *Bible historiale.* The latter, KBR 9001–2, inserts the lessons of the *Bible moralisée* into their biblical textual context, combining them with the *Bible historiale* in an additive fashion to produce a comprehensive biblical text supplemented by a multi-tiered exegetical program. In addition to the *texte, gloses, histoires,* and *incidents* – layers of text and commentary found in all *Bible historiale* manuscripts – KBR 9001–2 adds additional categories of interventions such as *questions* and *responses, exposicions, notables,* and *moralités* from a *Bible moralisée.* Moreover, the scribe who compiled it gestures beyond its text and commentary to an additional source of live, interactive assistance, encouraging its readers to pose their exegetical questions to flesh and blood experts: "La maniere comment l'en puisse tous ses sens appliquer, aux maistres demandez, et aussi la laisse car laissier la doy qui bien regarde les choses ci-dessus escriptes ou dites" ("As to how to apply all of these senses, ask the masters, and leave it be, for whoever looks carefully at the things written or said above should leave it aside," KBR 9001, fol. 20v). This gloss explicitly positions its lay reader – even one so powerful as King Charles VI of France, its most likely recipient – in the role of a student who should defer to the mediation of scholarly, professional readers.[9] While the quotation is unique to this fifteenth-century manuscript, it follows a trajectory that begins with Guyart's own constructed relationship between implied author and implied reader modeled on that of university master and student.

For the lay reader who had the access, ability, and will to read a *Bible historiale* manuscript (or to hear it read), the text and its material presentation encourage "patience," with all of the physical, psychological, moral, and theological connotations that word implied. Positioning the implied reader in the role of student is one prominent strategy the *Bible historiale* and its manuscripts use to train lay readers to acquire the focus and self-discipline needed to read long narrative texts, the humble obedience to direct their curiosity towards productive rather than unsuitable questions, and finally, the contemplative imagination to understand their own lives in the context of a long and expansive sacred history. "Patience" conceived in such terms connects interpretive practices to moral and spiritual ones in order to guide and constrain reading choices. Drawing from medieval as well as modern theories of literacies, reading experiences, and narrative temporality, the remainder of this chapter examines how certain features of the *Bible historiale*, including its structure, narrative techniques, illustrations, and manuscript format, work together to deter unwanted, "impatient" reading behaviours and to cultivate "patient" ones.

The (Readerly) Virtue of Patience

In modern English, the word and concept "patience" still carry many of the connotations of its Latin and medieval vernacular origins: it encompasses a lexical field describing personality traits and behaviours related to self-restraint, especially in reaction to pain, hardship, or otherwise unpleasant circumstances. Patience has a temporal value in that someone who is "patient" is willing to wait (where waiting is, in itself, understood as a kind of suffering) and is thus slow to anger, to complain, to make rash decisions, or to give up on a difficult task.[10] The Latin *patientia* and its medieval vernacular cognates share these meanings, but with some additional connotations deriving from its etymology from the verb *patior*, to suffer, endure, persevere, or submit to. Taken as a composite of its constituent meanings, "patience" allows people to bear adversity or subjugation for a sustained period of time without it breaking their will or self-control. Patience defers the negative emotions of fear, anger, restlessness, resentment, despair, and doubt in pursuit of a higher cause, with the hope of eventual reward or vindication in time.

In medieval Latin Christianity, patience is related to the cardinal virtue of fortitude (*fortitudo*) and is listed among the "gifts of the Spirit," based on Galatians 5:22: "Fructus autem Spiritus est caritas, gaudiam, pax, patientia, benignitas, bonitas, longanimitas" ("But the fruit of the Spirit is charity, joy, peace, patience, benignity, goodness, forbearance"). Early Christian treatises on patience attributed to the church fathers Augustine and Tertullian evoke Christ's suffering as the ultimate example of patience to be imitated with humility and obedience to God. They contrast that model of holy patience, cultivated through sustained practice and facilitated by God's grace, to the impatience that opens the way for people to sin out of inordinate anger, rebellion, or selfish desires.[11] *Patientia* appears frequently in the Vulgate translation of the Epistles in a variety of contexts: urging early Christians to remain steadfast in their faith even if they are persecuted for it, such as at 2 Corinthians 6:4, "But in all things let us exhibit ourselves as the ministers of God, in much patience, in tribulation, in necessities, in distresses"; to mentor and preach to fellow believers with patience, i.e., with humility, kindness, and persistence, as at 2 Timothy 4:2, "reprove, entreat, rebuke in all patience and doctrine"; or to emulate the patient, unwavering faith of biblical figures including prophets (Jas 5:10), Job (Jas 5:11), and Noah (1 Pt 3:20). Patience will sustain them as they wait for the return of Christ (2 Thes 3:5) and the fulfilment of the reward their faith promises: "But if we hope for that which we see not, we wait for it with patience" (Rom 8:25).[12]

Medieval and earlier Christian theologians usually described "patience" in moral terms: as a stoic response to hardship, as a compassionate and humble approach to preaching or asserting authority, or as the willing, trusting submission to the authority of God and church. They understood the practice of patience to apply to all human endeavours, including clerical and monastic, scholastic, and devotional approaches to reading the Bible. According to Saint Augustine, Saint Benedict, Hugh of Saint Victor, and other patristic and medieval authorities on the matter, reading the Bible required the discipline of a quiet, but actively engaged, mind. This is especially evident in the monastic meditative practice of *lectio divina,* which systematically moves from a close exegetical reading of a passage through the additional steps of personal reflection (*meditatio*), prayer (*oratio*), and spiritual contemplation (*contemplatio*).[13] While Guyart's translation does not explicitly promote or teach *lectio divina* or any other specific monastic or scholastic regimen for reading the Bible, such models do inform his choices in presenting the biblical text and guiding readers in its interpretation. Clerical translators and authors such as Guyart would have considered how their own clerical training in how to read the Latin Bible might best be simulated for lay readers in mediated vernacular translations, according to prevalent clerical ideas about those readers.

Correcting, or Pre-Empting, the Impatient Student

As we have seen in previous chapters, Guyart discusses and defends many of his choices in terms of what he thinks his readers want and need from a Bible translation or in terms of how they will interpret and respond to the text (such as their potential to "err" in reading the Book of Job, or their likely scepticism about how Jerome structures his Book of Esther).[14] Scribes – at least the more literate and more attentive ones – were perhaps the most intimate and active readers of the *Bible historiale* and, at the same time, of its audience.[15] Many such scribes and editors, such as those of Ghent UB 141 and KBR 9001–2 discussed above, add their own comments about their alterations or additions to their source manuscripts based on a shared belief that different vernacular versions of the Bible were necessary to suit different audiences with different literacies and reading habits, to fulfil different purposes for the same readers, or to address readers' changing needs at different life stages. Accordingly, textual and paratextual contents and their presentation varied considerably among manuscripts, with different selections of biblical books, abridged or in full, in prose or verse, with different kinds and amounts of commentary and visual illustration.[16] The Ghent UB 141 scribe's binary and implicitly hierarchical distinction between "impatient" readers who can only enjoy and understand short ("briefves") lessons and the more patient, curious readers who can and want to read longer narrative texts and commentary echoes some scribes' rationalizations for including the two different books of Job: one for "simple folk" who need a simple, direct moral lesson, and one for the more sophisticated and curious readers who are dissatisfied with the abridged version and want to read the whole story.[17] They evaluate the two translations in terms of the hypothetical readers whose needs would be poorly served by one version or the other.

Guyart's and his scribes' remarks about their target audiences exhibit, on the one hand, sensitivity to the real variability of levels of literacy and reading techniques among vernacular lay readers; on the other hand, they also reflect derogatory clerical stereotypes of lay readers as too ignorant, incompetent, or inattentive to understand complex texts.[18] Related to this trope of the undisciplined lay reader is another familiar stereotype from clerical contexts, the unruly or unreceptive student who fails to listen to the teaching *magister*, a scene that appears frequently in medieval iconography, especially in illustrated scholastic texts.[19] While not usually aimed at a primary audience of clerics or university students, illustrations in some manuscripts of the *Bible historiale* make use of this trope as an immediately recognizable schema of effective and ineffective textual study, where effectiveness requires patience: sustained attention, deference to authority, and a calm but positive affect, in contrast to the ineffective learners in the scene who become distracted, complain, or fall asleep.

In Royal 19 D 2, for instance, a running gag in the miniature cycle places here a Corinthian, there an Ephesian sleeping in the back row of Saint Paul's "lectures." Other impatient readers pull their hats over their eyes or whisper to a friend. In addition to providing comic relief, such visual representations model "good" and "bad" study behaviours with respect to both the authoritative "master" Paul and the text he speaks to them, which is presumably the epistle reproduced in the manuscript following the image. Thus positioned at the beginning of a self-contained segment of text (a letter, a book of the Bible), such images invite readers of the manuscript to see themselves in the group of Paul's students and to consider their own state of mind as they prepare to read or hear his lesson. After smiling, perhaps, at the sleeping student in the back, they are gently reminded of their own fatigue or distraction and drawn back to a more earnest and active state, prepared to receive – or better, eagerly consume – the text to follow. Other, less remarkable figures in the scene, who appear to be listening attentively or asking a question, gain positive value by contrast to the drowsy or disruptive reader-listeners. The latter, the images suggest, are those whose ears and minds are not open, because they are too eager to speak, too distracted by worldly cares, or so passive as to doze off, completely inert (Figure 5.1).

In a variation on the same theme, some manuscript illuminations in *Bible historiale* manuscripts depict biblical authors and authorities such

Figure 5.1 Paul instructing a group of disciples (one of whom is nodding off) in a miniature placed at the beginning of 2 Corinthians. Royal 19 D 2, fol. 487v. Source: https://www.bl.uk/manuscripts/. © British Library Board

as Paul and Moses, as well as their later scholarly translators and commentators (Jerome, Comestor, and Guyart), more explicitly in the role of university masters: they teach from a high chair behind a lectern or turntable full of books, as their clerkly students look up from their benches below.[20] This gesture visually translates, for lay readers, a clerical university model of engaging with biblical texts as students, who may ask questions of the text but ultimately defer to the interpretive mediation of clerical authority, personified in Guyart's narrative voice as well as in the layers of authoritative voices he mediates: Jerome, Comestor, the authorities Comestor cites (Augustine, Bede, Josephus), and the biblical authors whose words the others translate and interpret.

Deborah McGrady has argued that visual and textual representations of lay reading in late medieval manuscripts of the thirteenth to fifteenth centuries often combine monastic and scholastic models of reading – more specifically, the private devotional reading of *lectio divina* and the collective subordinate role of students in scholastic *praelectio* (lecture) – in order to define and constrain the lay reader's relationship to the text. As a result of increasing vernacular literacy and manuscript production and a parallel shift from the predominantly public oral performance of texts towards private or semi-private study, the autonomy and variability of individual lay reading threatened to undermine authorial and institutional control over the reception of texts. McGrady concludes that clerical authors, scribes, and artists employed textual and iconographical representations of monastic and scholastic reading to invite lay readers to place themselves in the role of student, even when practicing solitary reading, and to view the clerical author as an expert intercessory figure or *magister* to whom they should submit.[21]

In the *Bible historiale*, visual representations of scholastic *praelectio*, featuring Guyart, Comestor, Jerome, and biblical authors like Saint Paul in the chair of the university master, reinforce the terms in which Guyart establishes his own authority in relation to his would-be readers. As Rosemarie Potz McGerr suggests in the title of her article "Guyart Desmoulins, the Vernacular Master of Histories, and his *Bible historiale*," Guyart steps into the role of the scholastic author he translates: Peter Comestor, Master of Histories ("le maistre en histoires," as Guyart calls him), whose authoritative *Historia scholastica* was a standard university textbook of historical biblical exegesis and was undoubtedly a formative text in Guyart's own education.[22] Some later scribes draw attention to Guyart's perceived status as master in his own right: for example, in BnF fr. 15370, the scribe identifies Guyart not as an author or translator, but as "le maistre que la bible translatait" ("the master who translated the Bible," fol. 131r). Referring to Guyart's inclusion of Comestor's preface, which defines the levels of exegesis and emphasizes the value of historical exegesis as a foundation for understanding the Bible and the world, McGerr explains that "The vernacular reader, like the university student, enters the text through a discourse on the methodology of exegesis. [… T]his text was meant to be a teaching book in the scholastic method for a nonscholastic audience."[23]

Guyart places his readers in the position of students through his authoritative mediating voice, through his inclusion of scholastic content, and through his prescribed manuscript layout that adopts elements of scholastic glossed manuscripts by foregrounding the biblical text in larger script, followed by smaller script for the *histoires* and shorter glosses in the margins.[24] Even as later manuscript copies modified Guyart's envisioned format to more closely resemble other deluxe vernacular manuscripts (richly decorated and illustrated, with text in two uniform columns of *bâtarde* script), illustrations emphasizing the book's scholastic origins could compensate for those changes and encourage the reader to adopt the role, attitude, and behaviours of a student who patiently attends and defers to the judgment of the text's masterly voices. Such a role flatters lay readers by inviting them to see themselves within a learned book culture usually reserved for Latin-literate clerics. At the same time, however, Guyart's increased mediation of his Latin source texts reinforces the subordinate nature of the lay reader's position, whether this mediation consists of removing content he does not trust lay readers to interpret correctly or, as McGerr illustrates, of replacing Comestor's long expositions of non-Christian and heterodox perspectives (pagan, Manichean, Jewish) on the facts of the cosmos and the nature of God with simple statements that they are wrong.[25] Such changes reflect not only a cautious approach when introducing lay readers to alternative beliefs, but also a different understanding of the purpose of their religious education; unlike future clergy and masters of theology who study the *Historia scholastica* in Latin in a scholastic setting, the lay reader would never take the priest's or master's place in a role of teaching authority, and therefore did not necessarily need the knowledge base required to perform Christian apologetics, preaching, or exegesis.

In the student-like role assigned to them by the text and its manuscript presentation, readers are asked to embody patience in a particular way: submission to textual authority and the silent deferral of interpretation encouraged by the implied author and modeled by the patience of (the "Petit") Job and by the more cooperative students illustrated in manuscripts. A second, related aspect of readerly patience has to do with a more quotidian, but also theologically rich, association of "patience" with waiting and duration, effects of the *Bible historiale*'s linear narration and scholastic organization. This temporal consciousness is central to Guyart's construction of a historical Bible, in contrast to (for example) the Ghent UB 141 scribe's pedagogical strategy of "brevity," which dehistoricizes biblical narrative and restricts its interpretive possibilities. The central event of the Crucifixion in the *Bible moralisée* gives meaning to all that precedes and follows it in such a way that the reader is permitted an extemporal perspective from which historical time and narrative sequence both become irrelevant to meaning.[26] Herein lies the crux of what gives the *Bible moralisée* and the *Bible historiale* their respective forms and requires of the *Bible historiale*'s reader more "patience": the two traditions situate themselves differently with respect to time and readings of history. It is the primacy of history, I argue, that produces a quality in the text that demands and fosters "patience" in its reader through a constructed awareness of the passage of time.

Historia fundamentum est: **Reading Time in the *Bible historiale*[27]**

It may seem a banal observation to note, as the scribe of Ghent UB 141 does, that the *Bible historiale* is a much longer text than the *Bible moralisée*, that reading it in full would therefore take more time than reading a *Bible moralisée*, and that devoting more time to reading the Bible would require more patience. However, what makes time meaningful as an index and practice of patience when reading the *Bible historiale* is how time is consciously organized, interpreted, and felt. In the practice of *lectio divina*, time is experienced in the rhythm of the language as the reader meditates on the pronunciation of each syllable. In history, time is divided and ordered so as to make meaning of events through their past causes and future effects, and in Christological readings of biblical history, their figural relationships to one another. These two timelines – the individual time of the reader's progression through the text and the cosmic time the Bible purports to tell from Creation to Apocalypse – are bound together in the *Bible historiale*. It is a text whose structure and historical commentary both require sustained attention to the linear narration of events and draw readers' attention to their own historical time and its readability in the tradition of historical exegesis. The patience needed to learn to read history in this way is inseparable from the patience needed to trust and submit to the clerical authority of the text; the latter is a precondition for the former insofar as it structures the reading experience as a series of biblical readings alternating with historical analyses and questions for contemplation.

Time is brought to consciousness by being measured, and the measurement of time is a focal point of Guyart and of his scholastic source, Peter Comestor's *Historia scholastica*. Comestor's prologue, which Guyart translates between his own preface and the first verse of Genesis, offers a meditation on God's mansions. Comestor's analogy likens the Bible to God's dining hall, whose floor, walls, and roof represent the ways of reading it: history, allegory, tropology. History forms the foundation on which the other readings stand and thus becomes the focus of the *Historia scholastica* and *Bible historiale*. For Comestor, history is a function of time and can be further classified into three kinds of temporality. As Guyart translates it, "histoires est li fondemens, la quele est devisee en trois manieres, cest asauoir histoire annuele, qualendaire, et effimere" ("history is the foundation, which is divided three ways, namely annual, calendric, and ephemeral," BnF fr. 155, fol. 2r).[28] Whereas Comestor assumes his audience will understand these terms, the French translator adds an *incident* to further explain their meaning as well as the meaning of *incident* as a category of gloss:

> uns incidens. Histoire annele est une chose qui est faite en .i. an, kalendaire qui est faite en .i. mois, effimere qui est faite soudainement, cest en .i. iour ou en la partie d'un mois, et est apelee effimere a la semblance d'un poisson de mer qui le meismes jour qu'il est nez meurt ou tost apres. Et notez ci que incidens est une chose qui bien chiet dedens histoire et n'est mie de histoire. (BnF fr. 155, fol. 2r)
>
> (An *incident*: Annual history is something that happens within a year, calendric is that which happens within a month, ephemeral happens suddenly, that is, in one day or part of a month, and it is named "ephemeral" after an ocean fish that dies the same day it is born, or soon after. And note here that *incident* is something that falls inside history yet is not part of history.)

The short passage quoted above, which does not appear in Comestor's text, reveals how Guyart sees the cosmic time of years, months, and days measured by the movements of heavenly bodies as deeply intertwined with the human time of generations, lifespans, and life events, and also with the textual time of writing, reading, and making meaning of human and natural events through language.

As noted in chapter 3, Guyart's use of the word "history" (*histoire*, or its orthographic variants *hystoire* or *ystoire*) is multivalent. It can refer to historical time, as it does in the first half of the quoted passage; to the historiographic narration of past events, as in its common modern usage; to a narrative or "story," whether purporting to be factually based or not; to the historical sense of scripture and its exposition; to the specific title of Comestor's historical commentary, the *Historia scholastica*; or to the individual chapters or extracts of that text that Guyart intercalates between segments of translated biblical text and designates as separate from the Bible with the rubric "*histoire*." This conflation of meanings produces Guyart's puzzling definition of *incident* as something that falls within, but is not part of, history. His definition is etymological: the medieval Latin word *incidentia* derives from *caedo, caedere*, to cut or fall; the *incident* is the unexpected event that cuts into, falls into, or interrupts the background noise of time passing as expected. In Guyart's usage of the word, *incidents* can be part of yet outside of history in at least two ways: some instances of the word indicate Guyart's asides that interrupt the sections of commentary labeled *histoires* (as opposed to the *gloses* that interrupt the main biblical text); other *incidents* derive from asides given the same label in Comestor's text, and those usually pertain to non-biblical historical events (such as Greek or Egyptian history) inserted into the biblical timeline for synchronous comparison.

In a text that is usually precise with language, Guyart's multivalent use of the word and concept *histoire* points to a common medieval Christian (and, in some respects, Jewish) view of human history, first, as meaningfully connected to (cyclical) cosmic time through God's providence and validated by the religious ritual significance of liturgical calendars, seasons, and holy days; and, second, as readable for figural meaning (that is, events can symbolize, interpret, or prefigure other events).[29] The Bible is the basis, model, and archetype for this view of history and of time, and historical exegesis brings it into focus. Guyart's treatment of Comestor's prologue and his extended discussions of historical temporalities attune the implied readers' focus to time in the text, to the physical experience of reading it, and to an understanding of the rituals and events of their lives as connected to cosmic time. As Guyart's (false) etymology connecting the ephemeral to a fish's short lifespan suggests, to contemplate the passage of time is an exercise in patience that asks readers to contemplate their own mortality.

Such a measurement of time is built into the structure of the Bible itself, beginning with the six days of Creation by which the universe is spatially, sequentially, and conceptually organized. The Bible marks time in days, weeks, years, and generations counting from its beginning, and eschatological prophecies counting from its end. Specific durations of time take on meaning as a way to draw prophetic, figural, or symbolic associations between events. Three days pass before Job's silence breaks, before Jonah escapes the belly of the whale, and before Christ rises; forty days is the time Noah spends on the Ark, Moses on Mount Sinai, and Jesus fasting and resisting temptation. Time is not only counted, but felt: the messianic prophet waits, and the martyr endures.

From the Seven Ages of the World to the Seven Ages of Man to the seven-year cycles or "year-weeks" of the Old Testament, Guyart des Moulins's *Bible historiale* joins a long tradition of applying temporal divisions as an organizing principle of history, of concepts, and of texts after the model of the first week of Creation. The liturgical calendar already keyed extracts of biblical text to days of the year, imbuing them with added meanings and associations according to where they fall. In Guyart des Moulins's *Bible historiale*, the structure of the text takes on its own rhythm in which biblical time is drawn out by its periodic pauses – in the *histoires* and *incidents* intercalated between chapters or sometimes shorter segments of biblical text – to meditate on the duration of biblical epochs, events, and lives and on the numerological and eschatological significance of those measures of time. This rhythmic structure is most visible in Genesis, where *histoires* draw further connections between the (divinely created) astronomical divisions of time, the church's reckoning of time, and the finitude of human lives and histories, gesturing towards an apocalyptic end. After the fourth day of Creation (Gn 1:14–19), Guyart translates Comestor's explanations of how the moon and sun divide time into days and years, and how the church determines the annual calendar of 365 days and six hours. A running commentary in the *histoires* and glosses throughout Genesis collates information from Hebrew and Greek (Septuagint) biblical sources, commentators like Augustine, historians such as Josephus, and the apocalyptic writer Pseudo-Methodius to elucidate the exact chronology of biblical history: how long Adam and Eve were in paradise, the length of the "first age" from their creation to the Flood, and where Guyart's own generation falls on the long timeline between Adam's first day on earth and the Last Judgment.

Making meaning of the present in the context of biblical and universal history was of the utmost concern when Guyart des Moulins began his *Bible historiale* in 1291. Tripoli and Acre, the last crusader strongholds in the Levant, had just fallen to the Mamluks in 1289 and 1291, respectively, effectively ending the two-century-long Latin Christian fight for Jerusalem. Worn down by losses and increasingly critical of the crusading mission, contemporaries asked themselves why a just God would allow his faithful to suffer brutalities at the hands of their non-Christian foes or whether their ruin was deserved.[30] While translating Genesis 16 and its corresponding *histoire* that cites Pseudo-Methodius's prophecies of destruction to be wrought by Ishmael's descendants upon Christians in the East, the French cleric is reminded of recent events and departs from his source (the *Historia scholastica*) to add his own reflections on their significance.[31] Invested with prophetic and apocalyptic meaning, the events of the day – and the moral failings that contributed to them – form the backdrop against which he has undertaken to translate the Bible:

> "Li asne sauvages et les chievres seurmonteront toutes rages de bestes, et li nombres des debonnaires (c'est des c[r]estiens) sera par aus destruiz," aussi com ce fust a dire, "Gens sans loy (ce sont paien) destruiront les crestiens." Et de ce dist methodies des filz Hysmel (ce sont paien) qui … tenront la terre par iiii. semaines d'ans … et si ociront les prestres es sains lieus et es sains lieus gerront avec les fames et lieront leur chevaus aus sepultures des sains pour la mauvestié des crestiens qui adonc seront. Il semble que ceste chose soit avenue en la destruction d'Acre et de Triple et de toute crestienté dela la mer, car on set vraiement que Diex en a soufert la destruction pour les orribles pechez de la terre. Et el tens que cele

terre fu destruite fu cist livres commenciez a translater et en cele meismes annee. (BnF fr. 155, fol. 10r)[32]

("The wild asses and the goats will surpass all beasts in their wrath, and the number of the good (that is, the Christians) will be destroyed by them," as if to say, "People without the Law (that is, pagans) will destroy the Christians." And regarding this [prophecy], [Pseudo-]Methodius says of the sons of Ishmael (that is, pagans) ... that they will keep the land for four year-weeks ... and that they will kill priests in holy places, and in those holy places they will lie with women and tie their horses to the sepulchres of saints, all because of the wickedness of the Christians there. It seems as though this has come to pass in the destruction of Acre and Tripoli and all of Christendom across the sea, for it is known for a fact that God allowed their destruction as a result of the horrible sins of the land. And it was at the time when that region was destroyed that the translation of this book was begun, and in that very year.)

This brief commentary exemplifies two different methods Guyart employs (sometimes following Comestor, as he was trained, and sometimes on his own) to read history for interpretive relationships between events separated by time, in this case on ideological grounds. One approach looks for causal relationships, asking why the crusader settlements of Acre and Tripoli were destroyed and finding an answer in the Bible through a conventional association of Ishmael with Arabs and Muslims.[33] Situating the origin of the Crusades in Genesis serves to justify the conflict as inherited and inevitable even as it also condemns the crusaders for causing their own defeat through their sins; their "pagan" adversaries, meanwhile, are depicted as animalistic and mere instruments of God's judgment, lacking the human agency and responsibility of the Christian armies.[34] In a parallel second reading of the events, Guyart looks to a seventh-century apocalyptic prophecy and uses it as an interpretive lens to assign biblical meanings to recent events in order to predict their outcome: the Apocalypse of Pseudo-Methodius foretells twenty-eight years of Christian oppression under "Ishmaelite" rule before a Last Emperor would restore peace and usher in the seventh and last Age of Man with the arrival of the Antichrist.

Guyart's musings connect the biblical Ishmael to the crusading colonies founded by Saint Louis and recently conquered by the Mamluk Sultanate. He then reads those recent losses as marking a significant turning point in sacred history, and he ends by merging that chronology of recent events with that of the *Bible historiale*'s own origins: "it was at the time when that region was destroyed that the translation of this book was begun, and in that very year." This poignant irruption of Guyart's present and of the later present of the reader is a performative gesture: it inscribes the author, book, and reader as part of the history it tells in order to implicate the reader as a potential actor in that history. Even as this gloss looks back to the end of an era, it underscores the opening of a new one with the book's own genesis as Guyart des Moulins, son of a crusader, looks to the next generation of challenges and opportunities facing the church and finds them not in the East, but among his lay neighbours.[35] Guyart founds his translation on the premise that knowledge of ancient biblical history is necessary to interpret the current state of the world, and vice versa.[36]

The *Bible historiale* thus traces humans and human realities – languages, customs, political divisions, and identities – to their origins in the mythical past in an attempt to explain the present state of the religious, secular, and natural world and the medieval French reader's relationship to each. Genealogies, etymologies of words, invention narratives of new technologies, and the cataclysmic results of human failures supplement the origin stories already present in the Bible to tell a fuller, more universal history of the world. As a global narrative strategy, the historical Bible generates, with some degree of artifice, textual and temporal continuity by smoothing over gaps in time and stylistic differences of a biblical canon composed of disparate texts by many authors composed for various purposes in different cultural contexts. It bridges historical and narrative gaps by interpolating details from other sources or, as explored in previous chapters, extrapolating them via imaginative speculation. It synchronizes, in *ordo naturalis*, the Hebrew, Greek, Roman, and North African chronologies and genealogies that periodically cross paths in the Old Testament and converge with the early church.[37]

Translating from Comestor's prologue, and atypically retaining Comestor's *je* in translation (as Guyart usually converts Comestor's "I" into a third-person citation), Guyart explains:

Ore ay je donc commencié ceste oeurre a la description du monde que Moyses fist de nostre premier pere Adam et ay mené le ruissel des hystoires tressi a l'Ascencion Nostre Sauveur, et laissié aux plus sages de moy a exposer la parfondeur des misteres, lesquelx peuent et les choses anciennes raconter et nouvelles faire. Et dedens ces hystoires des peres ay je enté et mis moult des hystoires des payens qui dedens cest oeuvre sont incidens et qui appartiennent a la raison des temps des hystoires des peres devant diz. Et les ay cy dedans entées aussi comme le ruisseau qui ist d'une riviere raemplist toutes les fosses qu'il treuve au dehors de la riviere, et pource ne laisse mye la riviere son droit cours. (Paris, Bibliothèque nationale de France, MS fr. 20087 [BnF fr. 20087], fol. 1v)

(I have begun this work, according to the description Moses made of the world, with our first father Adam and have followed the flow of the histories up to the Ascension of our Saviour, and left it to those wiser than I, those who can tell old things and make new ones, to expose the depths of their mysteries. And inside these histories of the fathers I have inserted many histories of the pagans, which in this work are called *incidents,* and which belong to the chronology of the histories of the aforementioned fathers. And I have inserted them just as a stream that branches off from a river fills all the crevices it finds outside the river, and yet the river does not stray from its course.)

Like a river, the historical causality of events flows forward in time: while one is in the downstream flow of the river (the present), one sees it branching out into many paths with no clear vision of where they lead. Once one stands at the mouth of the river looking back (into the historical past), there is only one path back upstream to a single point of origin that gives coherent meaning to the branches. Simultaneous events in other parts of the world give dimension to the Hebrew Bible, which forms the main river, presented as the central thread of history from which everything else branches out. By depicting alternate worlds in symbiosis, synchronized to the same timeline, the *Bible historiale* completes salvation history. Imposing historical and textual continuity from the Christian present back to Creation and ancient Judaea also reinforces French Christian claims to biblical texts and lands.[38] The choice to ground the Bible historically does not detract from its allegorical, moral, and tropological interpretations – the "mysteries" Comestor and Guyart leave to "those wiser than I" – but on the contrary, invests history, and readers' place within it, with sacred meaning.[39]

The paradox by which historical time and moral-Christological time may coexist in Christian cosmology was famously elaborated by Saint Augustine. If divine omniscience effectively collapses time into an already complete eternity, human knowledge, as he reflects in book 11 of his *Confessions,* is attained in and through time. This attainment of knowledge happens on all three of Comestor's historic scales – the annual, the calendric, and the ephemeral – as well as in the larger scale of human generations. Comestor (and Guyart with him) cites Josephus in this context to suggest that people in the Old Testament lived longer because, without the benefit of a large body of knowledge passed down from the discoveries of their ancestors, they had more to learn and needed longer lives to make technological advances:

Josephus dist que nus ne doit mescroire ce c'on dit de la longueur de la
vie des anciens peres, car por les granz vertuz et les glorieuses sciences

qu'il ne cessoient d'aquerre en touz tens sans repos, si comme astronomie et geometrie, leur donna diex plus longues vies car autrement ne les peussent il mie avoir aquisses s'il n'eussent au mains vescu vi^c ans. (BnF fr. 155, fol. 8r)

(Josephus says that no one should doubt what is said about the lifespans of the ancient fathers, because it was for the great virtues and glorious sciences that they kept acquiring at all times, nonstop, such as astronomy and geometry, that God gave them longer lives. They could not have learned those things unless they lived for at least six hundred years.)

For Comestor's scholarly audience and Guyart's lay reader, this learning over time is largely an effect of language, measured by sounds and silences pronounced in sequence, a fact Augustine also observes in his meditation on the human experience of time.[40] Embedded in grammar, the awareness of passing time, which historical narrative sets out to reproduce, becomes a necessary medium of thought and expression; in Paul Ricoeur's words, following Augustine, "l'enjeu ultime aussi bien de l'identité structurale de la fonction narrative que de l'exigence de vérité de toute oeuvre narrative, c'est le caractère *temporel* de l'expérience humaine" ("what is ultimately at stake, both in the structural integrity of the narrative function and in the exigency of truth in every narrative work, is the *temporal* character of human experience").[41] The practice of reading the *Bible historiale* emphasizes that temporal character, both by its structure and its content.

Structurally speaking, combining the Bible with the *Historia scholastica* by alternating between segments of the Bible and related chapters of Comestor's commentary becomes for Guyart a way of unifying and dividing the Bible at the same time. The biblical text is nested within a dialogic framework in such a way as to divide it into discrete units of narrative "selon la bible" (as they are introduced in rubrics) interrupted by *histoires* that interpret, add context, or connect biblical history to recent events or current debates. The guiding conversations within the *histoires*, which cite the divergent opinions of Josephus, Bede, Eusebius, Augustine, and other historical and theological authorities as well as vague collective attributions like "the Hebrews" and "the pagans," become a critical apparatus as well as a coda for each unit of biblical text that signals a pause for reflection and debate between sections of narrative. The rhythm of this alternation between *texte* and *histoire* begins with the days of Creation, and while there is no reason to insist that readers would have chosen to read just one *texte* and its *histoire* per day, the routine of short, daily readings from scripture followed by priestly commentary is already embedded into readers' experience and the liturgical calendar (and a few manuscripts do include marginal annotations keying passages to the date they would be read during Mass).[42] With this rhythm and the translator's frequent interjections to remind readers of what they have read before and to build anticipation for what they will read later, the structure of the *Bible historiale* generates meaning through sequence. Its sequentiality, combined with its acute attention to the reckoning of time as a meaningful way to organize cumulative human knowledge and experience, makes time present to the patient mind, ever conscious of its waiting.

Rewarding (and Disciplining) the Curious Mind

When the scribe of Ghent UB 141 implies that the length of the *Bible historiale* makes it difficult to read for all but the most patient and curious lay readers, he may have had in mind KBR 9001–2, the expanded *Bible historiale* manuscript whose prefaces furnished material for his own, and which was exceptionally "prolix." In fact, it is the longest known copy of the *Bible historiale*, counting 822 folios in total, divided into two massive volumes measuring 460 x 325 cm. Not only was Guyart's *Bible historiale* a longer text than many of its vernacular alternatives such as the *Bible moralisée*, but its later expansions (introduced in chapter 1) lengthened Guyart's work up to three times its original length, from a single-volume work in its likely original form to the massive composite versions common in the fifteenth century. In addition to the stages of supplementation Samuel Berger categorized as the *Petite, Moyenne,* and *Grande Bible historiale complétée* based on their addition of different sets of biblical books from the *Bible du XIIIe siècle,* many late manuscript copies of the *Bible historiale* reflect even more complex and individualized efforts at mixing and matching the two translations, glossing programs, and other supplements such as litanies, prayers, and catechetic texts.[43]

The market demand for increasingly "prolix" Bibles lends support to the Ghent UB 141 scribe's assessment that the ideal reading public for the *Bible historiale* is the one that demands "longues et extendues escriptures," and wants to hear the Bible "plus a plain." While the most common types and stages of supplementation in the *Bible historiale* manuscript tradition reflect an increasingly clear preference for comprehensiveness based on a Latin canonical standard, Guyart's work had already "completed" the historical books of the Bible in his own way to make them into a fuller, more continuous, and more universal history.[44] As a multi-authored collection of multi-purpose texts composed over centuries, the Latin Christian biblical canon leaves gaps in time and is silent about places, communities, and events outside its scope.

Peter Comestor's *Historia scholastica*, as a stand-alone textbook and reference work for students, scholars, and preachers already familiar with the Bible, fills in those gaps by proposing answers to questions the Bible does not answer. Guyart's translation takes the logical next step to insert those questions and answers deemed of interest and value to his lay readers directly into the Bible, and to seek additional answers from other texts where Comestor's are lacking or unsatisfactory.

For example, to account for the unrecorded intertestamental period between Judas Maccabeus's death and the birth of Christ, Guyart translates Comestor's account of John Hyrcanus, which in turn is based largely on Josephus's histories; the material appears as if it were a book of the Bible, between 2 Maccabees and the Gospels. Later, in the Gospels after the Crucifixion, Guyart is struck by Comestor's silence about the destruction of Jerusalem, a point Guyart considers important for ideological as well as theological reasons. After what appears to be Guyart's own homily-like exposition of the significance of Christ crying on the way to Jerusalem as a sign of his dual human and divine nature, Guyart then consults and translates a passage from Josephus's *Antiquities of the Jews* to complete the history (rubrics in italics):

En ce lieu cy vueil je mettre l'exposicion de cest euvangile que Dieux plora sur la cité.
Ja soit ce que le maistre n'en parle point es Hystoires pour une merveilleuse chose que
josephus en racompte ... Tous les maulx et toutes les doleurs qui avindrent a la cité, Josephus le hystoriographe, c'est a dire l'escripteur des Hystoires des Hebrieux les racompte plainement et bien. Mais pource que moult de gens ne scevent pas l'ystoire que Josephus en fist, vous en voulons nous une petite partie recorder. (Royal 19 D 3, fols. 497v–498r)

(Here I would like to put the exposition of this Gospel in which God cried for the
city. It happens that the Master does not mention it at all in his Histories *due to a*
wondrous thing that Josephus says about it ... All the evils and all the sorrows that befell the city, Josephus the historiographer, that is, the writer of the *Antiquities of the Jews,* tells them fully and well. But because many people do not know the story that Josephus told about it, we would like to copy a small part of it for you.)

This last explanation for the insertion of the episode from another source – "because many people do not know the story" – echoes the scribe of Ghent UB 141 in invoking curiosity as a trait of the ideal reader of the *Bible historiale.* The reader's curiosity, or desire to hear the full story, is not a passive, innate personal quality (although degrees of it may certainly differ among individual readers), but a feeling that can be generated or amplified by storytelling techniques. We see this process at work in the above passage when Guyart stokes readers' curiosity about something that Comestor mysteriously "does not mention at all" but that is "wondrous" ("merveilleuse"), and that is not well known. Similar to how he presents his readers with the probably untrue but exciting apocryphal narratives (discussed in chapter 3), he offers his readers privileged access to a secret, a scandal, a sensational story.

Curiosity does not necessarily entail patience. In the wrong degree or directed at the wrong questions, curiosity can tend towards impatience: too little curiosity results in boredom, and unbounded curiosity that asks subversive or inappropriate questions fails to exercise proper restraint or deference to authority. The narrative framing of the *Bible historiale* puts curiosity and patience in cooperative tension, where the intellectual desires of curiosity are tempered and directed by patience. Patient curiosity asks productive questions and sustains reader engagement. This productive questioning and the expansive, encyclopedic text it produces in the *Bible historiale* parallels how questions drive narrative expansion and continuation in other kinds of medieval narrative (such as Grail cycles): unresolved questions about the unfinished quest, the undeveloped character, the unfulfilled desire, or unresolved contradiction inspire new stories in response.[45] Guyart takes advantage of such questions and their narrative-generating force by placing questions in the minds of his implied readers, asking those questions on their behalf, building up their desire to know the answer. Then, he answers those questions with explanatory narratives drawn from other texts (Peter Comestor's *Historia scholastica*, Josephus's *Antiquities of the Jews*, Jacobus de Voragine's *Legenda aurea*) or his own imaginative speculations. Questions such as "Why did Esau trade away his primogeniture so cheaply," "If the dove did not return to the ark, where did it go," "Why was Jesus so angry at the money changers in the temple," and "How did Herod die" all give rise to multiple modes of textual expansion, including the kind of speculative fiction-as-gloss discussed in chapters 2 and 3. Such questions lead Guyart to test various possibilities and explore each scenario. In the absence of a definitive answer, this strategy allows readers some freedom in choosing the most satisfactory explanatory story.

For the maintenance of faith orthodoxy, Guyart considers some questions off limits. There are questions lay readers should not ask, or that clergy should not answer for them, and in some cases, questions arise that he as translator must be careful not to even put in lay readers' heads. These concerns about where to draw the line between productive and subversive questioning generate an ongoing dialectic and narrative tension in Guyart's translation between expanding the text to satisfy readers' curiosity and truncating it to discourage questions or even to deny access to material that might inspire unwanted questions. We have seen this occur when Job's questioning of God's providence and justice are omitted from the "Petit Job," lest Job's words lead readers to interrogate their faith in God or the church's teachings about him.[46] Earlier in the *Bible historiale*, an *histoire* on Genesis, following the account of the Fall, directly addresses the kind of "foolish" question its readers should not ask. Guyart, translating Comestor, writes:

> Ci peut en demander pour quoi Diex lessa l'ome tempter, come il seust bien par devant qu'il charroit em peché. De ce et de moult tiex autres demandes dison nous, tant comme a ceste heure apertient, qu'il le voult ainsi. Et s'on demande pou quoi il le voult ainsi. C'est une fole demande de demander la cause de la volenté Dieu, comme il soit la souveraine cause de toutes causes. (BnF fr. 155, fol. 5v)
>
> (Here one might ask why God allowed man to be tempted, for he knew well in advance that he would fall into sin. In response to this and many other questions of this sort, we say, for the time being, that he wanted it that way. And if one asks why he wanted it that way, the cause of God's will is a foolish question to ask, as he is the sovereign cause of all causes.)

The implied reader, the "en" or "one" in the above passage, is "foolish" for the implied doubt, the obstinate scepticism of his question, like the "fool" who "said in his heart: There is no God" (Ps 52:1). This questioner, asking why God allowed things to go wrong in Eden, is a sort of Job figure – not the unquestioningly patient one depicted in the "Petit Job," but the one who, his patience tried, demands answers and challenges conventional teachings about God with probative questions that unnerve his pious, but unafflicted friends before getting a similar answer from God: God's will is inscrutable. The model of the ideal, wise, and "patient" reader is therefore one who is curious, asks fruitful questions of the text, and is willing to read long explanations; the patient reader also knows when to stop a line of questioning and accepts not always getting answers. As established here in Genesis and reaffirmed with the "Petit Job," this model lay reader is one who has tempered questions and accepts deferred answers with a patient ignorance that seeks to learn only what he or she is prepared to understand.

What we find in the *Bible historiale*, then, are three different kinds of responses to what happens at the end of questioning. Given the historical focus of his translation and commentary, Guyart opts not to apply one solution common in medieval exegesis, seen throughout Gregory the Great's *Moralia in Job*, for example, of furnishing allegorical interpretations of details that cause discomfort at the literal level. There are several other translation options available to him, however. He could tell the whole text and "prolixly" expound upon its more challenging points, as he frequently does throughout Genesis, when he examines the morality of Abraham lying about his wife or the drunken Lot sleeping with his daughters. Alternatively, he might excise the text that could result in problematic questions or interpretations, as in the Book of Job and the parable of the unjust steward in Luke 16, which Guyart omits because, he says, it is "not very profitable to the laity."[47] Finally, where he considers the text important but doubts readers' patience, he might ask and then answer the "foolish" questions with an authoritative voice that reminds readers of their duty to accept clerical mediation, as in the above-quoted answer as to why God allowed Adam and Eve to be tempted. As translator, Guyart exploits all of these options, adding explanatory commentary and narratives and subtracting biblical text according to the situation.

As we have seen in previous chapters, many scribes producing manuscripts of Guyart's work did not passively copy all of his translation choices, but actively reconsidered them and preferred different solutions to the challenges Guyart identified. The later manuscript tradition rejects some of Guyart's self-censoring choices, either supplementing or replacing Guyart's "abridged" Job, Proverbs, and combined Gospels with full translations of the Vulgate text. These changes might reflect reader demand as well as growing confidence on the part of clerical compilers involved in revising and expanding the *Bible historiale* in at least some lay readers' competence as well as their allegiance to the church and its core teachings. Layers of commentary, added as an alternative solution to ensure that curious readers get church-approved answers to their inevitable questions, add to the increasing "prolixity" of French Bible manuscripts over the course of the fourteenth and fifteenth centuries.[48] By the fifteenth century, patiently curious French Bible readers could have access to a *Bible historiale* that included all books of the Vulgate canon supplemented with a variety of glosses and commentary. The manuscript quoted at the beginning of this chapter, Ghent UB 141, represents an extreme counterexample in which a scribe, doubtful of his readers' patience, rejected the *Bible historiale* in favour of brief *moralités* that stand in for the biblical text and teach readers only what the scribe thinks they need to know.

With that being said, the owner of that manuscript probably also owned a *Bible historiale*, as did most owners of a *Bible moralisée* manuscript, and could have read both at different times and in different ways. To quote the epilogue to 2 Maccabees 15:38–40 as it appears in the Vulgate:

> … ego quoque in his faciam finem sermonis. Et si quidem bene, et ut historiae competit, hoc et ipse velim: sin autem minus digne, concedendum est mihi. Sicut enim vinum semper bibere, aut semper aquam, contrarium est; alternis autem uti, delectabile: ita legentibus si semper exactus sit sermo, non erit gratus. Hic ergo erit consummates.
>
> (I also will here make an end of my narration. Which if I have done well, and as it becometh the history, it is what I desired: but if not so perfectly, it must be pardoned me. For as it is hurtful to drink always wine, or always water, but pleasant to use sometimes the one, and sometimes the other: so if the speech be always nicely framed, it will not be grateful to the readers. But here it shall be ended.)

Part of this passage is rendered differently in the *Bible historiale* to read "tout aussi plaira aus lisans ceste oeuvre se la parole est bien ordenee" ("in this way, this work will please readers if the speech is arranged well," Royal 19 D 3, fol. 450v). This subtle reversal of the author's suggestion that his inconsistent writing style may be more pleasing to readers than perfection suggests that the very unevenness is, in fact, what it means for a text to be "bien ordenee." The thoughtful, well-timed alternation within a single text between literary "water" and "wine" is no longer an accident to be excused but a deliberate feature of the translation program.[49]

Curiously, the late thirteenth-century translator incorrectly attributes these remarks not to the chronicler(s) who composed 2 Maccabees, but to his direct source text and his model as a translator, Saint Jerome, stating that "ce sont ci les paroles saint Jherome, comment il s'escuse humblement de ceste eeure s'il y a aucune chose a reprendre en l'ordenance de ses paroles" ("These are the words of Saint Jerome, wherein he excuses himself humbly for this work if there is anything to criticize in the arrangement of his words," BnF fr. 155, fol. 133r). This passage and its attribution acknowledge the possibility and perhaps need for different ways of translating and retelling the Bible, even within the same translation. They also testify to the translator's assumed responsibility for producing a varied text that is "bien ordenee"; that is, its style and arrangement are varied according to the exigencies of the story to be pleasing to its target readers. Guyart's words in praising his model Jerome resemble the language he uses in reference to his own choices, such as when he defends his reorganization of the Book of Esther (*"S'en semblera a la laie gent l'istoire miex ordenee"*), or excuses his decisions in his prologues ("Si pri a touz ceus qui ces translacions liront que s'il i a aucune chose a reprendre en l'ordenance du roumans, qu'il m'aient pour escusé" ["And I ask all those who will read these translations that, if there is anything to criticize about the arrangement of its French, to excuse me"], BnF fr. 155, fol. 1r).[50] A firm link is thereby established in the reader's mind between Guyart's project and Jerome's, whose example, thus construed, he purports to follow in spirit even in those instances where he departs from it in diction, syntax, content, and narrative arrangement. As scribes, stationers, and patrons would quickly concur, various modes of translation, along with modes of reading, enhanced by various glossing programs, illustrations, and page layouts, permitted vernacular Bible readers to attain a richer understanding and enjoyment of the Bible, whether through several different Bibles or one perfectly customized one.

Conclusion: Asking the Right Questions

In a 2017 piece titled "Readers and their E-Bibles: The Shape and Authority of the Hypertext Canon," biblical scholar Bryan Bibb speculates about the effects of digital text formats and technologies on how both scholarly and lay readers interpret and interact with the Bible:

> The current shift from *codex* to *screen* will be every bit as decisive as the historic shift from *scroll* to *codex* in the Greco-Roman world, or the shift from hand-lettered to printed manuscripts in the late Middle Ages. It is not certain, however, that these changes will lead to more interpretive sophistication or biblical literacy among nonexpert readers.
>
> […] Two developments in biblical reading that may result in particular from the use of electronic Bibles are (1) unparalleled access to competing translations, and (2) shifting functional definitions of the biblical "canon." The definition and nature of "the Bible" will shift as people increasingly encounter the text outside the physical boundaries of the printed volume. Electronic platforms have the potential to destabilize traditional notions of what the Bible is and how it functions.[1]

Bibb's first "development" concerns how digital "tools" facilitate the comparative study of Bible translations, scholarly or otherwise. For example, expert and non-expert readers alike can use digital platforms to look for patterns that differentiate translations, or to read parallel translations together to better appreciate multiple meanings of a word or verse without needing to know the source language.[2] A wide range of online platforms offer such aids to private or scholarly study of the Bible: popular websites such as BibleGateway.com offer free and instant access to parallel translations and concordances, tools by which readers can compare versions in English or across languages, while more erudite applications (some paid) include additional tools for linguistic analysis and critical apparatuses to aid in the study of biblical source texts, translations, and their respective contexts.

Bibb's second point is more radical, suggesting that digital reading interfaces can fundamentally shift readers' relationship to the Bible and even their collective sense of what "the Bible" is. The most extreme, canon-destabilizing example in his study is a site called topverses.com, which tracks Bible citations on the internet and uses that data to rank quoted verses by popularity. He quotes an early version of their front-page copy: "You will like TopVerses because we sorted every Bible verse by popularity. Now search the Bible and find verses in a useful order. We counted how many times each Bible verse (all 31,105 of them) is referenced anywhere on the internet and then ranked them all! Join us on social media to share your faith one verse at a time."[3] Bibb leans towards technological determinism in his analysis: innovations like web data mining algorithms applied to the Bible via platforms like TopVerses destabilize the textual canon and change how readers interpret and use it. I concur with the idea that the format in which one reads the Bible profoundly affects the reading experience and, if enough people read the same version or use the same reading interface or technology, it can have an impact on shared notions about the text and its applications. My analysis of the *Bible historiale* has concerned itself precisely with the relationship between readers and the biblical canon as mediated by biblical formats and rewritings (which, in turn, are heavily influenced by the target culture's dominant ideologies and poetics, as in Lefevere's model).[4] However, I contend that this is a two-way relationship: in and of themselves, text formats and technologies do not typically revolutionize how people read and think of the Bible as much as those formats and technologies develop in parallel with and in response to what readers already do with the text.[5]

In Bibb's example, the Bible verse popularity ranking feature on Top-Verses does not invent a new way to read or use the Bible, nor does it claim to do so. Rather, just as the platforms that support comparative study of translations facilitate an approach to reading the Bible that was already favoured by some (mostly scholarly) readers for close study of the text, its language, and its reception history, TopVerses applies digital tools to facilitate practices of reading and citing the Bible that were already in use. In the quotation above, the site promises to put the Bible in a "useful" order, implying that it accommodates a "use" its users already have in mind. Long before TopVerses applied digital tools to reorganize the Bible according to its most cited verses, there already existed a long and widespread tradition of selectively memorizing and quoting Bible verses without the context of their surrounding text. This practice yields a default subcanon of "top" verses prioritized for their encapsulation of a key point of Christian doctrine, for their aesthetic qualities, or for their applicability to common life situations, for example.

Not only do clergy memorize oft-cited Bible verses for deployment in scholarly arguments or preaching (as they also did in the Middle Ages), but lay Christians have been known to memorize and quote well-known verses to perform their belonging to a faith community, a purpose that does not require a lot of textual, historical, or scholarly context. When, for example, former NFL player Tim Tebow inscribed significant verse numbers such as John 3:16 on his face paint during games, the citation might have prompted curious fans to look up the verse, but its main force was perhaps to signal community with viewers who knew the reference, shared his evangelical Christian identity, and endorsed the verse's succinct expression of a central tenet of Christianity.[6] Regardless of what purpose a reader might have in mind when looking for the most "quotable" or "must-know" Bible verses, TopVerses did not introduce or popularize this practice; it just accommodates an existing demand, making it easier for non-professional readers who are not initiated in the "most important" verses through traditional means (e.g., Sunday school, Bible study, religious education) to identify which verses they should have in their repertoire.[7] Moreover, while some readers may see memorizing a few popular verses as an adequate substitute for reading longer biblical texts, users of TopVerses who want a more comprehensive understanding of the Bible can and presumably do read the Bible in other formats as well.

Bibb's anxiety about how platforms like TopVerses might threaten "the biblical canon" aligns with a long history of backlash in response to the perceived "vulgarization" of literate culture and the various non-scholarly applications non-professional readers find for "high-culture" texts. At the extreme, such responses portray technologically expanded access to texts as not only reaching a larger and, on average, less educated audience, but as actively diminishing individual readers' literacy, intelligence, or moral fortitude. Early twenty-first-century debates about the rapid proliferation of web-based visual, digital, and social media and growing public access to it asked whether or not the internet was "making us stupid." Concerned critics implicated the quality of users' engagement with it as, in Nicholas Carr's terms, "impatient," "distracted," and "shallow," not unlike the scribe's somewhat disparaging portrait of his "impatient" lay readers in the prologue to the *Bible moralisée* in Ghent UB 141.[8] To be sure, media, languages, and communication technologies have the power to shape users' habits, expectations, and perspectives (and vice versa).[9] But what technologically deterministic histories

Figure 6.1 Statue of Tim Tebow at the Ben Hill Griffin Stadium at the University of Florida. Known for wearing biblical verse references on his black eye paint, Tebow is represented wearing "John 3:16" in the statue, as he wore in the 2009 national championship. Statue by Sandy Proctor. Photo credit: Janet E. Gomez (reproduced with permission).

of reading largely neglect is the continuous, transhistorical coexistence of multiple types of texts, media, and textual interfaces and correspondingly different ways to read and interact with them.[10]

What Bibb describes, with a hint of anxiety, as electronic platforms' "potential to destabilize traditional notions of what the Bible is and how it functions" might instead reveal just how unstable and contingent those notions are. Coming from a different perspective on how textual technologies affect readers' experience of biblical texts, Joshua Mann explores how reading formats and their associated paratexts prioritize some aspects of textual history and frequently erase others.[11] His analysis shows what our supposedly "traditional" ideas about the Bible owe to print conventions of representing biblical texts, and how those conventions (and digital versions that retain them) obscure significant information about the Bible's complex authorship, its diverse languages, material supports, and textual traditions, and its history of translation, transmission, and canon formation. Most modern printed Bible codices, he argues, reinforce the ostensible fixity and uniformity of the canon as a hermeneutic lens while downplaying other ways of understanding textual ontologies and intertextual relationships that may have been more highly valued in different cultural contexts and at different stages of textual transmission. As Mann demonstrates, conventional modern print Bibles signal by their bindings and by their uniform typography, page layout, and textual organization that they contain not a set of disparate documents, but a single book whose parts "belong together" as a unified whole, to be read together, in the same way, for the same purpose.

From Mann's perspective, "the canon" is not a hermeneutically neutral principle for framing and organizing biblical texts, and such an organization does not necessarily promote a more sophisticated or expert reading of the texts; rather, it facilitates some (already culturally valued) readings, purposes, and inquiries and precludes others. To avoid such limitations, he encourages creativity in designing digital interfaces to represent biblical texts and textual artefacts in ways that encourage user engagement with them, unbound by dominant editorial conventions and their universalizing assumptions about what the Bible is and how and why people read it. He points to some projects that challenge these conventions and assumptions, such as 3D renderings of ancient and medieval biblical scrolls, tablets, and manuscript codices, some with interactive viewing modes using augmented reality (that is, additional information such as translations and curatorial descriptions that users can toggle on and off) and immersive artistic visualizations of biblical narratives and descriptions. Such advanced technologies – and, for that matter, the standardizing effects of print that they disrupt – might seem far removed from medieval manuscript rewritings of the Bible, but Mann's underlying point about the hermeneutic choices of editorial paratexts has implications for how *Bible historiale* manuscripts represent the Bible to medieval readers as well as for how we, as modern readers, perceive and evaluate that mediation.

Medieval translators, scribes, artists, and bookmakers were deeply conscious of their hermeneutic choices when, with each new vernacular translation or "rewriting" and each new manuscript, they reconceptualized what a Bible should look like for its target reader. More often than not, scribes did not merely copy an exemplar of a unified, "standard" translation, but combined available translated texts to generate new composite versions that, in their estimation, best fit their readers' expectations and needs. As I have shown, the variability of manuscripts corresponds to different ideas about medieval French-language readers, about their literacies and their reasons for reading the Bible, and about what standard of canonicity mattered to these readers. At the same time as they catered to reader expectations, these manuscripts communicated learned knowledge and dominant cultural beliefs surrounding the Bible, its textual history, and its uses. The manuscript expression of these cultural beliefs about the biblical canon was not universal but shows some degree of variation and disagreement.

Guyart and later scribes, artists, and early print editors of the *Bible historiale* used a variety of innovative strategies to balance a theologically necessary textual coherence between Old and New Testaments with a conscientious accounting of the complexities of biblical textual history as they understood it. I have outlined in previous chapters some examples of these strategies, such as Guyart's citation of sources, his reflections on "Moses" as a biblical author and of Jerome as a translator, and his own meticulous documentation of his choices in relation to his source texts, as well as how later scribes explain their own modifications to Guyart's translation. In addition, some manuscript artists add visual cues to help viewers conceptualize the authorship and organization of the Bible as a set of individual books, grouped according to attributed author, genre, or purpose, and collected as parts of a whole with a unified message. One manuscript illustration reminds its viewers that the two-volume Bible in front of them represents, in fact, many different books; within the table of contents is painted a bookcase holding the first twenty-five books listed (Genesis to Baruch) as separate codices, each buckled shut in its own cubby, each cubby labeled with the title of the book.[12] Another manuscript copy, made for King Charles V of France, opens with a four-panel frontispiece that schematizes four sets of biblical books – Pentateuch, wisdom books, historical books, prophetic books – and their origins. In one panel, the artist whimsically represents the "divine inspiration" of Moses's purported authorship of the Pentateuch as God tossing the books at Moses, who crouches in a cave, hands in prayer, with the caption ".v. livres de la loy Moyse" ("five books of Moses's law"). With similar humour, the second panel represents the wisdom books in a parody of Solomon's judgment of the quarrelling mothers, with one of the women holding a sword, ready to sever a book – instead of a baby – in half (Figure 6.2).[13]

Premodern reading and its supports were quite diverse, personalized, and situational, and so were ways of thinking about them.[14] Many critics have already challenged histories of reading that describe medieval interpretive practices as monolithic at any one time within a given community and coexisting with other methods only during short bursts

Figure 6.2 Four-panel frontispiece introducing a *Bible historiale*. Top left, God tosses books representing the Pentateuch at Moses; top right, a parody of Solomon's judgment, representing the wisdom books attributed to Solomon. Paris, Bibliothèque de l'Arsenal, MS 5212, fol. 1r. Source: gallica.bnf.fr/BnF.

of change. Adrian Johns, for example, has disputed the notion of an abrupt and total break from manuscript to print "culture"; Walter Ong and Brian Stock, a break from orality to literacy; Brian Stock, again, from *lectio divina* to the more imaginative approach to reading he calls *lectio spiritualis*; and Robert Sturges, from linearity to circularity, to name just a few.[15] Even the same texts – say, biblical narratives – furnished material that was readily adapted to multiple formats catering to different literacies, different reading priorities, and different ways of interacting with and using the texts, whether for different target audiences or whether within a single book for a single reader.

For example, to recall my comparison of the two traditions in chapter 5, the same royal readers owned the *Bible historiale* and the *Bible moralisée*,

Figure 6.3 Example of a fully illustrated *Bible moralisée*, with biblical scenes and (in this case, Latin) captions describing them on the left, juxtaposed with the scenes' textual and visual moral interpretation on the right. Rows 1 and 3 also have a figural relationship to rows 2 and 4, with 1 and 3 representing Old Testament scenes and 2 and 4 their respective New Testament parallels. London, British Library, MS Harley 1527, fol. 5r. Source: http://www.bl.uk/catalogues/illuminatedmanuscripts/. © British Library Board

the former fostered a deep understanding of biblical history, while the latter, with its quotable short *moralités* and the juxtaposed images included in its royal manuscripts communicated lessons that were easily retained, reproduced, and redeployed as cultural currency in the medieval French court (Figure 6.3).[16] Both traditions had value not only to different readers with different literacies or preferences, but to the same readers in different contexts or for different purposes. Each proposes a different solution to the challenge of instructing non-expert lay readers in biblical lessons relevant to their lives and consonant with church teachings, in each case creatively adapting pre-existing tools and technologies to the perceived needs and literacies of their readers. The *Bible historiale* adopts, among other strategies, scholastic conventions of glossing and commentary, norms of vernacular preaching, and narrative modes of vernacular French fiction, while the illustrated *Bible moralisée* supports a mode of reading paralleled in church art, which similarly juxtaposed Old and New Testament scenes (sometimes accompanied by text) to emphasize allegorical and typological connections that frequent visitors to the church could easily remember and internalize. In this sense, like TopVerses, these Bible formats did not entirely invent or bring about a new way of reading the Bible, but rather "translated" pre-existing reader practices to a new medium that allowed for greater flexibility to customize their representation of inter- and intratextual relationships.

If the premodern Latin Church prioritized enforcing the boundaries between authorized and heretical interpretations of biblical texts, its authoritative authors and traditions also acknowledged and at times celebrated the diversity of readers and readings, as when Augustine, in *Confessions* 12.18, marvels at the many potentially true interpretations of individual verses, reaching beyond even what their human authors could have foreseen.[17] Sensitive to the variability of readers and of the cultural contexts in which they read, Guyart produced a translation that was itself adaptable to readers whose reasons for reading the Bible may have varied as much as their individual reading experiences did. As I have argued in the preceding chapters, the *Bible historiale* invites scribes to expand on and personalize it and lay readers to supplement it with their experience in church and their own imaginative embellishments of its stories. Its omission of material from the Latin Vulgate, from the truncated Book of Job to the absence of most non-historical books, left space for future manuscript compilers to fill those gaps using pre-existing translations, and they did. Its modular structure, according to which each book comprised a core *texte* translated from the Latin Vulgate supplemented with a range of paratextual elements (*gloses, incidents,* and *histoires,* prologues and translator's notes, miniatures and diagrams) allowed for the further addition or substitution of textual and paratextual elements, for example, combining the *Bible du XIIIe siècle* translation of Maccabees with Guyart's *histoires*, or adding new translations of Jerome's prologues to each book of the Bible, or additional glosses from a *Bible moralisée*.

Finally, the running dialogue Guyart constructs with his reader through his interventions in the *histoires, gloses*, and rubrics initiates a dynamic tension between two diametrically opposed reader behaviours. At times, this dialogue invites the implied reader to interrogate the text, to ask questions, and to complete the narratives in their imagination, while at other moments, it seeks to discourage readers' questions and active interpretation, even to the point of barring access to texts that might be read subversively. This tension also generates an implicit debate about the translator's gatekeeping role, a debate whose traces appear in the manuscript tradition as later scribes furnish previously self-censored material or supply interpretive glosses as a compromise solution to steer interpretation without shutting it down entirely.

In this dynamic tension that engages the reader's participation without fully ceding interpretive freedom, I also see a model for understanding broader tendencies in medieval narrative and manuscript-based textualities. Although non-religious literature did not carry the same stakes or consequences of misreading as did the Bible, reading and misreading feature prominently as themes in later medieval literature, from the recurring failed acts of reading (of art, of narratives, of dreams, of other people's feelings and motives) in the *Roman de la Rose* to the outsized power that the fictional readers in Machaut's *Voir dit* have in shaping the text, disseminating it, and driving the plot of the story. Christine de Pizan, somewhat like Guyart des Moulins, models in her translations and in her original works the reader who asks fruitful questions (in her *Cité des Dames*) and who projects herself into the narrative, visualizing its details and imagining her own emotional response (in *Heures de contemplacion*). Less like Guyart, she also frequently models the reader who adeptly challenges authorities and performs critical re-readings of misogynistic traditions taken for granted.[18] Glossed and "moralized" vernacular texts, including translations (such as *Ovide moralisé*), new editions of older vernacular texts (like *Roman de la Rose moralisée*), and newly composed texts (like *Epistre Othéa*) reapplied the framing apparatus of glossed Bible translations to other genres, giving readers one or more prescribed lenses through which to interpret what they read and dividing the text accordingly into discrete units of meaning. These and other fictionalized recreations of exegetical processes share much with the dialogic framing structure of the *Bible historiale*, where Guyart implicates his reader in a fictional dialogue with the translator and a host of cited authoritative voices about the preceding story.

The *Bible historiale* and its manuscript tradition offer a window into how changing ideas about the Bible shaped the form it took for lay vernacular French readers. We can see these changes over the course of the approximately two hundred years from its composition to its first printed edition, and even within the translator's own lifetime, as bookmakers had already begun the process of "completing" Guyart's translation by adding from another translation what he omitted, sometimes with new glossing programs to direct readers' interpretation. Conversely, perhaps deemed inappropriate in a canonical Bible, the apocryphal stories were omitted from most copies and replaced by the Apocalypse even in the earliest surviving copies. By the fifteenth century, it was common for a *Bible historiale* manuscript to contain the entire Vulgate canon with an assortment of paratexts considered useful for readers' understanding of the Bible, their religious education, and their religious practice.

Making the Bible French in Guyart des Moulins's *Bible historiale* meant not only translating its language, but also enacting a cultural translation for its primary target audience of medieval French-speaking lay aristocrats. It meant making biblical narrative intelligible for lay readers who lacked advanced education in theology; making it enjoyable to avid consumers of courtly French literature; and helping those readers apply biblical lessons to the practice of their faith and to their wider social and political lives. Through its manuscript transformations, we can see how the relationship between the Bible and its lay readers (and clerical perceptions of that relationship) varied among different readers and over time to reflect changing social conditions and shifting political ideologies. We observe how scribes, artists, and even readers who annotated their Bibles read biblical narrative through the lens of their life experiences and their other readings, and vice versa. Finally, we see that the Bible, despite its sacred status, was not immune to the textual fluidity and imaginative mediation common to medieval textualities, translation norms, and manuscript culture. On the contrary, it was a living text whose reading and manuscript transmission were embedded in the same social practices and relationships as any purportedly fictional text, subject to many of the same cultural pressures as so-called courtly literature of the same period.

Appendix: Table of Selected Manuscripts[1]

Shelfmark	Date, provenance	Classifications (1. Berger, 2. Sneddon)	Job version(s)	Contents
BnF fr. 155	1310–15 Made in Paris; later belonged to Charles, duc d'Orléans and entered royal collection	1. BH 2. BH (siglum C4)	"Petit"	BH (Guyart): Prefaces, Octateuch (Genesis, Exodus, Leviticus, Numbers, Deuteronomy, Joshua, Judges, Ruth), 1–4 Kings, abridged Proverbs, "Petit Job," Tobit, Jeremiah, Ezekiel, Daniel, Judith, Esther, 1–2 Maccabees, John Hyrcanus, Gospel harmony (*Historia evangelica* with extracts from Gospels), Acts Other: glossed Apocalypse
W 125–6	1380–1400 Made in Paris; first belonged to Jean, duc de Berry	1. GB, Duc de Berry 2. GB (siglum E3)	"Grand," "Petit"	BH: Prefaces, Octateuch, 1–4 Kings, "Petit Job," Tobit, Jeremiah, Ezekiel, Daniel, Judith, Esther, 1–2 Maccabees[2] BXIII: 1–2 Paralipomenon (Chronicles), 1–3 Esdras, "Grand

(*Continued*)

Shelfmark	Date, provenance	Classifications (1. Berger, 2. Sneddon)	Job version(s)	Contents
				Job," Baruch, Isaiah, Lamentations, Psalms, Proverbs, sapiential books, other major and minor prophets, Gospels, Pauline Epistles, Acts, Catholic Epistles, composite Apocalypse Other: Canticles, Litany; Romans is from a different translation with prologues from Peter Lombard's *Collectanea*
Ars. 5057–8	1400–13 Made in Paris; first belonged to Jean, duc de Berry	1. GB 2. GB (siglum J3)	"Grand," "Petit"	BH: Same books as W 125–6 BXIII: Same books as W 125–6 Other: Canticles
Royal 19 D 3	1411–12 Compiled and copied by Thomas du Val in Clairefontaine, Chartres	1. GB Prol. 2. BH w/ BHC Prol. Extracts (siglum A4)	"Petit", "Grand" (unconventional order, with Jerome's prologues, unique rubrics)	BH: Prefaces, Octateuch, 1–4 Kings, "Petit Job," Tobit, Jeremiah, Ezekiel, Susanna, Judith, Esther, 1–2 Maccabees, John Hyrcanus, Gospel harmony, Acts, apocryphal legends BXIII: "Grand Job," Psalms (Jean de Blois), sapiential books, other major and minor prophets, Pauline and Catholic Epistles, Apocalypse Other: Canticles, Jerome's prologues

Shelfmark	Date, provenance	Classifications (1. Berger, 2. Sneddon)	Job version(s)	Contents
BnF fr. 15370–1	1497–1517 Made in Franche-Comté for Simon de Rye and Jeanne de la Baume	1. GB 2. GB w/BH extracts and other additions (siglum P3)	"Grand" (with added glosses from *Moralia in Job*), "Petit"	BH: Prefaces, Octateuch, 1–4 Kings, "Petit Job," Tobit, Jeremiah, Ezekiel, Daniel, Judith, Esther, 1–2 Maccabees, John Hyrcanus, parts of Gospel harmony BXIII: 1–2 Paralipomenon (Chronicles), 1–3 Esdras, "Grand Job," Psalms, Proverbs, sapiential books, major and minor prophets, Gospels, Pauline Epistles, Acts, Catholic Epistles, composite Apocalypse Other: Additional glosses added to Job (Gregory the Great), Psalms (Augustine), Gospels and Epistles (various sources); prologues (Jerome's and others), litany, Canticles, prayers, catechism, "les .xii. abusion du siecle"
Brussels, KBR 9001–2	1400–10	1. BM + *moralités* 2. GB/BMa, some prol. (Siglum Z2)	"Grand" (glossed), "Petit"	BH: Octateuch, 1–4 Kings, "Petit Job," Tobit, Jeremiah, Ezekiel, Daniel, Judith, Esther BXIII: 1–2 Paralipomenon (Chronicles), 1–3 Esdras (Para. and Esdras w/prol.), "Grand Job,"

(*Continued*)

Shelfmark	Date, provenance	Classifications (1. Berger, 2. Sneddon)	Job version(s)	Contents
				Psalms, Proverbs, sapiential books, major and minor prophets, 1–2 Maccabees, Gospels, Pauline Epistles, Acts, Catholic Epistles, composite Apocalypse Non-standard prefaces (four senses of scriptures, lexicon), Raoul de Presles's Psalms, most books glossed from the *Bible moralisée* and other sources
Ghent, UB 141	1410–20	1. N/A 2. N/A Irregular *Bible moralisée*	N/A	French *Bible moralisée* text related to BnF fr. 167 and KBR 9001–2 glosses Other: KBR 9001–2 prefaces, additional passages in Genesis linking the week of Creation to the Seven Ages of Man (probably also from KBR 9001–2), commentary on Psalms linking them to Christ's (historical) life

Notes

Introduction

1 Pinsky, "On Translation." Pinsky follows this observation by commenting on how translation is also reading, in terms very pertinent to Guyart's approach to translating the Bible, as we shall see. Not coincidentally, Pinsky then goes on to explain how English literature emerged through translation from Latin in the Middle Ages.

2 For an account of pedagogical efforts, popularized in the 1970s and 1980s, to teach the Bible "as literature" in university curricula, and the resistance that movement faced from some Christians who understood such an approach as framing the Bible as fictional or "untrue," see French, "Teaching the Bible as Literature."

3 Alter, *The Art of Biblical Narrative*, 19. On the first point (rethinking what literature is), Alter cites Rosenberg, "Meanings, Morals, and Mysteries." Notably, Alter uses the word "fiction" to describe biblical narrative, suggesting in his chapter "Sacred History and the Beginnings of Prose Fiction" that it has more in common with epic (fictionalized history) than with modern historiographical norms.

4 Guyart's prologue relates that he began translating in June 1291 at the age of forty, finished in February 1294 (1295 new style), and was elected dean of his collegiate church of Saint Pierre d'Aire-sur-la-Lys in 1297. On Guyart's chapter, see Rouyer, *Recherches historiques*. There is no consensus on the spelling of Guyart's name, which appears in catalogues and scholarship in every combination of Gu[y/i]ar[t/d] "Desmoulins" or "des Moulins," sometimes hyphenated.

5 Various scholars and cataloguers have calculated different numbers of manuscripts depending on what is counted – for example, whether a two-volume set counts as one or two; whether to count fragments or copies

of individual books of the Bible, selective compilations or extracts in miscellanies, etc. The figure of at least 144 manuscripts (of vol. 1 or 2 or both) and twenty editions comes from Fournié, "Les manuscrits de la *Bible historiale*," and "Les éditions de la Bible historiale."

6 Deluxe manuscripts represent the vast majority of surviving copies containing substantial portions of the *Bible historiale*, at least until its first print editions in the late fifteenth century. Portions of the *Bible historiale* do also survive in less deluxe and self-copied miscellany manuscripts. For a fairly comprehensive catalogue of manuscripts and early print editions that include the *Bible historiale*, the *Bible du XIIIe siècle*, combinations thereof, and – most relevant in this context – fragments and extracts included in miscellanies of other kinds, see Sneddon, "A Critical Edition." On self-made manuscripts that included extracts of the *Bible historiale* and other biblical and devotional texts, often made by bourgeois or aristocratic women in the late Middle Ages and Renaissance, see for example, Corbellini and Hoogvliet, "Holy Writ and Lay Readers in Late Medieval Europe"; and Hoogvliet, "Nicole de Bretaigne."

7 On diglossia, see Ferguson, "Diglossia." On the specific context of medieval Latin–French diglossia and how it began to break down starting in the thirteenth century, see Lusignan, *Parler vulgairement*.

8 Guyart's comments on the Eucharist are quoted in full in chapter 4.

9 "Positionality" used in this context comes from standpoint theory, a way of accounting for intersubjective discourse based in part on Hegel's work and developed further in postcolonial theory, such as in Spivak, "Can the Subaltern Speak?" Standpoint theory is most commonly used today as a way of thinking through race, gender, and intersectionality. See for example, Rolin, "Standpoint Theory as a Methodology"; Allen, "Feminist Standpoint Theory"; and Harnois, "Race, Gender, and the Black Women's Standpoint." Some scholars of translation have, in recent decades, written about how translators' positionality affects the translation and reception of texts in a variety of contexts. One early and influential essay in this vein is Tymoczko, "Ideology and the Position of the Translator."

10 Despite the relatively small body of surviving evidence about how actual readers read the *Bible historiale* and other medieval Bible translations, a few scholars such as Margriet Hoogvliet, Sabrina Corbellini, and Geneviève Hasenohr have done important work on what the manuscripts and external sources can tell us about how people read them. See for example, Corbellini and Hoogvliet, "Holy Writ and Lay Readers in Late Medieval Europe"; and Hasenohr, "Religious Reading amongst the Laity in France."

11 Iser, *The Implied Reader*.

12 Lefevere, *Translation, Rewriting*.

13 Lefevere, *Translation, Rewriting*, 9. I do not systematically use Lefevere's terminology (rewriting, patronage, poetics, professional versus non-professional readers, etc.) throughout this book, but do find it an apt model for introducing my general approach to Guyart's (and other medieval translators', as applicable) and scribes' interventions as part of a cultural system that influences all interactions between writer/rewriter, text, and reader.

14 Guyart's prologue dedicates his translation to several entities and causes: for the good of his own soul, for his readers, for the glory of God and of the Virgin Mary, and for the public good. A comment at the end of this list suggests but does not name a specific patron (as well as an anticipated wider audience), where he says he translated "au profit de touz ceus qui ceste euvre verront et a la requeste d'un mien especial ami qui mout desire le profit de m'ame" ("for the good of all those who will lay eyes on this work and at the request of a good friend of mine who greatly desires the profit of my soul," BnF fr. 155, fol. 1r). Rosemarie Potz McGerr has proposed some plausible possibilities for the identity of Guyart's "friend" and patron, most notably Matthieu Wilkin (who preceded Guyart as dean of his collegiate church), Count Robert II of Artois, or Count Robert's daughter Mahaut (who is known to have owned an early copy of the *Bible historiale*, now lost). See McGerr, "Guyart Desmoulins."

15 Berger, *La Bible française*. While certain aspects of the book's approach and conclusions are outdated, it was the first scholarly work (and remains one of few) to offer an in-depth and mostly accurate comparative study of the manuscripts of eight different medieval French prose Bible translations.

16 Key works of scholarship in this tradition include Zumthor, *Essai de poétique médiévale*; Nichols, "Introduction: Philology in a Manuscript Culture"; and Cerquiglini, *Éloge de la variante*; as well as applied studies of manuscript traditions, such as Huot, *The Romance of the Rose*.

17 Salvador's partial online edition, which includes tools for linguistic analysis as well as Latin text for comparison (Vulgate and *Historia scholastica*) can be found at www.biblehistoriale.fr (under "Bases de données"). His books *Vérité et Écriture(s)* and *Archéologie et étymologie sémantiques* include, respectively, editions of Genesis (without *histoires*) and Exodus as appendices to his linguistic analyses of those texts. There is also a printed facsimile edition based on the British Library's digital images of London, British Library, MS Royal 19 D 3. The first volume (of four anticipated) was published in 2017 by Éditions des Saints Pères with the title *La Bible historiale: La Genèse, L'Exode, Le Lévitique, Le Deutéronome, Les Nombres, Josué, Les Juges, Les Roys*.

18 Berger, *La Bible française*, 109–220.

1. Making the French Bible, or Making the Bible French

1 Bible quotations in English are from the Douay-Rheims translation except where I have translated from the *Bible historiale* or where otherwise indicated. I have chosen Douay-Rheims because it translates the Latin Vulgate and is therefore closer than Hebrew- and Greek-based translations to the *Bible historiale* and to sources used by the Latin Christian commentators discussed herein.

2 Some of the earliest vernacular translations were produced not from Latin but from Hebrew and Greek source texts, such as the fourth-century Gothic Bible. See for example, Falluomini, *The Gothic Version of the Gospels and Pauline Epistles.* For some general overviews of medieval Bible translation in multiple European languages, see for example, Van Liere, *An Introduction to the Medieval Bible;* Corbellini, van Duijn, Folkerts, and Hoogvliet, "Challenging the Paradigms"; *The Cambridge History of the Bible,* vol. 2; and more recently, *The New Cambridge History of the Bible,* vol. 2.

3 Many manuscript copies of vernacular Bible translations and adaptations were owned by individual laypeople, while others belonged to royal or monastic libraries, and still others appear to have been used for preaching or for training clergy responsible for preaching to the laity. Some vernacular works containing material from the Bible – including the *Bible historiale* and its later printed editions – appear to envisage use by lay, clerical, and religious target audiences. Gustave Masson was among the first to study the use of vernacular translations in preaching contexts in his "Biblical Literature in France during the Middle Ages."

4 Special thanks to Christine Jablonski, conservator of historical monuments for DRAC-Bretagne, and to Xavier-Laurent Salvador for introducing me to the vernacular biblical inscriptions at Saint-Jacques in Merléac. For more about the church, its vernacular inscriptions from the Book of Genesis, and their relationship to medieval French Bible translations as well as to other biblical illustrations and inscriptions in medieval church buildings, see our collection, Salvador and Patterson, *Paroles et images sur le commencement.*

5 Jerome himself defines two models of translation as "word-for-word" (verbatim, or literal) and "sense-for-sense" (with a focus on meaning, translating whole sentences with syntactic and lexical flexibility). Based in part on Cicero's comments about translation, he defends his own translation style as "non verbum e verbo sed sensum de sensu" ("not word-for-word, but sense-for-sense"). However, as Rita Copeland has pointed out, his distinction should not necessarily be taken as a face value, unqualified endorsement of a Ciceronian rhetorical model of translation, but evaluated in the context of Jerome's larger body of work and his different approaches to biblical (for

which he does advocate for a somewhat more literal approach, informed by Christian hermeneutics) versus non-biblical translation. Copeland, *Rhetoric, Hermeneutics, and Translation in the Middle Ages*, 55.

6 Reiss and Vermeer, *Towards a General Theory of Translational Action*. A distinguishing feature of *skopos* theory is that it acknowledges that modes of equivalence (word- for-word versus sense-for-sense, or formal versus functional) are not always an adequate framework for describing translation practices because the source and target texts may differ in the functions they serve for their respective audiences. It also emphasizes the purposeful choices translators make in shaping the target text for its target readership. The Greek word *skopos* denotes a cluster of concepts including "target" and "goal" as well as "watcher" or "guardian."

7 On the well-known 1360 Middle Dutch History Bible translated by Petrus Naghel, see for example, Van Liere, *An Introduction to the Medieval Bible*, 197–8. As he notes, the French *Bible historiale* inspired similar "history bibles in languages as diverse as Dutch, German, Castilian, Czech and even Old Norse" (195). It is not entirely clear to what extent any of these translations may have been translated from French rather than Latin sources, but their structure and use of sources (mainly the *Historia scholastica*) very closely follow Guyart des Moulins's translation. A partial English translation (of Genesis) known as the *Historye of the Patriarks* appears to have been translated directly from Guyart's text into Middle English, as Mayumi Taguchi demonstrates in her side-by-side edition, *The Historye of the Patriarks*.

8 Most such misidentifications come from non-specialists in passing references or footnotes. However, even some otherwise expert scholarship based on accurate secondary sources has not only misconstrued what the *Bible historiale* is but has drawn inaccurate conclusions about the state of medieval Bible translation as a whole as a result of those misunderstandings. For example, James Morey, in an article surveying the influence of Peter Comestor's *Historia scholastica*, inaccurately claims (perhaps based on a misunderstanding of Berger's description) that Guyart combined his translation of the *Historia scholastica* with the earlier French Bible translation. On the contrary, Guyart translated large portions of the Bible himself, and his translation and glosses are clearly distinguishable from those of the *Bible du XIIIe siècle* (*BXIII*). Later scribes and bookmakers inserted some material from the earlier *BXIII*, but even in the combined versions, Guyart's translation is retained for most if not all of the historical books. There is no evidence that Guyart was aware of, much less relied on, the earlier translation. Morey, "Peter Comestor, Biblical Paraphrase, and the Medieval Popular Bible," 22.

9 Rouse and Rouse, "The Commercial Production of Manuscript Books," 109 and 113. Statistically speaking, they were probably right about it being a *Bible historiale*; why they do not consider the *Bible historiale* a Bible, despite some familiarity with its manuscripts, is a question I cannot presume to answer for them. They may have relied on other faulty descriptions of the *Bible historiale* that identify it as translating only Peter Comestor's *Historia scholastica*, or may exclude it based on its added commentary and departures from the Vulgate and modern biblical canons.

10 Characteristic of this style of historiography is the idea of history-as-*Bildüngsroman*, which casts a presumed-homogeneous culture as the protagonist in a sort of novelistic plot in which it evolves and matures at key turning points. See Thiesse, *La création des identités nationales*; Geary, "Writing the Nation." Thiesse and Geary mainly refer to a nineteenth-century trend of telling history through engaging (but nationalistic) narratives, inspired especially by the novels of Sir Walter Scott.

11 Conversely, the Middle Ages have been idealized in problematic ways based on different sets of aesthetic or political values projected onto them, from the Romantic poets and nineteenth-century nationalists to present-day white supremacists. Therefore, my goal is not to elevate the Middle Ages as inherently "good," but to acknowledge the limitations of historiography that, in both cases, seeks to establish continuity with past cultures by projecting modern values and identities onto them.

12 "Using the New Testament Recovery Version," 1. Bibles for America volunteers distribute these pamphlets (often on college campuses) with free copies of the New Testament Recovery Version, published by Watchman Nee and Witness Lee's Living Stream Ministry. Living Stream Ministry's web page "Translating the Bible" tells a somewhat less reductive history of Bible translation, but still inaccurately asserts that the fourteenth-century Middle English translation sometimes attributed to Wycliffe was "the first in Europe in nearly a thousand years."

13 The King James Bible translators did not claim divine inspiration for themselves. However, some proponents of the King James Only movement argue the KJV's superiority over other English translations on the grounds that it was uniquely inspired by God. Most extreme among these is the perspective represented by Peter Ruckman, who sees the KJV as directly revealed by God, and therefore not even really a translation. See White, *The King James Only Controversy*.

14 Andrew C. Gow has called this trope the "Protestant paradigm" in his "Challenging the Protestant Paradigm."

15 Robinson, *Translation and Taboo*, 78–9.

16 Robinson reads Aelfric's narrow concerns about signalling flawed Old Testament figures' moral failings in translation (for lay readers who, he

feared, might read them uncritically as role models without commentary) as a general rejection of translation. He then reads Thomas More's 1529 denunciation of translations by Tyndale and others as evidence of a broader, centuries-long hostility towards translation on the part of the Catholic Church (ignoring the specificity of Tyndale's and More's positions and the fact that Bible translation became more, not less, controversial during the Reformation). These examples certainly raise questions about navigating taboos in translation, but Robinson's conclusions about them are reductive and factually inaccurate.

17 Robinson, *Translation and Taboo*, 85.

18 Innocent III, "Epist. 141, to the Bishop of Metz," *PL* 214.0695b–0698d. Translation mine. The Bishop of Metz's letters are lost, but much of their content is quoted or paraphrased in Innocent's replies.

19 Innocent himself would later denounce the movement's founder, Valdes, as heretical at the Fourth Lateran Council in 1215. Valdes commissioned translations of the Bible (which do not survive), but this alone was not the reason for Innocent's decision. As Alexander Patschovsky notes, the translations commissioned by Valdes, and later, his followers, were produced by clergy and thus unlikely to have diverged from orthodox interpretations. Patschovsky further argues that, at least at this early stage, most Waldensians were not literate and likely learned about the Bible by listening to and memorizing parts of the translations. See Patschovsky, "The Literacy of Waldensianism."

20 Deanesly, *The Lollard Bible*, 34. See also Robson, "Vernacular Scriptures in France," 441. One clear example of how Deanesly's work has led later scholars to exaggerate church suppression of "real" Bible translations is chapter 2 of Morey, *Book and Verse*, 24–37. While acknowledging a large, varied corpus of biblical literature, he takes for granted Deanesly's conclusions and argues that only selective, usually paraphrased verse translations were "acceptable" to the church, and that the continent was more repressive than England with respect to Bible translation in general. While he notes the existence of the *Bible historiale* in several places in this book, he dismisses it as primarily a translation of the *Historia scholastica* and not really a Bible.

21 Deanesly, *The Lollard Bible*, 18–19.

22 Boyle, "Innocent III and Vernacular Versions of Scripture."

23 This also appears in Innocent's "Epist. 141, to the Bishop of Metz," *PL* 214.0695–0698. Here I quote Boyle's (partial) translation in "Innocent III," 101.

24 Boyle, "Innocent III," 106–7.

25 Arundel's Latin text appears in Wilkins, *Concilia Magnae Britanniae et Hiberniae*, 314–19.

26 I follow Kelly's use of the label "Middle English Bible" rather than "Wycliffite Bible" since his analysis credibly casts doubt on the Wycliffite authorship of the translations into Middle English, with the exception of a prologue appended to some copies. See Kelly, *The Middle English Bible*. Other key contributions on these points include Somerset, Havens, and Pitard, *Lollards and Their Influence in Late Medieval England*, as well as an anthology of primary source texts edited by Dove, *The Earliest Advocates of the English Bible*. Also of note in challenging the idea of Bible translation and dissemination as an inherent break from the medieval church – by examining the more pertinent question of exegetical authority – is Levy, *Holy Scripture and the Quest for Authority*.

27 According to book historians Lucien Febvre and Henri-Jean Martin, vernacular bibles printed before 1500 included eleven translations in German, three in Low German, four in Italian, and at least one each in French, Spanish, Flemish, and Czech; this count does not include psalters or other translations of individual biblical books, nor does it include the many more translations that circulated in manuscript form but were never selected for print. Febvre and Martin, *L'Apparition du livre*, 351. The one French translation was the *Bible historiale*.

28 The cardinals were divided over questions concerning vernacular translations. Pope Paul IV effectively banned them in 1559, but the *Index Tridentinus* of 1564 would relax this prohibition to permit translations made by Catholics, although both their sale and purchase required special authorization. On the Council of Trent's decision and the many French translations produced during this period, see "De Lefèvre d'Étaples à la fin du XVIe siècle," in Bogaert, *Les Bibles en français*, 47–106.

29 "No universal and absolute prohibition of the translation of the Scriptures into the vernacular nor of the use of such translations by clergy or laity was ever issued by any council of the Church or any pope." Hargreaves, "The Wycliffite Versions," 391.

30 See McGerr, "Guyart Desmoulins," 215; Salvador, *Vérité et écriture(s)*, 42–3; Billard and Hudson, *Heresy and Literacy*; Stock, *The Implications of Literacy*, 88–151.

31 Van Liere, *An Introduction to the Medieval Bible*, 203.

32 François, "The Catholic Church and Vernacular Bible Reading."

33 See Boyle, "Innocent III," and Sneddon, "A Critical Edition," 1: 28–35.

34 Copeland distinguishes between primary translations, which present themselves as translations, often with commentary, explicitly in service to or in dialogue with one or several source texts, and secondary translations, which are based on antecedent texts but are framed as independent textual creations. As she acknowledges, many medieval translations are not clearly

identifiable as one or the other, but exhibit features of both. See Copeland, *Rhetoric, Hermeneutics, and Translation*, 93–6.

35 For a survey of medieval verse translations of the Bible, see Bonnard, *Les traductions de la Bible*. J.R. Smeets has edited several of these; see *La Bible de Jehan Malkaraume* and *La Bible de Macé de la Charité*. For Herman de Valenciennes's work, see *Li Romanz de Dieu et de sa mere*.

36 On the Acre Bible, see Nobel, "Early Biblical Translators and Their Readers." On the *Bible du XIII* siècle*, see Sneddon, "The 'Bible du XIIIe siècle'." For more about all of the medieval prose translations, see Berger, *La Bible française*.

37 Berger, *La Bible française*, devotes a chapter to each of these.

38 Margriet Hoogvliet documents many of these abridged and fragmentary vernacular Bible forms and their varied uses in "The Medieval Vernacular Bible in French." Some of these are also discussed in Berger, *La Bible française*.

39 On printed editions of the *Bible historiale (complétée)* and their provenance, see Fournié, "Les éditions de la *Bible historiale*." On sixteenth-century personal, self-made copies of vernacular biblical and religious texts, see for example, Corbellini and Hoogvliet, "Holy Writ and Lay Readers in Late Medieval Europe"; and Hoogvliet, "Nicole de Bretaigne and a Collection of Religious Texts in French."

40 Several scholars have shown, based upon wills, library inventories, and similar documents that copies of the *Bible historiale* as well as other translations containing more than a single book of the Bible were most often simply recorded as "the Bible" or a "French Bible"; this is also corroborated by owners' inscriptions in manuscripts themselves. See for example, Sneddon, "The 'Bible du XIIIe siècle'," 1: 132 and 140.

41 Beer, *Medieval Translators and Their Craft*, 2.

42 Margriet Hoogvliet quotes Maurice Bogaert, Georges Duby, and Hervé Martin as examples of scholars whose projections onto the Middle Ages of modern ideas about the biblical canon and about translations have contributed to inaccurate assumptions about medieval Bible translation and the marginalization of their study in all their forms. Hoogvliet, "The Medieval Vernacular Bible in French," 283–5.

43 Philippe de Mézières, for example, counsels King Charles VI to read the Bible for personal improvement as well as for advice on governing and on war. See *Le Songe du vieil pelerin*, especially parts 2 and 3. Geneviève Hasenohr notes examples of priests recommending to young husbands to teach their young wives to read using the *Bible historiale* ("Religious Reading," 207 and 209).

44 In what I believe to be the most recent count, Éléonore Fournié has identified 144 individual manuscript volumes and fragments; her list is

most likely not exhaustive, and does not tend to include, for example, miscellanies that include parts of the *Bible historiale* alongside non-biblical materials. See "Les manuscrits de la *Bible historiale*." Since many of these manuscripts and fragments belong to two-volume sets, the number of unique copies of which at least one volume survives is closer to one hundred. For another, perhaps more complete, catalogue of manuscripts, see also Sneddon, "A Critical Edition," vol. 1. Sneddon's work includes both the *Bible historiale* and the earlier *Bible du XIIIe siècle* as well as miscellanies that contain extracts from these. Fragments, extracts, and second volumes can be difficult to categorize, since it was common to pair the *BXIII*'s second volume with a first volume consisting of either Guyart's translation or a combination of the two.

45 My use of the title *Bible historiale* throughout this book is restricted to vernacular Bibles that include significant parts of the translation given that title by Guyart des Moulins. This may include the expanded *Bible historiale complétée* and, where relevant, translations in other vernacular languages that are based on or retranslated from Guyart's text using the same sources and compositional structure. I do not follow the less common practice of using the term *Bible historiale* to refer to a much larger genre of medieval texts, across many languages, that compile stories from the Hebrew or Christian Bible alongside oral apocryphal traditions, with or without reliance on the *Historia scholastica* (indeed, some predating it). As an example of this broader use of the term, Moses Gaster uses "*Bible historiale*" to describe early predecessors (and potential sources) of the *Historia scholastica* in Hebrew and Slavonic languages; see Gaster, *Ilchester Lectures on Greeko-Slavonic Literature* and *Chronicles of Jerahmeel.*

46 Guyart's 1297 prologue introduces the work as the *Bible historiale*; he also offers the subtitle or alternative title *Histoires scolastiques* after the *Historia scholastica.*

47 The apocryphal narratives, discussed in chapter 3, are absent from almost all surviving manuscripts of the *Bible historiale*, whether "*complétée*" or not. They were omitted, intentionally or not, from an early exemplar that affected most lines of transmission.

48 It is not easy to pinpoint the exact origins of long-dominant modern translation norms of transparency and fluency, objectivity and anonymity – the idea that a translation should appear not to be a translation – but they certainly do not apply to medieval Latin–vernacular translation. They seem to find some support during the Renaissance but pertain most fully to the nineteenth and twentieth centuries. Recent translation theorists including (among others) Maria Tymoczko and Lawrence Venuti have advocated for greater visibility for translators and their work, as well as for translators to take overt responsibility for their agency in making decisions that will shape

a work's reception in translation. See for example, Tymoczko, *Enlarging Translation*; and Venuti, *The Translator's Invisibility*.

49 Copeland, *Rhetoric, Hermeneutics, and Translation*, 87–91.

50 Isidore of Seville, *Etymologiarum sive originum libri XX* 10.12; Copeland's translation, qtd. in *Rhetoric, Hermeneutics, and Translation*, 89–90. The entire definition reads: "Interpres, quod inter partes medius sit duarum linguarum, dum transferet. Sed et qui Deum [quem] interpretatur et hominum quibus divina indicat mysteria, interpres vocatur [quia inter eam quam transferet]."

51 Guyart identifies himself as a "prestre et chanoine" ("priest and canon") in his prologue, and his priestly functions explicitly inform his commentary and his manner of justifying his choices. A fair proportion of scholarship on the *Bible historiale* has focused on its didactic aims. Much of Xavier-Laurent Salvador's work discusses Guyart's methods of instruction from a linguistic standpoint, and Rosemarie Potz McGerr ("Guyart Desmoulins") explores the translator's reprisal of Comestor's role as a "Master" in his own right, adapted to a vernacular audience.

52 The two authors arrive at similar conclusions about the hegemonic discourse of *translatio*-as-metaphor by different paths. In "An Epistemology of Tension," Stahuljak traces the uses of the medieval *translatio* topos to talk about how its multiple metaphorical meanings (transfer of power, knowledge, relics, and texts) conflict with actual translation practices and "obscure the relations of power that take place in cultural and political translation" (37). Meanwhile, Tymoczko, in "Western Metaphorical Discourses," focuses on the lasting effects of these Latin and Romance metaphoric words for translation in limiting modern Western conceptions and practices of translation.

53 Stahuljak, "An Epistemology of Tension," 45–6.

54 Guyart seems to address two separate audiences: the laity ("laies gens") and a clerical public who would copy his work and might find occasion to correct or add to it. There are records of the *Bible historiale* being recommended by priests and chaplains to individuals looking to educate themselves or their families; see Hasenohr, "Religious Reading." It is also possible that some clergy may have relied on French translations to aid in preaching or to supplement their own weak Latin.

55 "Rather than supporting a view of medieval vernacular translations as wholesale simplifications, a detailed comparison of the *Bible historiale* and its Latin source brings to light a subtle interplay between the vernacular reader's desire for new material and the learned culture's concern for proper dissemination of knowledge." McGerr, "Guyart Desmoulins," 211. Later chapters discuss in more detail some of the translator's notes (as well as scribal rubrics), including some examples quoted in this paragraph.

56 Salvador, *Vérité et écriture(s)*, 48–9.

57 Salvador, *Vérité et écriture(s)*, 67. This notion of authorial *témoignage* follows from Salvador's earlier assertion that in the *Bible historiale*, "la vérité qui s'y exprime est avant tout celle d'un auteur qui fait acte de foi en offrant au texte la dimension de son mystère par son témoignage" (15). One has the impression, in the translator/narrator's *je* as a guarantor of truth and in Salvador's evaluation thereof, of an almost Derridian conception of *témoignage*: "je promets la vérité et je demande à l'autre de croire l'autre que je suis, là où je suis le seul à pouvoir en témoigner et où jamais l'ordre de la preuve ou de l'intuition ne seront réductibles ou homogènes à cette fiduciarité élémentaire, à cette 'bonne foi' promise ou requise … Il revient à dire 'crois à ce que je dis comme on croit à un miracle'." Derrida, *Foi et Savoir*, 96–7.

58 The notion of "implied author" as a constructed, narrating double for the author with whom the reader is to identify and agree goes back to Booth, *The Rhetoric of Fiction*. In the case of the *Bible historiale*, this is often a difficult identification given the distance Guyart's implied author adopts with respect to his implied reader in withholding information and suspending interpretation wherever he doubts the reader's understanding or consent. The resulting tension might more accurately be described by Wolfgang Iser's model built on a more conflictual relationship between (implied) reader and author. See Iser, *The Implied Reader*.

59 One might ask how we even know what Guyart translated and what he did not. Samuel Berger largely settled the question in his chapter on the *Bible historiale* in his 1884 *La Bible française*. His reconstitution of Guyart's translation is based on cross-manuscript comparisons of tables of contents, Guyart's prologue, self-references, cross references that linger in the text across copies even when the manuscript's contents no longer correspond to them, and through comparison with the *Bible du XIIIe siècle*, as well as other codicological and traductological clues.

60 Guyart des Moulins is thought, based on the gap between his latest signatures on chapter documents and the earliest of his successor's, to have died between 1312 and 1322, most likely in the latter years of that range, ca. 1320. However, it is unlikely that he participated in the alterations made to his work in Paris as early as 1312. On what is known about Guyart's life and death, see Morand, "Un opuscule de Guiard des Moulins," 498; on the dates and stages of supplementation of his work, see Berger, *La Bible française*, 187–99.

61 Berger, *La Bible française*, 188. While this manuscript is incomplete, Berger determines by comparison that its text matches another early *Bible historiale complétée* (1317) that may have been copied from it or shared an exemplar. Interestingly, this oldest surviving (maybe first) composite Bible of its kind

was produced not in a commercial workshop but by a cleric, who signs his name Roberto de Marchia, in prison (*in carcere*).

62 Berger's account of the two translations and the stages of their combination in Paris bookshops has been generally accepted by later scholars, with some corrections. Berger treats the *Bible du XIIIᵉ siècle* and the *Bible historiale* (including "*complétée*" versions) in parts 3 and 4 of *La Bible française*.

63 Sneddon, "The 'Bible du XIIIᵉ siècle'," 127–40; Quéreuil, *La Bible française du XIIIᵉ siècle*, 1–12.

64 See Sneddon, "A Critical Edition," 1: 239. I discuss some of the manuscripts with unique glossing programs in chapters 4 and 5 especially.

65 On the general patterns and stages of supplementation, see Berger, *La Bible française*, 187–99. For a more nuanced classification system, see vol. 1 of Sneddon, "A Critical Edition." Examples of manuscripts supplemented in unique ways are discussed in later chapters, and the Appendix at the end of this book outlines the contents of those manuscripts I have frequently cited or discussed in detail.

66 On this copy, Paris, Bibliothèque national de France, MS fr. 152 (BnF fr.152), and its unusual compilation, see Sneddon, "A Critical Edition," 1: 173, 229–33, 287 (entries 19, 48, 79).

67 Sneddon identifies twenty-nine complete or nearly complete manuscripts of the *Bible du XIIIᵉ siècle*, including some that are just one volume of a two-volume set. Some of these latter examples are second volumes paired with a volume 1 of the *Bible historiale complétée*, which complicates the count. See Sneddon, "A Critical Edition," 1: 141–202.

68 The rhetorical aim of promoting French Christian claims to biblical texts and lands is evident, for example, in Guyart's intertestamental section on the life of John Hyrcanus (based on Josephus's histories via Comestor's *Historia*), which symbolically passes "ownership" of biblical history from the Hebrews to the Christians with the prophesied end of the line of Hebrew kings. I discuss this and some other politicized readings of biblical history in chapter 5.

69 In noting this shift seen between Philippe VI's and Charles V's manuscripts, I do not mean to suggest that crusading ideologies had disappeared; rather, they are subsumed into new discourses during the Hundred Years War. On this point, see for example, Patterson, "Stolen Scriptures."

70 For a detailed description and the full digitized manuscript, see the British Library's online Catalogue of Illuminated Manuscripts, http://www.bl.uk/manuscripts/FullDisplay.aspx?ref=Royal_MS_19_D_I.

71 For a full description of this manuscript, see Véronique de Becdelièvre, "Français 5707," in *Le Catalogue BnF, archives et manuscrits*, Bibliothèque nationale de France, https://archivesetmanuscrits.bnf.fr/ark:/12148/cc784870. On the portrait and poem, see also Sherman, *The Portraits of Charles V*, 46–7.

72 Philippe, in his *Songe du vieil pelerin*, writes: "Que se dira de la grant devocion des autres roys preudommes, du benoist saint Loys, et derrainement de la devocion de ton pere Charles, humble et devost, qui chacun an par grant devocion lisoit, par maniere d'oroison, la Bible toute entiere? Et ainsi le fist xv ou xvi ans sans faillir." ("What can we say about the great devotion of other wise kings, from that of the blessed Saint Louis to, most recently, the devotion of your father Charles, humble and pious, who, every year, out of great devotion, read the whole Bible as a way of praying? He did that for fifteen or sixteen years without fail.") Philippe de Mézières, *Le Songe du vieil pelerin*, 2: 256; see also 2: 223.

73 On the Vérards' prolific publishing venture, see Winn, *Anthoine Vérard*, and McFarlane, *Antoine Vérard*. Again, on the printed editions of the *Bible historiale*, see Fournié, "Les éditions de la *Bible historiale*." Winn and Fournié both date the first edition to 1498. The editions were printed under several different titles.

74 All quotations herein from the 1517 Vérard edition (*Le premier [-second] volume de la Bible en françois*) are from Rosenwald 967. This edition employs two numbering systems; with the exception of the vol. 1 prologue, which precedes fol. 1, I refer to the folio ("feuillet") numbers at the top right of each verso rather than the quire signatures at bottom right.

75 While I am not aware of any official church decrees making this same claim requiring the lay faithful to read and study the Bible, the royal privilege granted to this edition with these prologues and the lack of evidence of any church effort to modify or censor them suggests that such a claim was not especially controversial either. Margaret Deanesly points to the absence of such claims in priests' manuals as evidence that the pre- and early-Reformation Catholic Church did not consider Bible reading to be important for the laity even where they allowed for it; however, she does not consider unofficial but non-controversial sources such as this one making the case that it was.

76 This movement, based on humanist ideals and a desire for church reform from within, fell under the disapproval of Rome but was afforded relative security by Marguerite de Navarre's support and, through her intervention, the protection of her brother François I. See Stephenson, *The Power and Patronage of Marguerite de Navarre*, 151–69.

77 Bogaert, *Les Bibles en français*, 27.

78 Whereas Guyart advocates, like Luther, for putting scriptures in the laity's hands and even seems to share the latter's criticism, though expressed in more tentative terms, for the sale of indulgences, the *Bible historiale* clearly presents itself as a supplement to, not a replacement for, the sacraments and doctrine of the church. Chapter 4 examines some cases in which the *Bible historiale* grapples with the risks of translating certain kinds of biblical text

(especially the Book of Job). On its careful negotiation between granting and restricting access to the Bible, see also McGerr, "Guyart Desmoulins."

79 On the concept of diglossia, i.e., the coexistence within a society of a "high" language thought of in terms of writing and grammar and reserved for respected functions of state, religion, literature, education, etc., and a "low" form thought of in terms of everyday speech and popular media, see Ferguson, "Diglossia." On how this diglossia began to dissolve in the later Middle Ages with increased use of vernacular French, see Lusignan, *Parler vulgairement.* Finally, on how the *Bible historiale* both helped elevate the status of the French language and contributed to linguistic change, see Salvador, *Vérité et écriture(s)*, 58.

80 In section 1.10.2 of *De vulgari eloquentia*, Dante, associating each Romance language with its characteristic literary genre(s), identifies French as the language of prose narrative and points to what he calls the "Biblia cum Troianorum Romanorumque gestibus compilata" ("the Bible compiled with the deeds of the Trojans and Romans") among the crowning achievements of the "lingua *oil*." Dante could be referring to the *Histoire ancienne jusqu'à César*, which incorporates biblical narratives.

2. Telling It Right: Confronting Reader Resistance

1 Parataxis (as opposed to hypotaxis) refers to a rhetorical or narrative style characterized by the lack of subordinating conjunctions (e.g., although, because) and transitional adverbs (e.g., therefore, however) that explicitly define the relationships between narrated events.

2 Alter, *The Art of Biblical Narrative*, 12.

3 I do not mean to assert that Guyart or his readers would have specifically known the *Jeu d'Adam*. Rather, I point to it as an example familiar to modern scholars of a broader tradition of medieval retellings of Adam and Eve (in drama, paintings, literature), which Guyart and his readers probably knew in some form.

4 Chapter 22 of Comestor's commentary on Genesis can be found in *Historia scholastica, PL* 128.1072c–1072d.

5 Jung, *Answer to Job*, 13–20. "Psychic realities" are influential concepts, stories, and characters that, even if fictional and understood as such, have real effects on the thought structures of cultures and the individuals within them.

6 A good example is Ars. 5059, which has seven miniatures of Adam and Eve from fol. 5v to 9v. These include, in order: the creation of Eve; a modest Eve covering herself as Adam points and seems to ask why (out of sequence compared to the text); God marrying Adam and Eve; Eve talking to the serpent, Adam with back turned; Adam and Eve sharing the fruit, their

arms repeating the gesture of the marriage scene; God chastising them and the serpent; and an angel chasing them from paradise as Eve holds her head in her hands and Adam reaches out to console her. The detail and expressiveness of faces and gestures in this series contrast sharply with the marked lack of pathos in the Genesis account and appear more in line with the speculative embellishments brought to the text by the *histoires* and glosses.

7 It is hard to prove anything about how these translations were received or experienced, but I would suggest that the verse translations lend themselves more to communal oral performance, not only for their rhyme and metre but for other markers of orality as well (such as narrative voice and oral formulae), whereas at least some prose translations, and especially the *Bible historiale*, envisage a more visual, intimate reading with their illustrations, diagrams, and cross references directing readers to manipulate the book in front of them. Of course, that does not preclude either type of text from being used in ways not envisaged by an author or scribe. On performance as a way of thinking holistically about the relationship between orality and writing in medieval texts, from their composition to their reception and reproduction, I refer the reader to Zumthor, "La performance: Oralité et écriture," chapter 2 of *La poésie et la voix*, 37–66.

8 On Herman de Valenciennes's *Romanz de Dieu et de sa mere* and its varied manuscript treatment, see Boulton, *Sacred Fictions of Medieval France*, 83–109. For an overview of medieval French verse translations, see Bonnard, *Les traductions de la Bible*.

9 I discuss the *Bible du XIIIe siècle* or *Old French Bible* and its relationship to the *Bible historiale* in the manuscript tradition in chapter 1. For a detailed account of its contents and likely origins, see Sneddon, "A Critical Edition," and for an overview of all of these prose translations, Berger, *La Bible française*.

10 Smeets, *La Chevalerie de Judas Macabé*, ll. 75–9. There are in fact two texts known as the *Chevalerie de Judas Macabé*, one anonymous (Pierre du Ries has been proposed as the author) and the other by Gautier de Belleperche. This edition is the anonymous one.

11 On horizons of expectations and how they are formed through prior reading habits, see Jauss, *Toward an Aesthetic of Reception*.

12 Jehan Malkaraume, *La Bible de Jehan Malkaraume*. I have retained the inconsistent use of tenses that lends the narration an oral, spontaneous quality; the use of the historic present for "binds" and "holds" seems almost to freeze the scene at its climax.

13 Discrepancy in pronouns is very common in the *Bible historiale*, whether as a deliberate choice or as a result of mistranslation, corruption in the source of translation, scribal error, correction, or hypercorrection; pronouns also

vary among *Bible historiale* manuscripts. In this case, no significant change of meaning is introduced by the two altered pronouns: in fact, the French version arguably makes more sense. The addition of adverbs of temporality or causation and of coordinating conjunctions where none were provided in Latin is also a common feature of the *Bible historiale*'s translation. Clive Sneddon has shown how this feature of French narration, which became common in the mid-thirteenth century, was imported to translations, and is the most prominent marker of a French vernacular "style" in otherwise straightforward translations, linking them to literary and stylistic conventions such as one finds in romances. See Sneddon, "Translation Technique." Salvador makes a similar case for many instances of *donc* in the *Bible historiale* being used as a way of giving the text its vernacular rhythm. See Salvador, *Vérité et écriture(s)*, 450–511.

14 Smeets dates the Jehan Malkaraume Bible to between 1270 and 1293; again, according to Guyart's prologue, he began the *Bible historiale* in 1291, finished it in 1295, and added the prologue to his final version in 1297. Jehan Malkaraume, *La Bible de Jehan Malkaraume*, 1: 18.

15 This double "I," typical of medieval texts composed for oral performance, is perhaps best exemplified by the recurring formula "or vos dirai" ("I will tell you"). Meanwhile, any commentary in this translation is unmarked, unattributed, as free indirect discourse, assumed under the same voice. The "je qui translatay" of the *Bible historiale*, in contrast, draws clearer distinctions between Guyart's narrative "I" and the "I" of biblical characters, narrators, his predecessor Jerome and other interlocutors (although some scribes add their own first-person comments without distinguishing their "I" from Guyart's).

16 "Domestication" is typically opposed to "foreignization," which deliberately retains a higher degree of source-text syntax, vocabulary, idiomatic expression, and cultural references. While Friedrich Schleiermacher was the first to apply these terms to translation, today they are most associated with the work of Lawrence Venuti, who advocates for foreignizing translation (particularly into English and other dominant or colonizing languages) to resist both the erasure of marginalized cultures and the minimization of the work of translators. Given that the *Bible historiale* is translating from a dominant, higher-prestige language into a vernacular one, Venuti's domestication/foreignization model does not apply in this way. See Venuti, *The Translator's Invisibility* and *The Scandals of Translation*. Eugene Nida illustrates his concept of dynamic equivalence with the example of J.B. Phillips's translation of Romans 16:16, "greet one another with a holy kiss," as "give one another a hearty handshake all around." Guyart's translation choices with respect to the Vulgate biblical text more closely fit what Nida calls "formal equivalence." See Nida, *Toward a Science of Translating*, 160. The

definition of formal equivalence occurs in the chapter titled "Principles of Correspondence," 156–92.

17 Guyart's lexical doubling involves using two words to convey multiple possible meanings of a word or, in some cases, adding a more familiar synonym after a rare word. I do not mean to downplay the significance of diction, syntax, and other linguistic features as meaningful translation choices in the *Bible historiale* or the *Bible du XIIIe siècle* with which it is often combined; these are indeed telling and have been treated in more detail by Clive Sneddon and Xavier-Laurent Salvador. Salvador, in his books *Vérités et écriture(s)* and *Archéologie et étymologie sémantiques* and in numerous articles, has expertly treated, among other questions, Guyart's use of neologisms and expressions of time and causality within the contexts of his didactic program and teleological framework. On the calques and lexical doubling specifically, see Salvador, "Les 'biblismes'."

18 See the chapter "The Reading Process: A Phenomenological Approach," in Iser, *The Implied Reader*, 274–94.

19 Guyart also cites "Saint Methodius" (possibly Pseudo-Methodius, whose Apocalypse is also cited with reference to prophecies concerning the descendants of Ishmael) in reference to Moses's silence about another son of Noah's and about the possibility that Adam and Eve had other children before Cain, among other topics.

20 Compare Esther in *Biblia Sacra iuxta Vulgatam versionem* and in Brenton, *The Septuagint with Apocrypha*.

21 The main text of the Hebrew version corresponds to chapters 1–10 in the Vulgate. The extra documents, taken from the Septuagint, are, in order: chapter 11: Mordechai's dream; 12: extended scene of Mordechai's revelation of the plot against King Ahasuerus; 13: King Ahasuerus's edict to all his provinces ordering them to kill all Jews (1–7) and Mordechai's prayer; 14: Esther's prayer; 15: extended version of the scene in which Esther goes to speak to the king in private, including God's intervention to turn "the king's spirit into mildness" (15:11); and 16: the king's letter reversing the edict from 13 and granting the Jews permission to prosecute their enemies.

22 Guyart is only aware that the source is Greek; Jerome indicates this much.

23 "Then Mordechai said: God hath done these things. I remember a dream that I saw, which signified these same things: and nothing thereof hath failed" (10:4–5).

24 Here and throughout, I use italics to indicate rubrics.

25 On the preservation of Latin phrases and Latinisms as a translation strategy to establish authority, see also Salvador, *Vérité et écriture(s)*.

26 For a close analysis of how *Bible historiale* manuscript illustration balances a high degree of personalization with an increasingly standardized list

of conventions and of scenes selected for illustration, see Flum, "Die Titelbilder der 'Bible historiale'." See also Fournié, *L'iconographie de la Bible historiale*, which focuses primarily on the miniature cycle of one manuscript, Brussels, Bibliothèque royale de Belgique, MS 9001–2 (KBR 9001–2). I discuss the expansions of the *Bible historiale*, including the insertion of material from the *Bible du XIIIe siècle*, in greater detail in chapter 1 and some specific manuscript examples in chapters 4 and 5.

27 For a fuller reflection on the *Bible historiale*'s textual and visual correspondences with contemporary churches, their art and ritual, and community uses, see Patterson, "La Bible française du moyen âge." I have translated or paraphrased parts of this section from that chapter.

28 Qtd. in Berger, *La Bible française*, 173.

29 The same schema is reproduced again on fol. 39r.

30 The symbolic interpretation occurs on fol. 29v.

31 Two of the many examples of manuscripts that represent churches or reliquaries instead of the tabernacle map are: Paris, Bibliothèque nationale de France, MS fr. 160, fol. 63r (ca. 1310–25), and Royal 19 D 2, fol. 68v.

32 Compare to Comestor's "Translatum est itaque regnum de Juda ad alienigenam, imminente Christi adventu." *Historia scholastica, PL* 128, 2 Mc ch. 22.

33 For further discussion of *Bible historiale* manuscripts and their appropriation of the Old Testament to promote the interests of France and its king, see Patterson, "Stolen Scriptures," and Kumler, *"Faire translater, faire historier."*

34 Bartz, Hanke, and Zumbült, *Pagina sacra*, 122–4. The manuscript's current owner is Joost R. Ritman; its medieval owners are unknown. Sneddon also describes it (as Ex-Phillipps MS 3668) in "A Critical Edition," 1: 445–6 (entry 178).

35 Sneddon, "A Critical Edition," 1: 341–4 (entry 109).

36 Sneddon, "A Critical Edition," 1: 446–7 (entry 179).

37 The first two of these quotations occur in many, but not all, copies; the third I find on fol. a.i.v of vol. 1 of the 1517 Vérard edition, Rosenwald 967. I have not compared other printings or editions.

38 On the idea of a generic "vernacular format" that developed in the early fourteenth century in the Paris bookshops, see Diamond, "Manufacture and Market."

39 The stages or levels of exegesis and their application by these authors are discussed in further detail in chapter 4.

40 Se l'escripture ne me ment,   If scripture does not lie,
   Tout est pour nostre enseignement   Everything is for our
                                          instruction

   Quanqu'il a es livres escript,   Once it is written in
                                          books,

Soient bon ou mal li escript. (ll. 1–4)	Whether good or bad.
Des le premier comencement	From the beginning
Du mont jusqu'à l'avenement	Of the world until the coming of
Jhesu Christ, qui pour nous requerre	Jesus Christ, who, in order to redeem us,
Vault descendre du ciel en terre,	Descended from heaven to earth,
Font ci mencion cestes fables,	All is told in these tales,
Qui toutes samblent mençoignables,	Which seem fictive,
Mes n'i a riens qui ne soit voir:	But there is nothing in them that is not true.
Qui le sens en porroit savoir,	Whosoever might know their meaning,
La veritez seroit aperte,	Will uncover their truth,
Qui souz les fables gist couverte. (ll. 37–45)	Which lay covered under fictions.

De Boer, *Ovide moralisé,* vol. 1. The date for this anonymous poem
   has been estimated around 1300.

41 Versions of *Barlaam and Josaphat* circulated in many languages during the
   Middle Ages, including Arabic, Georgian, and Ethiopic as well as Latin, Old
   French, Provençal, Catalan, Italian, and Middle English. Not all of these
   translations turn the titular characters into Christian saints, but most do.
   For the French version, see Gui de Cambrai, *Barlaam and Josaphat.*

42 The reference to Prometheus occurs in an *incident* at the end of Genesis 35,
   and the stories about Abraham's and Keturah's children and grandchildren
   and Hercules appear in a gloss on Genesis 25. The supposed son of
   Keturah, who built tabernacles in Libya and is the father of Hercules's wife
   "Ethee," is named "Affert" and credited as the namesake of the continent of
   Africa. The source of these non-biblical characters and stories is credited as
   Josephus, who is said to have sourced them from an earlier Jewish prophet
   or historian named Heddus.

43 Tubal-Cain's supposed invention of music using differently weighted
   hammers is recounted in an *histoire* on the generations of Cain (Gn 4:17–
   24); his sister is credited with inventing textiles. The Oedipal episode in
   Judas's life is part of a series of apocryphal narratives discussed in chapter
   3. As I explain there, this episode is not new to Guyart's translation but
   circulated in earlier Latin and vernacular versions; Guyart's direct source
   seems to be Jacobus de Voragine's *Legenda aurea* or *Golden Legend.*

44 "There are still others who delight to hear the words of God and to learn
of His works not because these bring them salvation but because they are
marvels ... What else can I call their conduct than a turning of the divine
announcements into tales?" Hugh of St. Victor, *Didascalicon: A Medieval
Guide to the Arts* 5.10, 134.

45 Aquinas, in *Expositio Super Job* 2, theorizes that God "speaks" in three ways,
only one of which involves "corporeal" human language. The other two
occur through the imagination (dreams and visions) and "intelligible
expression," i.e., direct transmission of knowledge to the intellect. In
the *Summa Theologica* 34.1, he also posits that "'to speak' is in God 'to
see by thought'." When applied to the Bible, this way of understanding
divine speech allows Aquinas to view the biblical authors' and translators'
work as one step removed from God's mind and independent in its
poetic expression, leading him to redefine the distinction between the
literal and mystical senses as one between human (i.e., of the biblical
authors) and divine intentionality, both accessible through the text. He
is not alone among medieval and patristic Christian and Jewish thinkers
to understand biblical "inspiration" in such a way, but his elaboration
of its mechanism is especially clear. Aquinas, *Expositio super Iob*; and in
translation, *Literal Exposition on Job*. See also Yocum, "Aquinas's *Literal
Exposition on Job*."

**3. Soothing Listeners' Ears: Narrative Aesthetics
and Poetic Faith**

1 For the French context, see for example, Boulton, *Sacred Fictions of Medieval
France*, which focuses on lives of Christ and the Virgin Mary. For a similar
overview of Middle English biblical literature, whose range includes some
relatively close translations as well as more divergent retellings based on Old
and New Testament and apocryphal materials, see Morey, *Book and Verse*.

2 Visi, "Introduction," *Retelling the Bible*, 21–30. The book's sections on
"Translation and Interpretation" and "Preaching and Teaching" are also
relevant to this discussion. "Retelling" as defined by Visi and the authors
in the collection shares much in common with Lefevere's "rewriting" (as
outlined in my introduction) but with emphasis on narrative and a broader
scope that includes visual arts and other non-textual media. See Lefevere,
Translation, Rewriting.

3 Lucie Doležalová presents the *Historia scholastica* itself as a kind of
"text-based" retelling of the Bible in "The Dining Room of God: Petrus
Comestor's 'Historia scholastica' and Retelling the Bible as Feasting,"
Retelling the Bible, 229–44.

4 Certain events, including those of the Crusades, played an important role in shaping these fictionalized retellings of the Bible. In particular, Saint Louis's acquisition of the Passion relics in 1238 inspired new literary fictions about the True Cross. In the years 1291–5 when Guyart des Moulins was working on his *Bible historiale*, the French crusaders had just been defeated and expelled from their settlements in Tripoli (1289) and Acre (1291). These defeats of the French crusaders bore special significance for Guyart; in chapter 5, I discuss his reflections upon these events and their meaning in universal Christian history in his translation of Genesis.

5 Éléonore Fournié's catalogue of manuscripts ("Les manuscrits de la *Bible historiale*") lists one other copy, namely London, British Library, MS Royal 19 D 4–5, as containing them; however, this appears to be an error, as I checked the digitized manuscript and did not find them there.

6 Berger, *La Bible française*, 175–7, 182–6. In terms of style, Berger points to the wording of the justifications for the stories' inclusion in rubrics ("mais je l'ai cy mise … ") as closely echoing Guyart's other notes present in all families of manuscripts (for example, compare to quotations justifying Job and Proverbs in chapter 4). We might also note that the interruptions demarcating scriptural from apocryphal episodes are consistent with Guyart's style throughout, and the sources (Comestor, Josephus, Bede) are the same authors he cites most frequently throughout the *Bible historiale*. In addition to the glosses and cross references mentioned by Berger, Sneddon discovered the apocryphal texts listed in at least one table of contents for Acts (apparently considered part of Guyart's Book of Acts) in Brussels, Bibliothèque royale de Belgique, MS II.987. See Berger, *La Bible française*, 50 n18; and Sneddon, "A Critical Edition," 1: 219–21 (entry 4).

7 The specificity of this manuscript is discussed in further detail in chapter 4. Thomas du Val's significant editorial intervention recalls that described by Huot, "The Scribe as Editor." Thomas du Val's programmatic revision of rubric chapter headings with a certain reader in mind – here, an educated lay reader who will be flattered by the implication that he or she can handle more difficult material than the ordinary person but who requires some moral orientation – has parallels with the scribes' use of rubrics in Paris, Bibliothèque national de France, MSS fr. 1569 and 1574, which Huot attributes to a courtly and a clerkly implied audience, respectively.

8 See, for example, BnF fr. 155, fol. 181v (qtd. in Berger, *La Bible française*, 176 n1), which states that the Life of Pilate comes after the Life of Judas. Thomas du Val includes a unique final rubric at the end of Acts naming their translator as "sire Guiart des Moulins, doian de l'Eglise S. Pierre d'Aire en l'eveschie de Terouane" ("Sir Guyart des Moulins, dean of Saint Peter's Church of Aire, diocese of Thérouanne," fol. 252r–v). This may have been meant to indicate which version of Acts was used (if Thomas was aware that

some copies substituted Acts from the *Bible du XIIIe siècle*), but could also suggest that the scribe, at least, understands Guyart's part of the translation to have ended here, before the apocryphal texts. Thomas du Val, as evidenced by his introductions to Job (see chapter 4), displays awareness of the piecework compilation that had produced the *Bible historiale* tradition as it had come down to him and, judging by the unusual combination of texts in his copy, was probably working from at least two exemplars with different contents.

 9 For full transcriptions of these texts and additional discussion of their likely sources, see Burgio, "Ricerche sulla tradizione manoscritta." Extracts of them are also provided in Berger, *La Bible française*, 182–6.

10 In addition to this conventional association between the Tree of Life and the True Cross, trees figure throughout the canonical Bible both as literal living objects and as prophetic or poetic signs. Various species of trees referenced in Deuteronomy, Kings, and Psalms acquire signifying power for their botanical properties and allusive depth. Proverbs and the prophecies of Ecclesiasticus, Isaiah, Jeremiah, Ezekiel, Daniel, the Minor Prophets, and the Apocalypse draw upon symbolic associations established for common trees as well as the Tree of Life. Explicit associations between the Tree of Life and the True Cross arc found elsewhere in medieval literature as well, such as in the anonymous thirteenth-century *Queste del Saint Graal.*

11 The *Legenda aurea* or *Golden Legend* dates, by all accounts, from the 1260s. It would be more fully translated into French in the 1330s by Jean de Vignay. Latin lives of Judas and Pilate similar to those included in the *Golden Legend* and *Bible historiale* circulated independently in religious miscellanies (perhaps, as Brandon Hawk has argued, intended as resources for preaching) at least as early as the 1160s. See Hawk, "The Literary Contexts." Guyart's version clearly translates primarily from the *Golden Legend* rather than earlier versions; the most obvious sign of this is Guyart's (modified) inclusion of Jacobus de Voragine's asides about the apocryphal nature of the stories.

12 This episode may summarize chapter 142 of the *Legenda aurea* on Saint Justina but is not associated with Julian in that text.

13 Jacobus de Voragine's version also treats Judas and Pilate as parallel figures, if in slightly different terms: "Now because Christ was betrayed and brought to his death by Judas due to greed, by the Jews due to envy, and by Pilate due to fear, we might consider the punishments that God inflicted on them for this sin. But you will find an account of Judas's origin and punishment in the legend of Saint Matthias, and the story of the Jews' punishment and downfall in that of Saint James the Less. What follows is what we read in a history, admittedly apocryphal, concerning the origin and punishment of Pilate." *The Golden Legend*, 1: 210–11.

14 Hawk, "The Literary Contexts"; Lim, "The Ages of Man." These articles are not based specifically on the French *Bible historiale* version of the stories, but on an earlier Latin version and a slightly later English translation (also based on the *Golden Legend*), respectively.

15 These stories' use of an evil character or action to cause or reveal a salutary effect recalls Barbara Newman's study of the *felix culpa* or "happy sin" and the "double judgment" it invites from its readers. Exemplified by Adam and Eve's sin that creates the precondition for redemption by Christ, Newman traces its redeployment as a common trope and plot device in medieval romance. See Newman, *Medieval Crossover*.

16 For a history and comparative study of the many versions and possible sources of the Holy Rood legends, particularly those beginning with Seth, see Quinn, *The Quest of Seth*.

17 Meyer, "Die *Geschichte des Kreuzholzes vor Christus*." The texts of the *Legende* (VI) and the *Historia* (I) are found on pp. 131–49 and 107, respectively. He also includes a Provençal translation of the *Legende* version. Note that Meyer's titles *Legende* and *Historia* have no relation to the *Legenda aurea* or *Historia scholastica*.

18 There is some overlap in episodes between the two versions Guyart translates and the one included in the *Golden Legend*, but many of their plot details and choice of episodes differ significantly. The one element Guyart seems to take from the *Golden Legend* rather than the other two Latin versions of the True Cross legends is his attention to signalling biblical versus apocryphal episodes, but his wording in doing so is quite different from Jacobus's. According to Meyer, the German *Bible historiale* (*Historienbibel*) inserts the *Golden Legend* version of the story in the "histoire" or "Geschichte" about Adam and Seth. Meyer, "Die *Geschichte*," 127.

19 The Acre Bible, also known as the Bible of Saint Louis for its likeliest first patron, as well as some manuscripts of the *Bible historiale* reference the Crusades in their text and illustrations and express support for them either implicitly (by visually associating the crusaders with biblical heroes) or explicitly. Royal 19 D 1 is in fact a crusading miscellany for Philip VI that includes battle narratives from the *Bible historiale*, and the *Bible historiale* manuscript, BnF fr. 152, depicts the armies in the Apocalypse carrying crusader shields (specifically the Templars' design of red crosses on white backgrounds). Guyart laments the recent fall of Tripoli and Acre in a gloss in Genesis, relating these losses to events described in the Apocalypse of Pseudo-Methodius (reproduced in chapter 5). The Acre Bible survives in Paris, Bibliothèque de l'Arsenal, MS 5211.

20 Meyer dates this version to the end of the thirteenth century or very beginning of the fourteenth; however, its appearance in the *Bible historiale*, at least if Guyart put it there, requires it to predate his completion of the

translation in 1295 and probably the beginning of his work in 1291. The 1260 date is based on its apparent borrowings from the *Legenda aurea*.

21 Quinn notes that this scene, in which The Queen of Sheba recognizes the wood's significance, but Solomon does not, seems to reflect a common medieval Christian view that the Queen of Sheba, wiser than the wise King Solomon, prefigures the superior wisdom of the pagans in more readily accepting Christ than the Jews did. See Quinn, *The Quest of Seth*, 65. The same scene takes on an even more anti-Semitic tone in the *Bible historiale*, which ends with the comment that the Jews crucified Christ.

22 Spacey, *The Miraculous and the Writing of Crusade Narrative*. On justificatory miracle stories attached to pillaged relics from Constantinople in particular, see especially pp. 57–61.

23 The Holy Rood legends' condensation of Old and New Testament continuity recalls a prophetic dream recounted in an *histoire* that occurs early in Guyart's Genesis: "Et quant Adam ne vit nule chose entre les bestes et les oisiaus semblable a lui, Diex l'endormi, ne mie de droit dormir, mais ainsi com s'il fust raviz, et dist on qu'il fu adonc en la souverainne court de Paradis, de quoi, quant il s'esveilla, il prophetisa de la conjunction Jhesucrist et sainte yglise et du deluge et du jugement a venir par feu, et le moustra apres et dist a ses enfans. Et quant Diex ot Adam endormi, il li osta une de ses costes s'en edefia une famme et l'amena a Adam et Adam l'apela si com devant est dit" ("And when Adam didn't see anything among the beasts and the birds that was like him, God put him to sleep, not regular sleep but as if rapt, and they say that he was in the sovereign court of paradise. When he awoke from [the sleep], he prophesied about the union of Jesus Christ and the Holy Church and the Flood and the Judgment by fire that was to come. And later he explained and told his children about it. And when God had put Adam to sleep, he took one of his ribs and built a woman out of it and brought her to Adam. And Adam named her as has already been said," BnF fr. 155, fol. 4v).

24 The first text in the series, the Life of Julian the Apostate, is not explicitly labeled as apocryphal; however, it does not directly concern characters or events of the Bible as the other stories do.

25 Salvador, *Vérité et écriture(s)*, 83–4. See also chapter 1 above for further discussion of Guyart's prologue and its construction of his "truthfulness" and authority.

26 "Nam circa 40 annos sunt multi Theologi infiniti et stationarii Parisiis ... , qui cum illiterati fuerint et uxorati, non curantes, non scientes de veritate textus sacri, proposuerunt exemplaria vitiosa, et scriptores infiniti addiderunt ad corruptionem multas mutationes." Hody, *De Bibliorum textibus originalibus*, 421, qtd. in Berger, *La Bible française*, 156.

27 Quotations from BnF fr. 155, fol. 1v. Guyart's remarks about clerics correcting his errors occur on the same folio: "Si pri a touz clers entandant escriptures qui cest ouvrage liront que s'il i treuvent a corriger que la lime de leur sens vueille limer mon rude engin et corrigier" ("So I ask all clerics who understand scriptures who will read this work, if they find anything to correct, that they should polish my rude skill with the file of their minds and correct it"). I quote and discuss both passages in chapter 1 as well.

28 For a discussion of the legal models for Guyart's prologues and their implications for a Bible translation, see Salvador, *Vérité et écriture(s)*, 65–7.

29 As Rosemarie Potz McGerr argues, Guyart does not include in his translation all of Comestor's references to pagan mythology, perhaps out of concern that his readers might erroneously retain them as true; however, he does include some, often noting what about them is false. See McGerr, "Guyart Desmoulins."

30 The second quotation is from Coleman, "Late Scholastic *Memoria* et *Reminiscentia*," 43.

31 In a few cases, Guyart raises the question of whether a story is only intended as a parable (which he defines as "par semblances" ["by analogy or metaphor"]), or if it is also a "true" story. He concludes, for example, that the story of the rich man and Lazarus is true because of its specificity: "Et ceste chose n'est mye tant seulement parabole, ains est vraie chose qui avint ainsi. Et ce sceit on bien par le nom du mendiant, qui y est nommez, et avoit nom Ladre, et estoit ou sein Abraham" ("And this is not just a parable but is a real [or true] thing that happened just as it is told. And we know that by the name of the beggar, who is named in the story, and his name was Lazarus, and he was in Abraham's bosom," Royal 19 D 3, fol. 492r). By contrast, he says of Christ's parable of the sower: "Et il parla moult a eulx en paraboles, cest a dire par semblances, et dit … " ("And he often spoke to them in parables, that is, through analogies … ," Royal 19 D 3, fol. 479v).

32 "Apocrypha" (with a capital A) can also refer more specifically to materials found in the Septuagint but not the Hebrew Old Testament and that are generally excluded from Protestant Bible canons. For a critical overview of these Apocrypha (or deuterocanon) and the history and circumstances of their inclusion or exclusion from the biblical canon in various Christian traditions, see for example, Goodman, *The Apocrypha*. This specific use of "Apocryphal" does not apply to the pre-Reformation Middle Ages.

33 Tóth, "Way Out of the Tunnel?" 47–70.

34 Augustine, *De civitate Dei*. Brandon W. Hawk also discusses this quotation in "Apocrypha and Fictionality," 254.

35 Hawk, *Preaching Apocrypha*, and "The Literary Contexts." I note his interpretation of the purpose of Judas's life above; Hawk mainly discusses

the other purposes in chapters 2 (Trinity) and 3 (other doctrinal matters) of *Preaching Apocrypha.*

36 Hawk, *Preaching Apocrypha,* 103–32.

37 Hevelone, "Preaching the Saints," and "Examining Saints' Lives and Sermons." On the question of the *Legenda aurea*'s initial audience and use, see also Ryan's introduction to his edition (*The Golden Legend,* xvii–xviii) and Boureau's introduction to *La légende dorée,* 21–5.

38 Orlemanski, "Who Has Fiction?" Orlemanski argues against modernist (and, to some extent, universalist as well) definitions of fiction, with special attention to that found in Gallagher, "The Rise of Fictionality."

39 Unlike fables and exempla, whose epigrammatic moral lessons are not essential to their understanding, the parable requires a key. Christ often speaks in enigmatic parables not only to elucidate but also to control his message, at times identifying the story's metaphoric referent only for his disciples.

40 For a discussion of literary inventiveness as idolatrous and the Devil's domain, as expressed by Tertullian and others, see for example, Leupin, *Fiction et Incarnation,* 1–85. The iconoclastic equivalency between artistic representation – figural and verbal – and idolatry largely goes back to the Old Testament's reductionist descriptions of pagan religions as image worship. For a discussion of literary fiction as a form of idolatry in Jewish thought, from the Torah and Talmud to contemporary literature, see Kauvar, *Cynthia Ozick's Fiction.*

41 Macrobius, *Commentary on the Dream of Scipio.*

42 On the appropriation and modification of Macrobius's taxonomy and defense of *fabula* by medieval commentators, including William of Conches and Peter Abelard, see Dronke, *Fabula.*

43 One finds these, for example, in *Aucassin et Nicolette*'s recurring stage directions for prose sections, "or dient et content et fablent" for spoken prose, perhaps distinguishing between dialogue and narration. Dufournet, *Aucassin et Nicolette.*

44 While Comestor does not grant the Hebrew "fables" the same authority as the more canonical written *historia,* he does not usually refute the historical truth of these oral, apocryphal tales either. If anything, the impersonal passive expression lends them an air of legitimacy. Guyart's use of the verb *dire* is not exclusively restricted to oral tradition – in fact he uses it sometimes to refer to authors of written texts as well – but his word choice implies no inherent judgment about the referential or fictional character of what is said.

45 For example, Peter Bietenholz, writing about a tendency in medieval literature to add imaginative flourishes to purportedly "non-fiction" genres such as histories, biographies, and sermons, concludes that "the distinction

between fact and fiction, *historia* and *fabula*, was particularly prone to be ignored, or at least neglected." Bietenholz, *Historia and Fabula*, 62. I find this characterization somewhat misleading for the reasons I explain.

46 There are other examples of texts – romances, saints' lives, even ostensibly biblical citations – that, for whatever reasons, are less concerned with maintaining these distinctions or interrogating the boundaries between them. For example, Brian Murdoch notes the example of a Breton verse Bible that integrates apocryphal material from the *Vita Adae et Evae* without any indication that it is not from the Bible. See Murdoch, *The Apocryphal Adam and Eve*, 232–3.

47 On the narratological concepts *temps de l'histoire* and *temps du récit* as well as diegetic versus extradiegetic levels of narration, see Genette, "Discours du récit."

48 Rubric: "*Or laisse Moyses la generacion Esau dont il n'est cy nul mestier de mettre, si iray avant a l'istoire, comment Joseph fu vendu et enuoyé en Egipte selon la B[ible]*" ("*Now Moses leaves the generations of Esau, but there is no need to put them here, so I am going to move ahead in the story to how Joseph was sold and sent to Egypt according to the Bible*," W 125, fol. 25v).

49 Ainsworth, *Jean Froissart*, 46–50.

50 Froissart defends his preferred narrative style ("cronique historiée") in the following terms: "Se je disoie: 'Ainsi et ainsi en avint en ce temps,' sans ouvrir ne esclarcir la matere qui fut grande et grosse et orrible et bien taillie d'aler malement, ce seroit cronique non pas historiée, et se m'en passeroie bien, se je vouloie; or ne m'en vueille pas passer que je n'esclarcisse tout le fait ou cas que Dieu m'en a donné le sens, le temps, le memoire, et le loisir de cronissier et historier tout au long de la matiere." ("If I were to say, 'Such and such happened at that time,' without elaborating on or clarifying the event, which was big and fat and horrible and bound to go badly, this would be a non-historiated chronicle, and then I could move on quickly if I so wanted; but I don't want to rush through it without any clarification, given that God has given me the intelligence, the time, the memory and the leisure to chronicle and historiate the whole account.") Froissart, *Chroniques*, 13: 222, qtd. in Ainsworth, *Jean Froissart*, 47. Janet Coleman reads fictionalizing elements in Froissart as an affirmation of a late scholastic and ultimately Augustinian historiographical ideal of recuperating inner truths or *anamnesis*, the remembering of universal truths that the soul forgets when it takes corporeal form. As the "facts" of history are unavailable to the senses, remembering them involves tapping into the soul's eternal memory to imaginatively reconstruct and visualize the distant past. See Coleman, "Late Scholastic *Memoria*," 22–44.

51 In Antoine and Bartolémy Vérard's 1517 edition of Jean de Rély's recension of the *Bible historiale*, we read: "A la louenge de dieu le createur et de

sa tressacre mere finist le premier volume de la grant bible en francois historiee et corrigee auec le psaultier" ("To the praise of God the Creator and of his very holy Mother was this first volume completed of the Great Bible in French, historiated and corrected with the Psalter," fol. 165v). Old and Middle French usage of "historier" refers interchangeably to both verbal narrative and visual artistic representation; Godefroy lists "raconter en historien," "représenter (un événement) en un tableau, une tapisserie," and "Par extens., orner d'enjolivements" as meanings for "historier." Godefroy, *Dictionnaire de l'ancienne langue française.*

52 For a set of interesting explorations of the relationship between canonicity and apocrypha through the lens of modern fan fiction, see Uhlenbruch and Ammann, "Fan Fiction and Ancient Scribal Cultures." I do not mean to suggest that conformity to everyday phenomenal reality does not matter at all in the stories; rather, it is secondary to the norms governing widely known and accepted biblical stories.

53 Iser, *The Fictive and the Imaginary.*

54 Aristotle treats the relationship between sense perception, imagination, and the cognitive processes of conscious thought in his *De anima,* particularly in sections 2 and 3. Aristotle, *De Anima (On Soul).*

55 Vance, *Mervelous Signals,* 336.

56 Gerson, *Oeuvres complètes,* 450. Extract and translation qtd. from Boulton, *Sacred Fictions,* 5.

57 See for example, Christine de Pizan, *Heures de contemplacion.* This edition publishes Christine's text as well as Gerson's *Petit traictié de la mort et passion de Nostre Seigneur Jhesucrist,* which is a main source for Christine's version. I write about Christine's rewriting of Gerson's text in Patterson, "Christine de Pizan, Translator and Translation Critic."

58 The Life of Julian, like those of Pilate and Judas, could have been displaced from its original order, since this prologue, which appears to serve as a general introduction to the collection, appears at the start of the second story. The absence of the Genealogy, another textual supplement mentioned alongside the apocryphal narratives in tables of contents, also presents the possibility of another omitted introductory rubric. It is unclear whether the Life of Julian would have been identified explicitly as apocryphal or understood as such; the *Legenda aurea* does not insist upon the apocryphal nature of the Julian episodes as it does with Judas and Pilate, so Guyart simply may have been following his source.

59 Compare to Jacobus de Voragine: "Thus far we have quoted the aforementioned apocryphal history: let the reader judge whether the story is worth the telling." *The Golden Legend,* 213. This and the following examples are in plain brown ink, with no rubrication or underlining.

60 Emphasis mine. The whole comment reads: "So far, however, what we
   have set down comes from the aforesaid apocryphal history, and whether
   it should be retold is left to the reader's judgment, though probably it is
   better left aside than repeated." Jacobus de Voragine, *The Golden Legend*,
   168. The Latin reads: "Hucusque in praedicta hystoria legitur, quae utrum
   recitanda sit, lectoris arbitrio relinquatur, licet sit potius reliquenda quam
   asserenda." Jacobus de Voragine, *Legenda aurea*, ch. 45.
61 Guyart does occasionally adopt a stance similar to Jacobus de Voragine's,
   that is, addressing an intermediary reader, whether copyists or clergy who
   might be using it in their preaching or private or public reading with lay
   patrons, or, for that matter, potential critics. However, he also seems to
   expect lay readers to encounter his text directly, and most of his direct
   addresses reflect this.
62 Coleridge, *Biographia Literaria*, 2: 6.
63 Karnes, "The Possibilities of Medieval Fiction," 210. My interpretation of
   Guyart's treatment of apocryphal stories differs slightly from Karnes's take
   on marvels in travel literature in that, unlike in most of her examples,
   Guyart does seem (to me) to encourage a posture of wilful belief coexisting
   with doubt rather than a completely unresolved potentiality or hypothetical.
   This small nuance may be attributable to the religious nature of the stories'
   intended effect.
64 Jacques de Vitry, *Historia orientalis* cap. 90, 374, qtd. in Karnes, "The
   Possibilities of Medieval Fiction," 214.
65 Justice, "Did the Middle Ages?"
66 Justice, "Did the Middle Ages?" 12.
67 Justice, "Did the Middle Ages?" 13. Justice bases this description of belief on
   Aquinas's *De veritate* q. 14 a. 1.
68 See Coleman, "Late Scholastic *Memoria*."
69 The passage continues, noting that Bede's and Eusebius's accounts are
   not helpful in resolving the issue, as they report only that Pilate faced
   some misfortunes and died by his own hand, without mention of exile (or
   prison).
70 On the Gospel of Nicodemus as a source for Robert de Boron's *Roman de
   l'Estoire du Graal* (*Joseph d'Arimathie*) and other medieval French vernacular
   literature, see O'Gorman, "The *Gospel of Nicodemus*."
71 Hugh of St. Victor, *Didascalicon: A Medieval Guide to the Arts* 5.10, 134.

**4. Les paroles dont je vous ay fait mention: The *Bible historiale*'s Two
   Books of Job**

 1 A version of this chapter was previously published as Patterson,
   "Interpreting Job's Silence."

2 Cf. also verse 1:22. Here, as usual, I quote from Douay-Rheims for English translations of the Latin Vulgate (except, of course, for direct translations of the *Bible historiale*).

3 My biblical citations use Vulgate chapter and verse numbers, which do not necessarily correspond to those found in *Bible historiale* manuscripts or certain modern translations. Most BH manuscripts number forty-one chapters in the "Grand Job" (combining chapters 4 and 5), instead of the Vulgate's forty-two . Of the manuscripts quoted in this chapter, Royal 19 D 3 corrects this and reorders books to match the Vulgate order.

4 Guyart's *histoire* here follows the story told in Gn 19:31–5 and translates Comestor's chapter 53 ("de incestu Lot") of his commentary on Genesis. Similar moral evaluations of what did and did not constitute sin (and how grievous it was) follow stories of other morally questionable actions by Old Testament figures, such as when Abraham lies about Sara being his wife (Gn 20:2).

5 Compare to Comestor's chapter 30 ("de causa diluvii"). *Historia scholastica*, *PL* 128.1081c.

6 The *Historia scholastica*, completed between 1169 and 1173, was a set text, along with Peter Lombard's *Sentences* and the glossed Bible, in the theological schools by 1228. Comestor, as highly regarded for his teaching as his writing, was elected dean of Troyes in 1147 and named chancellor of Paris in 1160. He mentions Peter Abelard and John of Tours as mentors but was also influenced by Peter Lombard and the Victorines, the school associated with Hugh and Richard of Saint Victor. See Smalley, *The Study of the Bible*, 196–242; Daly, "Peter Comestor: Master of Histories"; and Luscombe, "Peter Comestor."

7 See especially chapter 1 for an overview of the *Bible historiale*'s contents, sources of commentary, compilation choices, and various manuscript layouts.

8 On the institutionally constructed authority of licit Bible translations, Xavier-Laurent Salvador explains that "au treizième siècle, date à laquelle se composent les premières grandes traductions en prose, la différence entre une Bible officielle et une Bible hérétique se trouve justement dans l'originalité de cette composition qui proteste sa fidélité non pas à l'esprit du texte original, mais à la vérité des enseignements universitaires qui ont été bâtis autour." Salvador, "Une autre définition de l'étymologie," 667 n15.

9 The *Historia* mentions Job only briefly in its exposition of Gn 22:21 (HS Gn 58) to say that Job's homeland, Hus or Uz, was named after one of Nachor's sons. While "abridged" by Guyart, the Book of Proverbs was fully translated in the *Bible du XIIIe siècle*. It also circulated in other versions, including the Anglo-Norman prose translation with commentary edited in Hunt, *Les Paroles Salomun*, based on Paris, Bibliothèque national de France, MS fr.

24862. The introduction of that edition describes some other prose and verse translations as well.

10 Copies containing both books of Job and the full Book of Proverbs sometimes remove "mout abregies" and change the singular nominative "li livres Job" to read "les livres Job," reflecting both the diminishing use of case distinctions in the fourteenth and fifteenth centuries and the recognition of the presence of two versions of the book. *Bible historiale* tables are not always emended to match actual contents.

11 I discuss in more detail Guyart's treatment of the Book of Proverbs in Patterson, "*Solomon au feminin.*" Guyart's Proverbs omits or transforms numerous references to the importance of learning and study, emphasizing instead moral prudence. It also entirely omits chapter 31 on good wives.

12 Dell, *The Book of Job as Sceptical Literature.*

13 Disagreement among translations amplifies this uncertainty. In many copies of the medieval "Grand Job" translation (to be discussed shortly), 39:35 reads "J'ai ditte une chose et la moye voulenté je ne l'eusse mie ditte et je ne adjousteray pas autre chose plus" ("I have said something, and I wish that I had not said it, and I will add no more," Ars. 5057, fol. 231r; similar in W 125, fol. 232r and Royal 19 D 3, fol. 255v). In a "corrected" version of the same text in BnF fr. 15370, which more closely follows the Vulgate, Job's recantation is more explicitly partial: "Je ay diz chose que je voulsisse que je n'eusse mie dit et une autre esquel je n'esjosteray plus" ("One thing I have spoken, which I wish I had not said: and another, to which I will add no more," fol. 130r; Douay-Rheims trans.). Modern English translations from Hebrew vary, but with similar ambivalence: for example, the Revised Standard Version (numbered 40:5) reads: "I have spoken once, and I will not answer; twice, but I will proceed no further."

14 Verse 42:7: "Vous ne parles mie droiture devant moy come Job mon sergent" ("You have not spoken the thing that is right before me as my servant Job hath," Ars. 5057, fol. 231r; Douay-Rheims trans.).

15 Robert Eisen notes that between 900 and 1500, at least seventy-six Jewish commentaries on Job were produced, a figure he credits to Frank Talmage. Eisen, *The Book of Job in Medieval Jewish Philosophy*, 4. The greater quantity of Jewish (as opposed to Christian) Job commentaries speaks in part to the freedom allowed in that tradition to read Job in a positive or negative light, allowing a greater number of viable positions in the debate surrounding him, including very traditionalist ones. Whereas Job's personal sins are usually treated as either irrelevant or nonexistent in Christian traditions, much of the Jewish commentary admits the possibility that he is an unreliable narrator, untruthful about or unaware of past sins (as suggested by Eliphaz).

16 Simonetti and Conti, *Job*, xvii–xix.

17 Smalley, *The Study of the Bible*, 301–2.

18 Douay-Rheims: "For I know that my Redeemer liveth, and in the last day I shall rise out of the earth. And I shall be clothed again with my skin, and in my flesh I will see my God. Whom I myself shall see, and my eyes shall behold, and not another: this my hope is laid up in my bosom." These lines were read by Jerome, and by Christian thinkers using his translation, as having Job announce the resurrection of the dead; many later translations (cf. KJV, NIV, RSV, etc.) read instead "he [my Redeemer/defender] will stand upon the earth." As evidence of the ambiguity of these words in Hebrew, Jewish commentator Saadiah Gaon's ninth-century *Book of Beliefs and Opinions* reads, instead of "*Redemptor*," "the favoured of God" and interprets the lines as referring to the survival of Job's story through future generations. For more on the varying interpretations of these lines, see Eisen, *The Book of Job in Medieval Jewish Philosophy*, 40–1; and also Sargent-Baur, *Brothers of Dragons*, 2–3.

19 Gregory I, *Morals on the Book of Job*, vol. 1, preface to bk. 4, ch. 2, p. 178.

20 This disclaimer responds to Job's apparent death wish ("So that my soul rather chooseth hanging, and my bones death," 7:15): "Now who that is in his right senses could believe that a man of so high praise, who in a word, we know, received from the Judge of that which is within the reward of the virtue of patience, settled amidst his afflictions to finish his life by strangling? ... Yet doubtless whereas the literal words when set against each other cannot be made to agree, they point out some other meaning in themselves which we are to seek for, as if with a kind of utterance they said, Whereas ye see our superficial form to be destructive to us, look for what may be found within us that is in place and consistent with itself." Gregory I, *Morals on the Book of Job*, vol. 1, epistle, sec. 3, p. 8.

21 Job is not explicitly said to be Jewish (nor is there any indication to the contrary), and as Robert Eisen remarks, there is little, if any, Jewish specificity to the book, adding to his universal appeal (*The Book of Job*, 10–12). Gregory claims Job – and all of Hus – to be Gentile, prefiguring universal salvation: "because as our Redeemer came to redeem both Jews and Gentiles, so He was willing to be prophesied of by the lips both of Jews and Gentiles, that He might be named by either people [*utrumque populum*], Who was at a future time to suffer for both." *Morals on the Book of Job*, vol. 1, preface to pt. 1, ch. 2, para. 5, p. 18. Latin source: Gregory I, "Moralium Libri, sive expositio in librum Job."

22 Aquinas, *Literal Exposition on Job*, 442.

23 Aquinas, *Literal Exposition on Job*, 441.

24 On Aquinas's and Maimonides's parallel readings of Job-as-student, see Yaffe, "Providence in Medieval Aristotelianism." See also the same author's

introduction to the *Expositio* in *Literal Exposition on Job*, esp. 4–6. Both Maimonides and Aquinas take Job to be both right and wrong in different aspects; Maimonides criticizes him for being too Aristotelian (to the point of denying providence) and Aquinas chides him for seeming so.

25 "The opinion attributed to *Job* is in keeping with the opinion of Aristotle; the opinion of *Eliphaz* is in keeping with the opinion of our Law; the opinion of *Bildad* is in keeping with the doctrine of the Muʿtazila; the opinion of *Zophar* is in keeping with the doctrine of the Ashʿariyya." Maimonides, *The Guide of the Perplexed* 3.23. Maimonides comes down on the side of Elihu (or Eliu), who may be, as Eisen suggests, more Aristotelian than Job (*The Book of Job*, 70).

26 The full passage reads, in Bliss's translation of Gregory's *Moralia*: "But his friends, who, while acting as his counselors, at the same time inveigh against him, are an express image of heretics, who under shew of giving counsel, are busied in leading astray; and hence they address the blessed Job as though on behalf of the Lord, but yet the Lord does not commend them, that is, because all heretics, while they try to defend, only offend God. Whence they are plainly told, and that by the same holy man *I desire to reason with God; first showing that ye are forgers of lies, ye are followers of corrupt doctrines.*" [Jb 13:3–4.] According to which it appears that these by their erroneous notions stood a type of heretics, whom the holy man charges with adhering to a creed [*cultui*] of corrupt doctrines." *Morals on the Book of Job*, vol. 1, preface to pt. 1, ch. 6, para. 15, p. 27.

27 Augustine elaborates (in the *Confessions, On Christian Doctrine*, etc.) a theory of scriptural reading dependent on the recognition of and submission to the need for grace to navigate the contradictions of scripture and avoid the pitfalls of a too-literal, "carnal" (for Augustine, Jewish) reading. As Stephen Nichols has argued, this "mediated reading," redoubled in the person of the pedagogue, transforms Old Testament prophets (whose direct transmission of God's word threatened the Augustinian semiotics of fallen language) into Christian saints. The saint's deeds may then be read through the double mediation of Christ and of the exegete/hagiographer's reformulation. See Nichols, "Prophetic Discourse." In this light, Job's calls for mediation and his paradoxical status as a prophet whose theophany only reinforces the opacity of divine language facilitate his adoption as a Christian saint.

28 Gregory I, *Morals on the Book of Job*, vol. 1, preface to pt. 1, ch. 6, para. 15, p. 27.

29 Innocent III, "Epist. 141, to the Bishop of Metz," *PL* 214.0695–0698. On these letters, often mentioned in histories of Bible translation, see especially Boyle, "Innocent III and Vernacular Versions of Scripture"; and on their Waldensian context, see Patschovsky, "The Literacy of

Waldensianism." I discuss misapplications of this letter in modern scholarship in chapter 1.

30 Thouzellier, "L'emploi de la Bible," 144, 153–6. See also her book *Catharisme et valdéisme en Languedoc*.

31 Thouzellier, "L'emploi de la Bible," 144 and 154.

32 Smalley summarizes a letter from a member of the Victorine community that lists Job alongside the Psalms and the Canticles as having no literal meaning (*The Study of the Bible*, 88–9, 301).

33 On the steps of supplementation and the approximate dates of the earliest surviving manuscripts containing each, see Berger, La Bible française, 187–99 and 210–20; Sneddon, "A Critical Edition" 1: 2–3.

34 The "Grand Job" begins: "Uns homme estoit en la terre Hus qui avoit nom Job, et cil homme estoit simple et droitturiez et crenoit Dieu … " (W 125, fol. 221v). The "Petit Job" begins: "En la terre de Hus fus un homs qui avoit a nom Job qui estoit simples et droiturier et Dieu doutant … " (W 125, fol. 232v). The *Bible historiale*'s "Petit Job" is not to be confused with a pictorial series of the same name (common in Books of Hours), nor with the "Pety Job," Richard Hampole's mid-fifteenth-century English poem based on the Office of the Dead (in fact, the verses Hampole adapts are absent from the *Bible historiale*'s "Petit Job").

35 Rare exceptions, such as one identifying the Behemoth as the Devil at 40:10, tend to efface the exegetical work behind them, reducing the word and its metaphorical or allegorical derivation to interchangeable synonyms. The equivalency "Beemoth (c'est le deable)" reflects an interpretation shared by Gregory the Great and Thomas Aquinas, among others.

36 The five that include only the "Grand Job" (and not the "Petit") are: Paris, Bibliothèque national de France, MS fr. 156 (BnF fr. 156); Paris, Bibliothèque national de France, MS fr. 15391 (BnF fr. 15391), which is misbound at the start of Job; Jena, Universitätsbibliothek, MS E1 and Oxford, Bodleian Library, MS Bodley 690, both unique in their contents; and Oxford, Corpus Christi College Library, MS 385, hand copied from a print edition that did include the "Petit Job," reportedly for François I. See Sneddon, "A Critical Edition," 1: 272–5, 275–8, 221–6, 419–21, 392–5 (entries 68, 70, 45, 158, 140). Sneddon's dissertation catalogue actually lists 161 manuscript copies, print editions, fragments, and extracts of the *Bible historiale* and *Bible du XIIIe siècle*; my figure of eighty includes only those "BH" and "BHC" copies complete enough to contain any version of Job and only the two main Vérard editions, upon which the others are based. I have excluded incomplete Bibles, the *Bible du XIIIe siècle*, and duplicate editions. On the other hand, my numbers include the Pierpont Morgan manuscripts, which Sneddon mentions but did not examine for his dissertation.

37 Again, on Berger's classification of *Bible historiale (complétée)* manuscripts, see his *La Bible française*, 157–220. I also summarize these stages of supplementation in chapter 1.

38 Sneddon cites two copies containing only the "Grand Job," BnF fr. 156 and fr. 15391, as representing an interim stage in development, along with The Hague, Koninklijke Bibliotheck, MS 71 A 23, the earliest to include both versions of Job, dating around 1320. He suggests that a common exemplar must have had only the "Grand Job" but offers no conclusive evidence to support this scenario over the equally likely case of an individual decision made in BnF fr. 156 to omit, vis-à-vis its source, the "Petit Job" as redundant. See Sneddon, "A Critical Edition," 1: 9, 22–3.

39 Guyart's biblical chapter titles, where included, are usually derived from Comestor's; wherever he translates biblical text not discussed by Comestor (such as Job), he comments that the book has no chapter titles. The *Bible du XIIIᵉ siècle* only provides chapter numbers, but summary titles are often added for consistency's sake when the same texts are incorporated into the *Bible historiale*.

40 For more information about the provenance and contents of the manuscripts I discuss herein and use as representative source texts for most quotations from the *Bible historiale*, see the Appendix. BnF fr. 155 is one volume, and Royal 19 D 3 consists of vols. 1 and 2. The other shelf marks refer to two-volume sets. For manuscript descriptions, see Berger, *La Bible française*, 157–86 and 212–20; Fournié, "Les manuscrits de la *Bible historiale*"; and, in greater detail, Sneddon, "A Critical Edition," 1: 203–497.

41 Compare to the same note in BnF fr. 155, fol. 1, quoted earlier in this chapter: "J'ensuis du tout et ensuivrai le Mestre en Histoire en toute s'ordenance sauve ce que les paraboles Salemon et li livres Job ne sont mie contenuz en Hystoires, mais je les ai mis en cest livre, mout abregies, pour la bonté d'aus." The Augustinian scribe of Royal 19 D 3, Thomas du Val, identifies himself in a colophon: "Cy fine l'Apocalipse qui est le darrenier livre de la Bible, escript et parfait par les mains de frere Thomas du Val, prestre et chanoine profes de l'Abbaye Nostre Dame de Clerefontaine ou dyocese de Chartres, l'an de la nativité Nostre Sires Jhesucrist mil cccc et onze ieii, Deo gracias, le vendredi .xxe. jour du mois de feuvrier. Priez pour lui" ("Here ends the Apocalypse, which is the last book of the Bible, written and completed by the hands of Friar Thomas du Val, priest and professed canon of the Abbey of Notre Dame de Clairefontaine in the diocese of Chartres in the Year of Our Lord 1411, thanks be to God, on Friday, 20 February. Pray for him," fol. 604r).

42 "Notez cy que le Maistre que la Bible translatait autrement ce livre Job et le abregait. Maiz pour la perfection et toute la Bible avoire le Roy Charle le Quint le fit translater tout au long avec les livres de Paralipomenon, Ezdras

et Neemie que le Maistre avoit laissier a translater" ("Notice here that the Master who translated the Bible [translated] this Book of Job differently and shortened it. But for the sake of completion and having all of the Bible, King Charles V had the whole thing translated along with the books of Paralipomenon, Esdras, and Nehemiah, which the Master had declined to translate," fol. 131r). While it is conceivable that Charles V requested that these books be included in his copies, he was not the first to have them added to the *Bible historiale*, much less the first to have them translated since they come from the mid-thirteenth-century translation. Charles V did also commission a different translation of the Bible by Raoul de Presles. See Berger, *La Bible française* for both the estimated dates by which these additions appeared in *Bible historiale complétée* manuscripts (part 3) and comparisons to Raoul de Presles's and other later translations (part 4).

43 These scribal notes cast doubt on Sneddon's theory that the "Petit Job" was retained erroneously, since at least some scribes present conscious reasons for retaining both. Sneddon, "A Critical Edition," 1: 273.

44 This note is common in late copies; a similar note appears in Ars. 5057, fol. 231v.

45 This misunderstanding likely stems from Guyart's ambiguous use of the word "histoire." The opening table of contents for BnF fr. 152 describes the censored section of the "Petit Job" as follows: "Comment Job commencha a parler. Si laisons chi tous les autres capitles jusques au xl.ii^e. pour le grant mistere des paroles que Job parla et li .iii. ami Job parlerent et que diex parla. Et revenons al hystorial selonc Hystoires" ("How Job began to speak. Then we will skip the rest of the chapters up to 42 on account of the great mystery of the words that Job and his friends and God spoke. And we shall return to the historical [part] according to the *Historia*," fol. 2r).

46 Gregory I, *Morals on the Book of Job*, bk. 4, ch. 1, p. 183.

47 Most copies of the *Bible historiale* that I have examined have rubrics similar to W 125's in the "Grand Job" (if they contain the "Grand Job").

48 The Vulgate chapter numbers given here match Royal 19 D 3 but not W 125.

49 This manuscript is described in great detail in Berger, "Une Bible Franc-Comtoise."

50 "Il est permis de croire, jusqu'à preuve du contraire, qu'elle a été composée avec soin (on pourrait dire avec amour) par un père de famille pour l'instruction de ses enfants. Les prières, le catéchisme, l'histoire profane des temps bibliques et la légende, l'histoire naturelle de la Bible et le commentaire édifiant s'y rencontrent pour faire de ce livre universel une sorte d'encyclopédie de la piété domestique, une véritable *Bible de famille*." ("It is reasonable to believe, absent proof to the contrary, that it was composed with care [one might even say with love] by a father for the

education of his children. The prayers, the catechism, the secular history of biblical times and legend, the natural history of the Bible, and the edifying commentary come together to make this universal book a sort of encyclopedia of domestic piety, a true *Family Bible.*") Berger, "Une Bible Franc-Comtoise," 140. Simon and Jeanne would go on to have eighteen children. Samuel Berger was born in 1843, the eldest of five children, in "nostre Franche-Comté" to Protestant pastor Eugène Berger. Samuel and his brother Philippe were both pastors in addition to their academic careers, so this portrait of the de Rye and de la Baume family may be informed by some nostalgia. Francois Laplanche, "Berger, Samuel," *Dictionnaire du monde religieux dans la France contemporaine: 5. Les Protestants,* 65–6.

51 Most notae in this copy are marked "no[ta]" in dark ink, *bâtarde* script, usually drawing attention to glosses rather than the main text; later marginalia in cursive and humanist scripts appear on fol. 352r (also on Apocalypse). On fol. 261v, a gloss on 2 Maccabees 12 (on praying for the dead) is marked by a row of roughly drawn horizontal lines at the edge of each line of text.

52 "And that on the last day … " is verse 19:25; the unmarked return to the text results in an ungrammatical sentence, so I supply the verb "lives" from "vit," occurring just before the gloss.

53 The start of this gloss is not identified; glosses in this copy are marked irregularly, sometimes merging seamlessly into the main text.

54 Sargent-Baur, *Brothers of Dragons,* 56–62. See also Besserman, *The Legend of Job in the Middle Ages.*

55 This verse is similar in all versions of the "Grand" and the "Petit Job." That some owners of the *Bible historiale* did, in fact, look to it for practical wisdom is suggested by copies such as BnF fr. 152, where *maniculae* mark axioms in the sapiential books on matters such as raising and marrying off children, providing for the poor, and presiding with justice over legal cases. In Royal 19 D 2 (not 3, the Thomas du Val manuscript discussed earlier in this chapter), passages pertaining to confession and the brevity of life are marked in the "Grand Job."

56 "*Militia*" (warfare) is alternately translated "*chevaucheur*" (W 125, fol. 223v) or "*chevauchée*" (Ars. 5057, fol. 222v).

57 A 1486 incunable's censorship of passages suggesting predestination further indicates the extent to which Job, despite being widely promulgated as a moral example, remained theologically controversial and deemed unsuitable for vernacular audiences who might be seduced by unsuitable doctrines. See Pierre de Nesson, *Les vigiles des morts (XVe s.),* 11. John Calvin would later treat predestination in Job in a series of sermons in 1554.

58 Griselda's story was previously told by Boccaccio and Petrarch, among others. Some versions present the story as an unironic model for wifely

obedience, and some (particularly Petrarch), compare it to Job as an example for all to emulate with respect to God. Boccaccio's and Chaucer's versions present an ambivalent treatment of the tale, its protagonist, and its social lessons and can be said to simultaneously hold up a dangerous model for women and critique it. Boccaccio's version criticizes the jealous Gualtieri and the social disparities that allow him to abuse his power over his wife, and hints that perhaps Griselda might have done better to leave him. Chaucer's Clerk is more explicit both in openly presenting resistance as an alternative and in highlighting the story's intertextual relationship with Job: "Men speke of Job, and moost for his humblesse,/As clerkes whan hem wel endite" (vv. 932–3). Chaucer, *The Canterbury Tales*. Ann Astell has argued that Chaucer's subversive Griselda is a direct, corrective response to what she sees as a gendered reading on Gregory's part, namely the allegorizing suppression of Job's "feminine" cries in order to preserve the framing narrative's image of a masculine, self-restrained saint or (she suggests) epic hero. Astell, "Translating Job as Female"; see also Astell, *Job, Boethius, and Epic Truth*. On the likelihood that the *Bible historiale* was a source for Chaucer's biblical material, see Johnson, "The Biblical Characters of Chaucer's Monk." Johnson's evidence is inconclusive, but it is an attractive possibility for Chaucer's ironic juxtaposition of two models of Job. On Boccaccio's and Petrarch's alternative readings of the Griselda story in parallel with the Book of Job, see Lorenzini, "Petrarch and Boccaccio."

59 The Grand Job renders these verses: "celui qui estrive a Dieu" (39:27, BnF fr. 15370, fol. 130r); "mettray jugement devant luy et empliray ma bouche de increpation" (23:4, BnF fr. 15370, fol. 127v).

60 Villon, *Le Testament Villon*, ll. 103–4. On Villon's reading of and use of allusions to Job, see Sargent-Baur, *Brothers of Dragons*.

61 This gloss varies slightly among manuscripts but is present in some form in all copies of the *Bible historiale* I've seen containing Guyart's translation of Leviticus, which is one of the few books of the Bible that Comestor quotes almost in its entirety as he comments on it; as a result, Guyart mostly just translates it as is from the *Historia scholastica*.

62 For this fabliau, with a delightful facing-page modern English translation, see Dubin and Bloch, *The Fabliaux*, 872–85.

63 Allan and Burridge, *Forbidden Words*.

64 For more detailed definitions and examples of these translation strategies in response to tabooed material, see for example, Lawton, "For the Gentleman and the Scholar."

65 The omitted material is from Comestor's *Historia evangelica* (part of the *Historia scholastica*), chapter 152, "*De Eucharistia data discipulis, et non Judae*," which simply rehearses the priests' words in preparing and administering the Eucharist. Comestor's work was aimed at the education of priests and

clerics; while much of that education would then be passed on to the laity through their preaching, Guyart clearly deemed this part of their education unsuitable for a secondary, lay audience.

66 For examples and discussions of French-language missals (made to assist parishioners in following the Mass) that specifically omit the words of the consecration, sometimes with explanations echoing Guyart's, see Peignot, *Catalogue d'une partie des livres*, 56 (concerning a missal made for Blanche of Navarre); Delaissé, "A Liturgical Problem"; and Hadley, "Camouflaging and Echoing the Latin Mass."

67 Macy, "The Theology of the Eucharist," 375–8.

68 This caution, seen in omissions, deliberate opacity, and direct rebuttals against unwanted beliefs, is evident throughout the *Bible historiale* and has been noted by McGerr (in "Guyart Desmoulins"), among others. McGerr's analysis is most interested in Genesis, but she also remarks briefly on the self-censorship of Job and more general issues arising from Bible translation.

69 "Cy trespasse je l'euvangile de villico iniquitatis, car elle n'est mye moult proufitable a laye gent" ("Here I am skipping the Gospel on the unjust steward [left in Latin], for it is not very profitable to the laity," Royal 19 D 3, fol. 500v). The translator's motive is not explained, but this parable, found in Luke 16, has an unclear moral lesson. Not only does Christ not interpret this parable in the account provided in Luke, but his apparent praise of the steward's example leaves the reader with many questions about what exactly is being praised about the steward's ruse to please both his lord and his lord's debtors and about the spiritual significance of the parable. Church fathers proposed a variety of interpretations; for a brief overview of these, see for example, "The Unjust Steward (Luke 16:1–9)" in "Parables," *The Catholic Encyclopedia*, http://www.newadvent.org/cathen/11460a.htm.

5. The Patient Reader

1 See chapter 4 for a full discussion of Guyart's treatment of the Book of Job, scribes' alternative strategies for presenting it to a lay audience, and the implications of both approaches for medieval lay readers.

2 On the "ideal reader" as one who is compliant, readily accepting the rhetorical and ideological positions adopted by the narrator of a text, see for example, Rabinowitz, "Truth in Fiction." Again, the notion of the "implied reader" comes from Iser, *The Implied Reader*.

3 John Lowden was the first to recognize the KBR manuscript's borrowings from the *Bible moralisée*, and he makes a compelling case in favour of it being the exemplar, with some modifications, for the prefaces and some other portions of Ghent UB 141. As he explains: "In Ghent UB 141, in the

prologue on the four methods of exposition of scripture, the author, while not naming himself, appears as 'le translateur de ce present livre.' He takes credit for authorship ('ay je fait un petit traictié au commencement de ce livre') and apostrophises readers in the first person ('qu'ils vueillent mon ignorance supporter et me tenir por excusé quant a ceste petite euvre'); the other additional texts avoid the first person. But in fact, not only was the author of the preface in Ghent UB 141 not the 'translator of the present book' (the French text of which goes back to BnF fr. 167), he was not even the author or translator of the first preface, nor of the 'little treatise' that follows. What he actually did was, for the most part, merely adapt texts he found already translated in a *Bible historiale*. But, and this is crucial, these were not the standard prefaces or texts of the *Bible historiale* tradition, but texts now found in only a single Bible, KBR 9001–2 (B), where they take the place of the usual prefaces: 'Pour ce que le diable … ,' 'A honourable pere … ' and 'En palais du roy et d'empereur … '." Lowden, "The *Bible Moralisée* in the Fifteenth Century," 100.

4 There exist broader and narrower definitions of the *Bible moralisée* tradition, which may include up to fifteen manuscripts and may be further divided according to visual format, language, and textual family. Current scholars casually familiar with the *Bible moralisée* usually associate the term with its use by John Lowden and other prominent art historians who have tended to focus on the seven fully illustrated copies made for French royalty. These, beginning with the earliest thirteenth-century models in Latin, are arranged in a grid pattern with eight miniatures per page with textual captions in French and/or Latin. In spite of Lowden's article on Ghent UB 141 and other later incarnations that are influenced by the *Bible historiale* and tend to adopt a two-column text format with only occasional miniatures (like the *Bible historiale*), in his *Making of the Bibles Moralisées*, he promptly dismisses this family of manuscripts as "an offshoot" and defines the *Bible moralisée* genre more narrowly by its earlier, fully illustrated format (1: 2–4). Four remaining manuscripts not related to Ghent UB 141 but adopting a relatively modest illumination program are also mostly sidelined in his foundational work. Lowden's restriction of the term to the seven fully illustrated copies departs from the opinions of earlier scholars like A. de Laborde and Reiner Haussherr who included all fifteen; ultimately, as Lowden admits, the title is not one that most medieval authors or scribes used (other than the scribe of Ghent UB 141), but rather "a convenient twentieth-century construct." Lowden, *The Making of the Bibles Moralisées*, 1: 4. For the purposes of my argument here, I (like the scribe) call Ghent UB 141 a *Bible moralisée*, even though it does not reproduce the illustration format familiar to many scholars.

5 Lowden also quotes and discusses this passage in "The *Bible Moralisée* in the Fifteenth Century," 101–2. My transcription and translation are based on the manuscript, however, and differ from Lowden's in a few places, for example substituting "s'esjoissent" for "se sioissent" and moving a comma from after to before "procedans."

6 "Cy commence le premier livre de la bible moralisee translatee de latin en francois," qtd. in Lowden, *The Making of the Bibles Moralisées*, 1: 2. Reiner Haussherr is responsible for this discovery; the term was retroactively applied to the more familiar eight-medallion format by Paulin Paris and A. de Laborde.

7 Salvador, "Les 'biblismes'," 10. Explained in more detail: "Nous appellerons donc 'biblisme' un ensemble d'unités à l'intérieur d'un lexique actualisées dans le discours d'une Bible traduite provoquant l'illusion d'un sens, tout en conservant l'opacité étymologique. C'est ainsi que la Bible, quoique traduite, demeure un sanctuaire fermé aux profanes." ("Thus I use the word 'biblism' to describe a set of internal lexical units, actualized in the discourse of a translated Bible, that produce the illusion of meaning while preserving etymological opacity. This is how the Bible, even in translation, remains a sanctuary closed off to the profane.") Salvador, "Les 'biblismes'," 15. Salvador cites numerous cases of Hebrew proper nouns whose meaning is connected to the destiny of that person or place, where Guyart alludes to the connection without proffering a translation for the name that would allow the reader to trace the derivation of meaning; one can only accept the result with a sense that something has been "lost in translation." This even happens where Jerome has attempted to translate the wordplay into Latin, such as the Hebrew formation of the word for "woman," which has the same root as "man," which Jerome has rendered as *vir/virago*. Guyart retains, but does not explain, the Latin reference: "Et Adam dit: 'C'est oz est ozes de mes os et c'est char de ma char. Ceste sera appellée virago car elle est prise et faite d'omme'" (qtd. in Salvador, "Les 'biblismes'," 10).

8 For a detailed comparison of Ghent UB 141 and KBR 9001–2 and the former's reliance on the latter, see Lowden, "The *Bible Moralisée* in the Fifteenth Century," 90–113.

9 Several cataloguers have plausibly proposed that Charles VI, who was king when the manuscript was made in the first decade of the fifteenth century, was the recipient of KBR 9001–2, and I agree that the evidence, such as the manuscript's annotations and illustrations, including a presentation scene to a king who resembles King Charles VI as represented elsewhere, supports this identification. See Fournié, *L'iconographie de la* Bible historiale, 26; and Gaspar and Lyna, *Les principaux manuscrits*, notice 189.

10 For example, the Merriam-Webster Dictionary defines "patient" as: "1. bearing pains or trials calmly or without complaint, 2. manifesting forbearance under provocation or strain, 3. not hasty or impetuous, 4. steadfast despite opposition, difficulty, or adversity, 5. a. able or willing to bear – used with *of,* b. SUSCEPTIBLE, ADMITTING // *patient* of one interpretation." "Patient," Merriam-Webster Online, https://www.merriam -webster.com/dictionary/patient#etymology.

11 Tertullian, "Of Patience," 3: 707–17; Augustine, "On Patience," 3: 527–36. The attribution of the latter is uncertain but is presented in the *Nicene and Post-Nicene Fathers* collection as most likely belonging to Augustine's sermons.

12 English translations quoted from Douay-Rheims; in all cases, "patience" is translated from "patientia" in the Vulgate.

13 On medieval practices of *lectio divina,* see Robertson, *Lectio divina.* While medieval authors rarely explicitly use the word "patient" or "patience" when describing the practice, modern commentators frequently do. For example, Dan Burke, an author, speaker and leader of multiple organizations devoted to lay Catholic spiritual formation, writes in his blog that *lectio divina* "will require deliberate patience," and the United Church of Christ website instructs its readers that they will need "patience and an open mind." Burke, "A Guide to Lectio Divina"; "Lectio divina," United Church of Christ.

14 For further discussion of these examples, see especially chapters 4 and 2, respectively.

15 Thomas du Val is the scribe of Royal 19 D 3, a manuscript discussed in previous chapters for its interpretive rubrics in the Book of Job and its unique inclusion of the apocryphal stories after Acts. On scribes as both readers and (re)writers, see for example, Dagenais, *The Ethics of Reading,* 170; and Deborah McGrady's further distinction between "intermediary" and "inventive" readers in *Controlling Readers,* 9–10. In terms of her taxonomy, most of my examples would tend towards the "intermediary" type.

16 On "paratextes," see Genette, *Seuils.*

17 These examples and their manuscript contexts (BnF fr. 15370, fol. 130v and Royal 19 D 3, fol. 244v) are discussed more fully in chapter 4.

18 For additional examples of such clerical expressions of disdain or anxiety towards (perceived) lay reading practices, but in the secular context of the *Rose* debate, see McGrady, "Reading for Authority," 154–7. Negative representations of lay readers, particularly by the clerical vernacular author Guillaume de Machaut, are also a major subject of McGrady's *Controlling Readers.*

19 One oft-cited example is an author portrait in a manuscript of the *Liber ethicorum des Henricus de Alemannia,* in which the author is depicted lecturing

to a room full of men and women, among whom some listen attentively or read along in their books, while others nod off, talk to one another, or seem distracted, looking elsewhere. Berlin, Staatliche Museen Preussischer Kulturbesitz, Min. 1233.

20 A very clear example of this version, where Paul teaches his letters in a university setting, can be found in W 126, fol. 216r. Guyart himself appears in a master's chair with a lectern or turntable of books in some of his author portraits, sometimes with and sometimes without students. Some author portraits emphasize instead a didactic priestly persona, as in Ars. 5057, fol. 1, where Guyart (or perhaps Comestor or Jerome) preaches to a group of women from a raised pulpit. Representations of authors as scholastic masters are not limited to Bibles or translations of scholarly Latin texts; Boccaccio, for example, is represented similarly in some manuscripts of his works.

21 McGrady, *Controlling Readers*, 22–44.

22 There is no definitive record of Guyart's education, but it seems likely that he was trained in the cathedral school at Saint Pierre d'Aire-sur-la-Lys, where he began as a choirboy in his youth and later served as a canon, priest, chapter historian, and dean. On what is known about Guyart's life and career, as well as another text he wrote about the chapter's ownership of half of Saint James the Greater's skull, see Morand, "Un opuscule de Guiard des Moulins."

23 McGerr, "Guyart Desmoulins," 227–8.

24 I quote from and discuss Guyart's description of this intended manuscript layout and its varied implementation in manuscripts in chapter 1.

25 McGerr, "Guyart Desmoulins," 225–7.

26 Ghent UB 141 is somewhat ambivalent on this last point; its format, and the scribe's apparent assumption that it will be read orally, impose a greater degree of sequentiality. At the same time, the fact remains that when encountering any given passage, each of which pairs an Old Testament scene to its moral interpretation, the reader need not remember the prior passages in order to understand this one. By dampening the role of memory in constructing connections among parts of the text, the passage of time, or *durée*, becomes less perceptible both in terms of the actual time spent reading or listening and in the long-term mental representation of history.

27 "History is the foundation." Peter Comestor, *Historia scholastica*, *PL* 128.1053. Comestor describes a house, or palace, as a metaphor for exegesis, with history at its foundation.

28 Comestor's text reads: "Historia fundamentum est, cujus tres sunt species: annalis, kalendaria, ephimera."

29 On how medieval historiographers discursively apply figural and biblical models to make social meaning of events, see for example, Spiegel, *The Past as Text*, and "Memory and History."

30 While he was able to identify specific examples of self-defeating conduct on the Christian side (broken treaties, lawless mercenaries, and infighting between the Genoese and Pisans in Acre), Ludolph of Suchem, a half century later, colours the defeat with an ominous tone of divine vengeance. "Indeed," he confirms, "we read in the stories of the loss of Acre that because of the sins of the people thereof the four elements fought on the side of the Saracens." Ludolph of Suchem, *Description of the Holy Land*, 57, repr. in Brundage, *The Crusades*, 270.

31 Chapters 11–14 of the late seventh-century Apocalypse of Pseudo-Methodius foretell a series of wars and disasters in the Middle East and Mediterranean and the decades-long oppression of Christians by the Ishmaelites (identified with Arabs). A Last Emperor hailing from Greece would restore peace and finally relinquish his crown at the True Cross, signalling the Antichrist's imminent arrival. Written in Syriac but translated early into Greek, the work was attributed in the Middle Ages to Saint Methodius of Olympus, a church father martyred in 312. Palmer, Brock, and Hoyland, *The Seventh Century in the West-Syrian Chronicles*, 222–42. Comestor cites Pseudo-Methodius in chapter 49.

32 This passage is sometimes cited as supporting the composition date of 1291 (as given also in the prologue), but little note has been made of its interpretation of events.

33 The identification of Ishmael as a common ancestor of Arabs generally and of Prophet Muhammad in particular is common in Islamic traditions as well as in medieval Christian and Jewish readings of Genesis. However, the Mamluk armies were not predominantly Arab and probably would not have identified themselves as Ishmaelites.

34 This representation of the culturally and ethnically heterogenous Mamluk armies, subsumed under the impossibly broad category of "pagan," associated with the singular biblical figure of Ishmael and depicted as animalistic in nature and without individual agency or moral personhood, fits a pattern in the European Christian racialization of Muslims as described by Geraldine Heng in chapter 3 of *The Invention of Race*.

35 A letter dated 1247 identifies Guyart's father Jean as a magistrate's sergeant and one-time crusader. Morand, "Un opuscule de Guiard des Moulins," 497.

36 Some other examples linking contemporary to ancient history in the *Bible historiale* include notes about the location of relics and artefacts, explanations of church practices and their origins in Hebrew traditions, and an alleged recent blood libel in Germany. This latter is reproduced in Berger, *La Bible française*, 175. The origins of more banal things are

explored in the *Bible historiale* as well, such as the invention of underwear: "Si devons nous savoir que les homes n'avoient adoncques eu nulles brayes. Semiramis fu une femme qui trouva premierement les braies des hommes" ("Let us note that men did not have underwear at that time. Semiramis was a woman who first invented men's underwear," Ars. 5057, fol. 16v).

37 I discuss a few other examples of these crossing chronologies and genealogies in chapter 2. *Ordo naturalis,* in medieval rhetorical terms, refers to narrative that imitates the chronological sequence of the events recounted and is most associated with history. It is opposed to *ordo artificialis,* which manipulates narrative time using flashbacks, foreshadowing, *in media res,* and other techniques for artistic effect. The historical Bible could be said to primarily follow *ordo naturalis,* although the doubled time of prophecy occasionally interjects the possibility of an extemporal perspective and the implied coherence of a divine Author. On *ordo naturalis* and *historia,* see for example, Green, *The Beginnings of Medieval Romance,* 96–102. As Green points out, however, *ordo naturalis* is by no means limited to "history," but is common in all kinds of medieval narrative (98); meanwhile, historians such as Froissart strategically employ both *ordo naturalis* and *ordo artificialis* in order to emphasize different kinds of relationships between events.

38 For more about how manuscripts of the *Bible historiale* make specifically French claims to biblical texts and lands as part of a crusading ideology that also extends to the Hundred Years War, see Patterson, "Stolen Scriptures."

39 This way of reading all events in parallel with, and in the same fashion as, those recounted in the Bible had a long tradition, and it was especially pertinent to crusading rhetoric. On the development of a sacred hermeneutics of *historia* that interpreted contemporary events (and their narration in historical as well as fictional narrative) through the lens of Christ and within the framework of salvation history, see Nichols, *Romanesque Signs.*

40 Augustine, *Confessions.* Consider, for example, section 11.11.13, which contrasts human experience of time as a sequence of events against God's eternity, in which nothing passes but everything coexists, and then his discussion at 11.27 of time experienced through speech, giving the example of metred verse.

41 Ricoeur, *Temps et récit,* 1: 17 (my translation). Ricoeur's first chapter is dedicated to Augustine's meditations on time and eternity as a countermodel to Aristotle's *Poetics.*

42 It is not clear to what extent the *Bible historiale* or other vernacular Bible translations might have been integrated into the Mass in some way by priests or parishioners. What is abundantly clear, however is that the translator and scribes saw the *Bible historiale* as going hand in hand with the Latin Mass and the Hours. For example, the first verses of each psalm are often bilingual, as are certain passages in the Gospels and the Lord's Prayer (with detailed

explanations of some of the Latin words), as if to cue readers to match the French text with what they are hearing or have heard in Mass. Clive Sneddon has noted one copy of the *Bible du XIIIe siècle*, Paris, Bibliothèque national de France, MS fr. 899, and one of the *Bible historiale (complétée)*, London, British Library, Add. MS 15247, in which passages have been explicitly cued to the liturgical calendar. He concludes that some readers must have used these texts either for personal devotion or possibly to follow along during Mass. Sneddon, "The 'Bible du XIIIe siècle'," 136.

43 Berger, *La Bible française*, 109–220. While oversimplified to some extent, Berger's categories are useful in describing general trends of *Bible historiale* manuscript production and are still used by researchers, curators, and librarians to describe the manuscripts of the *Bible historiale* in catalogues and other scholarship. See chapters 1 and 4 for further discussion of these patterns. Examples of texts that include additional glossing programs and supplementary materials include BnF fr. 15370–1, discussed in chapter 4 for its use of the *Moralia in Job* to gloss the Book of Job, and KBR 9001–2, mentioned in this chapter for its insertion of text from the *Bible moralisée* as an additional layer of moral glosses to supplement Guyart's historical ones. For a summary of the contents of these and other manuscripts quoted and discussed in this book, see the Appendix.

44 See chapters 1 and 4 for a fuller discussion of these supplementations.

45 On how questions drive medieval narrative, following a template common in myths (which, in Losada Goya's definition, would include biblical narrative as a story that is taken as true and that purports to explain realities in the world), see Losada Goya, "La nature mythique du Graal."

46 See chapter 4.

47 "Cy trespasse je l'euvangile de villico iniquitatis, car elle n'est mye moult proufitable a laye gent" ("Here I am skipping the Gospel on the unjust steward, for it is not very profitable to the laity," Royal D 3, fol. 500v). I also discuss this briefly in chapter 4.

48 Chapter 4 discusses some examples of such added commentary on the Book of Job.

49 I am reading this difference in translation to suggest – in keeping with Guyart's assumption that the comment belongs to the translator Jerome – a value placed on variety in narration throughout the Bible as unified by the translator, as opposed to its earlier context as a modesty topos comparing the writing style of 2 Maccabees against other historical/biblical accounts by other authors, that is, that if it is not as eloquently written, there is no harm, since readers grow bored with a lofty style if it is overused. Where the text of Maccabees derives from the *Bible du XIIIe siècle*, the epilogue closely resembles the Vulgate and Douay-Rheims.

50 See chapter 2 for a discussion of the Esther example.

Conclusion: Asking the Right Questions

1 Bibb, "Readers and Their E-Bibles," 256–7, 258.
2 Reading multiple translations simultaneously can reproduce what Kwame Appiah calls "thick translation," a method of critical translation where the translator does not simply choose one of several translation options for a multivalent word and accept a semantic loss, but instead indicates alternative meanings and layered connotations (provided in brackets) to give readers a more complete understanding of the source text. Appiah, "Thick Translation."
3 Bibb, "Readers and Their E-Bibles," 262.
4 On rewriting as a model for the ways professional readers mediate texts for non-professional readers, through translation, editing, teaching, etc., see Lefevere, *Translation, Rewriting*. I discuss his model of rewriting as it applies to the *Bible historiale* in the introduction.
5 Representative of this point of view, in which reader behaviours, reading cultures, and reading technologies mutually shape one another, is Chartier, "Communautés de lecteurs."
6 "For God so loved the world that he gave his one and only Son, that whoever believes in him shall not perish but have eternal life" (Jn 3:16). This practice of citation as a means of signalling community and confessing faith is more widespread than Tim Tebow; for example, numerous Christian retailers sell T-shirts and bumper stickers citing "John 3:16" (and in some cases, other verses) without the referenced biblical text.
7 My reference to "non-professional" (as opposed to "professional") hearkens back to Lefevere's use of this distinction in defining how rewriting works, i.e., how professional readers shape the transmission of texts for non-professional readers, as I explain in my introduction. See Lefevere, *Translation, Rewriting*, 1–19.
8 See, most notably, Carr, *The Shallows*. I thank Andrew Pigott for this reference. While I disagree with Carr's value judgment against digital media, one compelling (and convincing) aspect of his argument is the extent to which repeated use of these "tools for thinking," as he calls them, effects measurable physical and neurological changes in our brains (1–57). The "making us stupid" quotation refers to his related article "Is Google Making Us Stupid?" I discuss the example of Ghent UB 141 in chapter 5.
9 While not a central concern of the present argument, others have written about parallels between medieval manuscripts and present-day web pages, media, and applications and how they relate to reading practices and experiences; in some cases, scholars also turn these studies back around to the question of how best to represent medieval manuscripts digitally. See for example, Gillespie, "Medieval Hypertext"; Carlquist, "Medieval Manuscripts,

Hypertext and Reading"; and Nichols, *From Parchment to Cyberspace*. On the Ghent UB 141 manuscript, see chapter 5.

10 Representative of technological determinism as it relates to reading (and one of Carr's main sources) is Eisenstein, *The Printing Press as an Agent of Change*.

11 Mann, "How Technology Means." I thank my colleague Bridget Whearty for the reference.

12 Paris, Bibliothèque Mazarine, MS 313, fol. 1v. The image in question represents the first twenty-five books, up to Baruch, with the "Petit" and "Grand Job" combined as a single book. I have not seen the physical manuscript, of which no complete digitized copy is available, but only the digital image of fol. 1v publicly available on the "Bibliothèque virtuelle des manuscrits médiévaux," https://bvmm.irht.cnrs.fr. However, Clive Sneddon, who has consulted the manuscript, notes in his catalogue that neither the illustration nor the table of contents continue on fol. 2r, such that the full contents of the second volume, now lost, are unknown. Sneddon, "A Critical Edition," 1: 397. My attention was drawn to this illustration by a tweet that included a photo of the manuscript illustration: Emily Steiner (@PiersatPenn), "Quite unusual: the artist has *painted* the 25 books used as sources for the text (a Bible Historiale). Paris, Bibl. Maz. ms. 0313 (c. 1415)," Twitter, 24 March 2017, https://twitter.com/PiersatPenn /status/841747108789121025.

13 Paris, Bibliothèque de l'Arsenal, MS 5212, fol. 1r [Ars. 5212]. The "regular" version of this scene – where one of two quarrelling mothers is about to cut the disputed baby in half – appears in the frontispieces of many *Bible historiale* manuscripts, most often introducing the second volume, which usually starts with Proverbs (attributed to Solomon in the Middle Ages). The other two images in the frontispiece of Ars. 5212 do not employ the same kind of humorous play on books but offer more conventional representations of selected scenes from the historical and prophetic books, respectively. The complete manuscript has been digitized and can be viewed on Gallica: http://gallica.bnf.fr.

14 On circumstantial reading that seeks, through identification, to apply biblical material to the reader's particular condition, one thinks of the model of Augustine's famous vision in *Confessions* 8.12, in which he is guided to Romans 13:13 and 14:1, verses that seem to speak directly to his own struggle with doubts and temptations. On this question, see also Hugh of St. Victor, *Didascalicon: A Medieval Guide to the Arts* 5.6–10, and Dagenais, *The Ethics of Reading*, Introduction and chapter 2.

15 See Johns, *The Nature of the Book*, 1–57; Ong, "Orality, Literacy, and Medieval Textualization"; Stock, *The Implications of Literacy*, 12–87; Stock, *After Augustine*, chapter 7: "Lectio Spiritualis," 94–123; and Sturges, *Medieval*

Interpretation, 5–6. Sturges actually proposes a shift from determinacy to indeterminacy instead but admits a more nuanced transition than some of his predecessors, one that allows for the commingling of modes in the late Middle Ages as well as within a single text.

16 The *Bible moralisée* is best known in its eight-panel illustrated format as represented in deluxe royal copies, but these represent only seven of the fifteen surviving manuscripts of its text (as its manuscripts differ in their specific contents and in their language, which may be French or Latin or both). I discuss this in more detail in chapter 5.

17 "So what difficulty is it for me when these words [of Genesis] can be interpreted in various ways, provided only that the interpretations are true? What difficulty is it for me, I say, if I understand the text in a way different from someone else, who understands the scriptural author in another sense? In Bible study all of us are trying to find and grasp the meaning of the author we are reading, and when we believe him to be revealing truth, we do not dare to think he said anything which we either know or think to be incorrect. As long as each interpreter is endeavouring to find in the holy scriptures the meaning of the author who wrote it, what evil is it if an exegesis he gives is one shown to be true by you, light of all sincere souls, even if the author whom he is reading did not have that idea and, though he had grasped a truth, had not discerned that seen by the interpreter?" Augustine, *Confessions* 12.22 (31), 261.

18 See Patterson, "Christine de Pizan, Translator and Translation Critic."

Appendix: Table of Selected Manuscripts

1 Sources for information presented in this table include Berger, *La Bible française*, 210–20; Sneddon, "A Critical Edition," 1: 128–490; Fournié, "Les manuscrits de la *Bible historiale*"; Lowden, "The *Bible Moralisée* in the Fifteenth Century"; and Randall and Oliver, *Medieval and Renaissance Manuscripts in the Walters Art Gallery*. BH=*Bible historiale (non complétée)*, BXIII=*Bible du XIIIe siècle*, BM=Bible moyenne, GB=Grande Bible, BHC=*Bible historiale complétée*. Sneddon classifies some manuscripts in the "Petite Bible" and "Bible Moyenne" categories as type "a" or "b" depending on which, if any, versions of Titus and Revelation/Apocalypse they contain, hence "BMa" for KBR 9001–2 (see Berger and Sneddon). I have only included in this table manuscripts discussed at length or cited frequently.

2 Only the glosses for 1–2 Maccabees in W 125–6 are from Guyart's translation, contrary to Sneddon's assessment that both text and glosses are. The text is markedly different, deriving most likely from the *Bible du XIIIe siècle*.

Bibliography

Académie des Inscriptions et Belles-Lettres. *Histoire littéraire de la France, ouvrage commencé par des religieux Bénédictins de la Congrégation de Saint Maur, et continué par des membres de l'Institut (Académie des Inscriptions et Belles-Lettres).* Paris: Imprimerie nationale, 1733–1999.

Ainsworth, Peter F. *Jean Froissart and the Fabric of History: Truth, Myth, and Fiction in the* Chroniques. Oxford: Clarendon Press, 1990.

Allan, Keith, and Kate Burridge. *Forbidden Words: Taboo and the Censoring of Language.* Cambridge: Cambridge University Press, 2006.

Allen, Brenda J. "Feminist Standpoint Theory: A Black Woman's Review of Organizational Socialization." *Communication Studies* 47, no. 4 (1996): 257–71.

Alter, Robert. *The Art of Biblical Narrative.* New York: Basic Books, 1981.

Appiah, Kwame Anthony. "Thick Translation." *Callaloo* 16, no. 4 (1993): 808–19.

Aristotle. *De Anima (On Soul).* Translated by David Bolotin. Macon, GA: Mercer University Press, 2018.

Astell, Anne W. *Job, Boethius, and Epic Truth.* Ithaca, NY: Cornell University Press, 1994.

– "Translating Job as Female." In *Translation Theory and Practice in the Middle Ages,* edited by Jeanette M.A. Beer, 59–69. Kalamazoo: Medieval Institute Publications, Western Michigan University, 1997.

Augustine. *Confessions.* Translated and edited by Henry Chadwick. Oxford: Oxford University Press, 1998.

– *De civitate Dei.* Edited and translated by P.G. Walsh. Aris & Phillips Classical Texts. Liverpool: Liverpool University Press, 2005.

– *De magistro liber unus.* Sancti Aureli Augustini Opera, sect. 6, pars 4. Edited by Guenther Weigel. Corpus Scriptorum Ecclesiasticorum Latinorum 77. Vienna: Hoelder-Pichler-Tempsky, 1961.

– "On Patience." Translated by H. Browne. In *Nicene and Post-Nicene Fathers*, edited by Phillip Schaff, First Series, 3: 527–36. 14 vols. Buffalo: Christian Literature Publishing, 1887.

Bartz, Gabriela, Marion Hanke, and Beatrix Zumbült. *Pagina sacra: Bibles and Biblical Texts 1050–1511*. Stalden: Dr. Jörn Günther Rare Books AG, 2011.

Bates, Robert Chapman. *L'Hystore Job, adaptation en vers français du "Compendium in Job" de Pierre de Blois*. Yale Romanic Studies 14. New Haven, CT: Yale University Press, 1937.

Beer, Jeanette, ed. *A Companion to Medieval Translation*. Leeds: Arc Humanities Press, 2019.

– *Medieval Translators and Their Craft*. Studies in Medieval Culture 25. Kalamazoo: Western Michigan University Press, 1989.

Berger, Samuel. *La Bible française au Moyen Âge: Étude sur les plus anciennes versions de la Bible écrites en prose de langue d'oïl*. Paris: Imprimerie nationale, 1884.

– "Une Bible Franc-Comtoise en l'an 1500." *Mémoires de la Société d'émulation de Montbéliard* 13 (1881): 128–41.

Besserman, Lawrence L. *The Legend of Job in the Middle Ages*. Cambridge, MA: Harvard University Press, 1979.

Bibb, Bryan. "Readers and Their E-Bibles: The Shape and Authority of the Hypertext Canon." In *The Bible in American Life*, edited by Philip Goff, Arthur Farnsley, and Peter Thuesen. Oxford: Oxford University Press, 2017. E-book.

Bibles for America. "Using the New Testament Recovery Version: An Illustrated Guide." 2009.

Biblia Sacra iuxta Vulgatam versionem. Edited by R. Weber. 4th ed. Stuttgart: Deutsche Bibelgesellschaft, 1994.

Bibliothèque nationale de France. *Le Catalogue BnF, archives et manuscrits*. https://archivesetmanuscrits.bnf.fr/pageAccueil.html.

Bietenholz, Peter G. *Historia and Fabula: Myths and Legends in Historical Thought from Antiquity to the Modern Age*. Brill's Studies in Intellectual History 59. Leiden: Brill, 1994.

Biller, Peter, and Anne Hudson, eds. *Heresy and Literacy, 1000–1530*. Cambridge Studies in Medieval Literature 23. Cambridge: Cambridge University Press, 1994.

Boccaccio, Giovanni. *The Decameron*. Edited by G.H. McWilliam. 2nd ed. London: Penguin, 1995.

Bogaert, Pierre-Maurice, ed. *Les Bibles en français: Histoire illustrée du Moyen Âge à nos jours*. Turnhout: Brepols, 1991.

Bonnard, Jean. *Les traductions de la Bible en vers français au moyen âge*. Paris: Imprimerie nationale, 1884.

Booth, Wayne C. *The Rhetoric of Fiction*. Chicago: University of Chicago Press, 1961.

Boulton, Maureen Barry McCann, ed. *The Old French "Évangile de l'Enfance": An Edition with Introduction and Notes*. Toronto: Pontifical Institute of Mediaeval Studies Press, 1984.

– *Sacred Fictions of Medieval France: Narrative Theology in the Lives of Christ and the Virgin, 1150–1500*. Woodbridge, UK: D.S. Brewer, 2015.

Boureau, Alain. *La légende dorée: Le système narratif de Jacques de Voragine (1298)*. Paris: Éditions du Cerf, 1984.

Bowers, Jeffrey S., and Christopher W. Pleydell-Pearce. "Swearing, Euphemisms, and Linguistic Relativity." *PLoS One* 6/7 (2011). https://www .ncbi.nlm.nih.gov/pmc/articles/PMC3140516/.

Boyle, Leonard E. "Innocent III and Vernacular Versions of Scripture." In *The Bible in the Medieval World: Essays in Memory of Beryl Smalley*, edited by Katherine Walsh and Diana Wood, 97–107. Studies in Church History: Subsidia 4. Oxford: Blackwell, 1985.

Bozzolo, Carla, and Ezio Ornato. *Pour une histoire du livre manuscrit au Moyen Âge: Trois essais de codicologie quantitative*. Textes et études: Équipe de recherche sur l'humanisme français des XIVe et XVe siècles 2. Paris: Éditions du Centre national de la recherche scientifique, 1983.

Brenton, Lancelot C.L., trans. and ed. *The Septuagint with Apocrypha: Greek and English*. London: Samuel Bagster and Sons, 1851; repr. Hendrickson, 2009.

Brundage, James. *The Crusades: A Documentary Survey*. Milwaukee: Marquette University Press, 1962.

Burgio, Eugenio. "Ricerche sulla tradizione manoscritta delle vite antico-francesi di Giuda e de Pilato. III: Le 'histoires apocrifes' nella 'Bible Historiale.'" *Annali de ca' Foscari* 37 (1998): 153–213.

Burke, Dan. "A Guide to Lectio Divina: What It Is and How It Helps Prayer Life." *Spiritual Direction* (blog). 21 April 2012. https://spiritual direction.com/2012/04/21/what-is-lectio-divina-and-will-it-help -my-prayer-life-a-guide-to-lectio-divina.

Camille, Michael. "Visualising in the Vernacular: A New Cycle of Early Fourteenth-Century Bible Illustrations." Special issue on English Gothic Art, *The Burlington Magazine* 130, no. 1019 (February 1988): 97–106.

Carlquist, Jonas. "Medieval Manuscripts, Hypertext and Reading. Visions of Digital Editions." *Literary and Linguistic Computing* 19, no. 1 (April 2004): 105–18.

Carr, Nicholas. "Is Google Making Us Stupid? What the Internet Is Doing to Our Brains." *The Atlantic*, July/August 2008. http://www.theatlantic.com /magazine/archive/2008/07/is-google-making-us-stupid/6868/.

– *The Shallows: What the Internet is Doing to our Brains*. New York: W.W. Norton, 2010.

The Catholic Encyclopedia. New Advent, 2009. http://www.newadvent.org
/cathen/11460a.htm.

Cerquiglini, Bernard. *Éloge de la variante: Histoire critique de la philologie.* Paris:
Seuil, 1989.

Charles d'Orléans. *Poésies.* Edited by Pierre Champion. Classiques français du
Moyen Âge. Paris: Librairie ancienne, 1923.

Chartier, Roger. "Communautés de lecteurs." In *Culture écrite et société: L'ordre
des livres XIVe–XVIIIe siècle,* 133–54. Paris: Albin Michel, 1996.

Chaucer, Geoffrey. *The Canterbury Tales.* In *The Riverside Chaucer,* edited by
Larry Dean Benson. 3rd ed. Boston: Houghton Mifflin, 1987.

Christine de Pizan. *Heures de contemplacion sur la Passion de Nostre Seigneur
Jhesucrist.* Edited by Liliane Dulac and René Stuip. Paris: Champion, 2017.

– *Le livre des fais et bonnes meurs du Sage Roy Charles V.* Edited by Suzanne
Solente. Paris: Champion, 1936; repr. 1940.

Coleman, Janet. "Late Scholastic *Memoria* et *Reminiscentia,* Its Uses and
Abuses." In *Intellectuals and Writers in Fourteenth-Century Europe,* edited by
Piero Boitani and Anna Torti, 22–44. Tübingen: Gunter Narr, 1986.

Coleridge, Samuel Taylor. *Biographia Literaria; or Biographical Sketches of My
Literary Life and Opinions.* 2 vols. London: Rest Fenner, 1817.

Copeland, Rita. *Pedagogy, Intellectuals, and Dissent in the Later Middle Ages:
Lollardy and Ideas of Learning.* Cambridge Studies in Medieval Literature 44.
Cambridge: Cambridge University Press, 2001.

– *Rhetoric, Hermeneutics, and Translation in the Middle Ages: Academic Traditions
and Vernacular Texts.* Cambridge Studies in Medieval Literature 11.
Cambridge: Cambridge University Press, 1991.

Corbellini, Sabrina, and Margriet Hoogvliet. "Holy Writ and Lay Readers
in Late Medieval Europe: Translation and Participation." In *Texts,
Transmissions, Receptions. Modern Approaches to Narratives,* 281–94, edited by
A.P.M.H. Lardinois, Sophie Levie, and J.A.L. Hoeken. Leiden: Brill, 2014.

Corbellini, Sabrina, Mart van Duijn, Suzan Folkerts, and Margriet Hoogvliet.
"Challenging the Paradigms: Holy Writ and Lay Readers in Late Medieval
Europe." *Church History and Religious Culture* 93, no. 2 (2013): 171–88.

Dagenais, John. *The Ethics of Reading in Manuscript Culture: Glossing the Libro De
Buen Amor.* Princeton, NJ: Princeton University Press, 1994.

Daly, Saralyn R. "Peter Comestor: Master of Histories." *Speculum* 32, no. 1
(January 1957): 62–73.

Deanesly, Margaret. *The Lollard Bible and Other Medieval Biblical Versions.*
Cambridge Studies in Medieval Life and Thought. Cambridge: The
University Press, 1920.

De Boer, Cornelis, ed. *Ovide moralisé, poème du commencement du quatorzième
siècle, publié d'après tous les manuscrits connus.* 5 vols. Verhandelingen der

Koninklijke Akademie van Wetenschappen te Amsterdam. Afdeeling Letterkunde. Nieuwe Reeks, Deel 15, 21, 30, no. 3, 37, 43. Amsterdam: Johannes Müller, 1915–38.

Delaissé, L.M.J. "A Liturgical Problem at the End of the Middle Ages: The 'Missale Gallicum.'" In *Litterae Textuales. Essays Presented to G.I. Lieftinck*, edited by J.P. Gumbert and M.J.M de Haan, 4: 16–27. 4 vols. Amsterdam: A.L. van Gendt, 1972–6.

Dell, Katharine J. *The Book of Job as Sceptical Literature*. Beihefte zur Zeitschrift für die alttestamentliche Wissenschaft 197. Berlin: De Gruyter, 1991.

Derrida, Jacques, and Michel Wieviorka. *Foi et Savoir, suivi de Le siècle et le Pardon*. Points. Paris: Seuil, 2000.

Diamond, Joan. "Manufacture and Market in Parisian Book Illumination Around 1300." *Europäische Kunst um 1300: Acten Des XXV. Internationalen Kongresses für Kunstgeschichte* 6, no. 6 (1986): 101–10.

Dictionnaire du monde religieux dans la France contemporaine: 5. Les protestants. Edited by André Encrevé. Paris: Beauchesne, 1993.

Doležalová, Lucie. "The Dining Room of God: Petrus Comestor's 'Historia scholastica' and Retelling the Bible as Feasting." In *Retelling the Bible: Literary, Historical, and Social Contexts*, edited by Lucie Doležalová and Tamás Visi, 229–44. Frankfurt: Peter Lang, 2011.

Doležalová, Lucie, and Tamás Visi, eds. *Retelling the Bible: Literary, Historical, and Social Contexts*. Frankfurt: Peter Lang, 2011.

Dove, Mary, ed. *The Earliest Advocates of the English Bible. The Texts of the Medieval Debate*. Exeter: University of Exeter Press, 2010.

Dronke, Peter. *Fabula: Explorations into the Uses of Myth in Medieval Platonism*. Mittellateinische Studien und Texte 9. Leiden: Brill, 1974.

Dubin, Nathaniel E., and R. Howard Bloch. *The Fabliaux: A New Verse Translation*. New York: Liveright, 2013.

Dufournet, Jean, ed. *Aucassin et Nicolette: Édition critique*. 2nd ed. Paris: Garnier-Flammarion, 1984.

Eisen, Robert. *The Book of Job in Medieval Jewish Philosophy*. Oxford: Oxford University Press, 2004.

Eisenstein, Elizabeth L. *The Printing Press as an Agent of Change: Communications and Cultural Transformations in Early Modern Europe*. Cambridge: Cambridge University Press, 1979.

Falluomini, Carla. *The Gothic Version of the Gospels and Pauline Epistles: Cultural Background, Transmission and Character*. Berlin: de Gruyter, 2015.

Febvre, Lucien, and Henri-Jean Martin. *L'Apparition du livre*. Paris: Albin Michel, 1958; repr. 1971 and 1999.

Ferguson, C.A. "Diglossia." In *Language and Social Context: Selected Readings*, edited by Pier Paolo Giglioli, 232–51. Harmondsworth, UK: Penguin, 1972.

Flum, Thomas. "Die Titelbilder der 'Bible historiale.' Zwischen Standardisierung und Personalisierung." *Mittelalter* 18, no. 1 (June 2013): 62–86.

Fournié, Éléonore. "Les éditions de la *Bible historiale*. Présentation et catalogue raisonné d'éditions de la première moitié du XVIe siècle." *L'Atelier du Centre des recherches historiques, revue électronique de la CRH* 3, no. 2 (2009). https://acrh.revues.org/1832.

– "Les manuscrits de la *Bible historiale*." *L'Atelier du Centre de recherches historiques, revue électronique de la CRH* 3, no. 2 (2009). https://acrh.revues.org/1830.

– *L'iconographie de la* Bible historiale. Turnhout: Brepols, 2012.

François, Wim. "The Catholic Church and Vernacular Bible Reading, Before and After Trent." *Biblicum Jassyense* 4 (2013): 5–37.

French, R.W. "Teaching the Bible as Literature." *College English* 44, no. 8 (1982): 798–807.

Froehlich, Karlfried, Margaret T. Gibson, and Adolph Rusch, eds. *Biblia Latina cum Glossa Ordinaria: Facsimile Reprint of the Editio Princeps, Adolph Rusch of Strassburg 1480/81*. Turnhout: Brepols, 1992.

Froissart, Jean. *Chroniques de J. Froissart*. Edited by Siméon Luce, Gaston Raynaud, and Léon Mirot. Paris: Mme J. Renouard, 1869.

Gallagher, Catherine. "The Rise of Fictionality." In *The Novel*, vol. 1: *History, Geography, and Culture*, edited by Franco Moretti, 336–63. Princeton, NJ: Princeton University Press, 2006.

Gaspar, Camille, and Frédéric Lyna. *Les principaux manuscrits à peintures de la Biliothèque royale de Belgique*. 2 vols. Brussels: Bibliothèque royale Albert Ier, 1937.

Gaster, Moses. *Chronicles of Jerahmeel; Or the Hebrew Bible Historiale*. London: The Royal Asiatic Society, 1899.

– *Ilchester Lectures on Greeko-Slavonic Literature and its Relation to the Folk-Lore of Europe During the Middle Ages*. London: Trübner, 1887.

Geary, Patrick. "Writing the Nation: Historians and National Identities from the Nineteenth to the Twenty-First Centuries." In *The Middle Ages in the Modern World: Twenty-First Century Perspectives*, edited by Bettina Bildhauer and Chris Jones, 73–86. Oxford: Oxford University Press, 2017.

Genette, Gérard. "Discours du récit." In *Figures III*, 71–273. Paris: Seuil, 1976.

– *Seuils*. Collection Poétique. Paris: Seuil, 1987.

Gerson, Jean. *Oeuvres complètes de Jean Gerson. Introduction, textes et notes par Mgr Glorieux*. Edited by Palémon Glorieux. 10 vols. Paris: Desclée, 1960–73.

Gillespie, Vincent. "Medieval Hypertext: Image and Text from York Minster." In *Of the Making of Books: Medieval Manuscripts, Their Scribes and Readers: Essays Presented to M.B. Parkes*, edited by P.R. Robinson and R. Zim, 206–29. Aldershot, UK: Scolar Press, 1997.

Godefroy, Frédéric. *Dictionnaire de l'ancienne langue française et de tous ses dialectes du IXe au XVe siècle*. Classiques Garnier Numérique. http://www.classiques-garnier.com/numerique-bases/index.php.

Goodman, Martin, ed. *The Apocrypha.* The Oxford Bible Commentary. Oxford: Oxford University Press, 2001.

Gow, Andrew C. "Challenging the Protestant Paradigm. Bible Reading in Lay and Urban Contexts of the Later Middle Ages." In *Scripture and Pluralism. Reading the Bible in the Religiously Plural Worlds of the Middle Ages and the Renaissance,* edited by Thomas J. Heffernan and Thomas Burman, 161–91. Studies in the History of Christian Traditions 123. Leiden: Brill, 2005.

Green, Dennis Howard. *The Beginnings of Medieval Romance: Fact and Fiction, 1150–1220.* Cambridge Studies in Medieval Literature 47. Cambridge: Cambridge University Press, 2002.

Gregory I. "Moralium Libri, sive expositio in librum Job." *Patrologia Latina.* Edited by J.-P. Migne, 75.0509–1160. Alexandria, VA: Chadwyck-Healey, 1996. http://pld.chadwyck.com/.

– *Morals on the Book of Job.* Translated and edited by James Bliss. 3 vols. in 4. A Library of the Fathers of the Holy Catholic Church. Oxford: J.H. Parker, 1844.

Gui de Cambrai. *Barlaam and Josaphat: A Christian Tale of the Buddha.* Translated and edited by Peggy McCracken. New York: Penguin Classics, 2014.

Guillaume de Lorris and Jean de Meun. *Le Roman de la Rose.* Edited by Félix Lecoy. 3 vols. Les Classiques français du Moyen Âge. Paris: Champion, 1983.

Guyart des Moulins. *La Bible historiale: La Genèse, L'Exode, Le Lévitique, Le Deutéronome, Les Nombres, Josué, Les Juges, Les Roys.* Edited by Xavier-Laurent Salvador. Cambremer: Éditions des Saints Pères, 2017.

Hadley, Margaret E. "Camouflaging and Echoing the Latin Mass in an Illuminated French-Language Missal." In *Postcolonising the Medieval Image,* edited by Eva Frojmovic and Catherine E. Karkov, 62–88. New York: Routledge, 2017.

Hamburger, Jeffrey F. "Rewriting History: The Visual and the Vernacular in Late Medieval History Bibles." *Zeitschrift Für Deutsche Philologie* 124 (2005): 260–308.

Hamilton, Bernard. "The Cathars and Christian Perfection." In *The Medieval Church: Universities, Heresy, and the Religious Life: Essays in Honour of Gordon Leff,* edited by Gordon Leff, Peter Biller, and R.B. Dobson, 5–23. Studies in Church History, Subsidia 11. Woodbridge, UK: Published for the Ecclesiastical History Society by the Boydell Press, 1999.

Hargreaves, Henry. "The Wycliffite Versions." In *The Cambridge History of the Bible,* vol. 2: *The West from the Fathers to the Reformation,* edited by G.W.H. Lampe, 387–415. Cambridge: Cambridge University Press, 1969.

Harnois, Catherine E. "Race, Gender, and the Black Women's Standpoint." *Sociological Forum* 25, no. 1 (March 2010): 68–85.

Hasenohr, Geneviève. "Religious Reading amongst the Laity in France." In *Heresy and Literacy, 1000–1530,* edited by Peter Billard and Anne Hudson, 205–21. Cambridge: Cambridge University Press, 1996.

Hawk, Brandon W. "Apocrypha and Fictionality." *New Literary History* 51, no. 1 (Winter 2020): 253–7.

– "The Literary Contexts and Early Transmission of the Latin *Life of Judas*." *Journal of Medieval Religious Cultures* 44, no. 1 (2018): 60–76.

– *Preaching Apocrypha in Anglo-Saxon England*. Toronto: University of Toronto Press, 2018.

Heng, Geraldine. *The Invention of Race in the European Middle Ages*. Cambridge: Cambridge University Press, 2018.

Herman de Valenciennes. Li Romanz de Dieu et de sa mere *d'Herman de Valenciennes, chanoine et prêtre (XIIe siècle)*. Edited by Ina Spiele. Leiden: Presse universitaire de Leyde, 1975.

Hevelone, Suzanne. "Examining Saints' Lives and Sermons: Jacobus de Voragine on Mary Magdalene and Peter Martyr." *Medieval Sermon Studies* 51 (2007): 89–91.

– "Preaching the Saints: The *Legenda aurea* and Sermones de Sanctis of Jacobus de Voragine." PhD diss., Boston College, 2010.

Hoogvliet, Margriet. "The Medieval Vernacular Bible in French as a Flexible Text: Selective and Discontinuous Reading Practices." In *Form and Function in the Late Medieval Bible*, edited by Eyal Poleg and Laura Light, 283–306. Library of the Written Word 27. Leiden: Brill, 2016.

– "Nicole de Bretaigne and a Collection of Religious Texts in French: Bibliothèque de l'Arsenal, MS 5366 (15th century)." *Digital Philology* 5, no. 2 (2016): 160–81.

Holton, Amanda. "Which Bible Did Chaucer Use? The Biblical Tragedies in the Monk's Tale." *Notes and Queries* 253, no. 1 (March 2008): 13–17.

The Holy Bible, Douay-Rheims Translation. Rockford, IL: Tan Books, 1899; repr. 1971.

The Holy Bible: Recovery Version. "Translating the Bible." Living Stream Ministry. 2018. http://www.recoveryversion.bible/translation.html.

Hugh of St. Victor. *Didascalicon: A Medieval Guide to the Arts*. Edited and translated by Jerome Taylor. Records of Western Civilization, Sources and Studies 64. New York: Columbia University Press, 1961.

– *Didascalicon de Studio Legendi, a Critical Text*. Edited by Charles Henry Buttimer. Studies in Medieval and Renaissance Latin. Washington, DC: The Catholic University Press, 1939.

Hody, Humphrey. *De Bibliorum textibus originalibus, versionibus graecis, & latina vulgata*. Oxford, 1705.

Hunt, Tony, ed. *Les Paroles Salomun*. Anglo-Norman Text Society 70. Manchester: Anglo-Norman Text Society, 2012.

Huot, Sylvia Jean. *The Romance of the Rose and its Medieval Readers: Interpretation, Reception, Manuscript Transmission*. Cambridge: Cambridge University Press, 1993.

– "The Scribe as Editor: Rubrication as Critical Apparatus in Two Manuscripts of the *Roman de la Rose*." *L'Esprit créateur* 27, no. 1 (1987): 67–78.

Innocent III. "Epist. 141, to the Bishop of Metz." *Patrologia Latina*. Edited by J.-P. Migne, 214.0695–0698. Alexandria, VA: Chadwyck-Healey, 1996. http://pld.chadwyck.com/.

Iser, Wolfgang. *The Fictive and the Imaginary: Charting Literary Anthropology.* Baltimore: Johns Hopkins University Press, 1993.

– *The Implied Reader: Patterns of Communication in Prose Fiction from Bunyan to Beckett.* Baltimore: Johns Hopkins University Press, 1974.

Isidore of Seville. *Etymologiarum sive originum libri XX.* Edited by W.M. Lindsay. 2 vols. Oxford: Clarendon Press, 1911; repr. 1962.

Jacobus de Voragine. *The Golden Legend: Readings on the Saints.* Translated by William Granger Ryan. 2 vols. Princeton, NJ: Princeton University Press, 1993.

– *Legenda aurea: Vulgo historia lombardica dicta.* Edited by Johann Georg Theodor Grässe. 3rd ed. Breslau: G. Koebner, 1890.

Jacques de Vitry. *Historia orientalis.* Edited and translated by Jean Donnadieu. Turnhout: Brepols, 2008.

Jauss, Hans Robert. *Toward an Aesthetic of Reception.* Translated by Timothy Bahti. Theory and History of Literature 2. Minneapolis: University of Minnesota Press, 1982.

Jehan Malkaraume. *La Bible de Jehan Malkaraume.* Edited by Jean-Robert Smeets. Assen: Van Gorcum, 1978.

Johns, Adrian. *The Nature of the Book: Print and Knowledge in the Making.* Chicago: University of Chicago Press, 1998.

Johnson, Dudley R. "The Biblical Characters of Chaucer's Monk." *PMLA: Publications of the Modern Language Association of America* 66, no. 5 (1951): 827–43.

Jung, C.G. *Answer to Job.* Translated by R.F.C. Hull. Cleveland: Meridian Books, 1960.

Justice, Stephen. "Did the Middle Ages Believe in Their Miracles?" *Representations* 103, no. 1 (Summer 2008): 1–29.

Karnes, Michelle. "The Possibilities of Medieval Fiction." *New Literary History* 51, no. 1 (Winter 2020): 209–28.

Kauvar, Elaine M. *Cynthia Ozick's Fiction: Tradition and Invention.* Jewish Literature and Culture. Bloomington: Indiana University Press, 1993.

Kelly, Henry Ansgar. *The Middle English Bible: A Reassessment.* Philadelphia: University of Pennsylvania Press, 2016.

Kluxen, Wolfgang. "Maimonides and Latin Scholasticism." In *Maimonides and Philosophy: Papers Presented at the Sixth Jerusalem Philosophical Encounter, May 1985*, edited by Shlomo Pines and Yirmiahu Yovel, 224–32. Archives internationales d'histoire des idées 114. Dordrecht: M. Nijhoff, 1986.

Kumler, Aden. "*Faire translater, faire historier*: Charles V's *Bible Historiale* and the Visual Rhetoric of Vernacular Sapience." *Studies in Iconography* 29 (2008): 90–135.

Lachs, Samuel Tobias. "The Source of Hebrew Traditions in the *Historia scholastica*." *The Harvard Theological Review* 66, no. 3 (July 1973): 385–6.

Landow, George P. *Hypertext: The Convergence of Contemporary Critical Theory and Technology*. Parallax: Re-Visions of Culture and Society. Baltimore: Johns Hopkins University Press, 1992.

Lawton, Phillip. "For the Gentleman and the Scholar: Sexual and Scatological References in the Loeb Classical Library." In *Expurgating the Classics: Editing Out in Greek and Latin*, edited by Stephen Harrison and Christopher Stray, 175–96. London: Bristol Classical Press, 2012.

Lefevere, André. *Translation, Rewriting, and the Manipulation of Literary Fame*. Translation Studies. New York: Routledge, 2017.

Leupin, Alexandre. *Fiction et Incarnation: Littérature et théologie au Moyen Âge*. Idées et Recherches. Paris: Flammarion, 1993.

Levy, Ian Christopher. *Holy Scripture and the Quest for Authority at the End of the Middle Ages*. Notre Dame, IN: University of Notre Dame Press, 2012.

Lim, Gary. "The Ages of Man in Two Middle English Oedipus Narratives." *Studies in Philology* 116, no. 1 (2019): 1–34.

Lorenzini, Simona. "Petrarch and Boccaccio: The Rewriting of Griselda's Tale (*Dec.* 10.10). A Rhetorical Debate on Latin and Vernacular Languages." *Heliotropia* 16–17 (2019–20): 205–27.

Losada Goya, José Manuel. "La nature mythique du Graal dans Le Conte du Graal de Chrétien de Troyes." *Cahiers de Civilisation Médiévale* 52, no. 205 (2009): 3–20.

Lowden, John. "The *Bible Moralisée* in the Fifteenth Century and the Challenge of the *Bible Historiale*." *Journal of the Warburg and Courtauld Institutes* 68 (2005): 73–136.

– *The Making of the Bibles Moralisées*. 2 vols. University Park: Pennsylvania State University Press, 2000.

Ludolph of Suchem. *Description of the Holy Land and of the Way Thither*. Translated by Aubrey Stewart. London: Palestine Pilgrims' Text Society, 1895.

Luscombe, David. "Peter Comestor." In *The Bible in the Medieval World: Essays in Memory of Beryl Smalley*, edited by Katherine Walsh and Diana Wood, 109–29. Oxford: Blackwell for the Ecclesiastical History Society, 1985.

Lusignan, Serge. *Parler vulgairement: Les intellectuels et la langue française aux XIIIe et XIVe siècles*. Études médiévales. 2nd ed. Montreal: Presses de l'Université de Montréal, 1987.

Macé de la Charité. *La Bible de Macé de la Charité*. Edited by J.R. Smeets, P.E.R. Verhuyck, A.M.L. Prangsma-Hajenuis, H.C.M. Van der Krabben, and R.L.H. Lops. 7 vols. Leiden: Universitaire Pers, 1967–82.

Macrobius. *Commentary on the Dream of Scipio*. Edited by William Harris Stahl. Records of Civilization, Sources and Studies 48. New York: Columbia University Press, 1952.

Macy, Gary. "The Theology of the Eucharist in the High Middle Ages." In *A Companion to the Eucharist in the Middle Ages*, edited by Ian Christopher Levy, Gary Macy, and Kristen Van Ausdall, 365–98. Leiden: Brill, 2012.

Maimonides, Moses. *The Guide of the Perplexed*. Translated by Shlomo Pines. Chicago: University of Chicago Press, 1963.

Mann, Joshua L. "How Technology Means: Texts, History, and Their Associated Technologies." *Digital Humanities Quarterly* 12, no. 3 (2018). http://digitalhumanities.org/dhq/vol/12/3/000398/000398.html.

Marguerite de Navarre. *Heptaméron*. Edited by Simone de Reyff. Paris: Flammarion, 1982.

Marie de France. *Lais de Marie de France*. Edited by Laurence Harf-Lancner and Karl Warnke. Lettres gothiques. Paris: Librairie générale française, 1990.

Marsden, Richard, and E. Ann Matter, eds. *The New Cambridge History of the Bible*, vol. 2: *From 600 to 1450*. Cambridge: Cambridge University Press, 2012.

Masson, Gustave. "Biblical Literature in France during the Middle Ages: Peter Comestor and Guiart Desmoulins." *The Journal of Sacred Literature and Biblical Record* 8 (1866): 81–106.

McFarlane, John. *Antoine Vérard*. London: Chiswick Press, 1900.

McGerr, Rosemarie Potz. "Guyart Desmoulins, the Vernacular Master of Histories, and His *Bible historiale*." *Viator* 14 (1983): 211–44.

McGrady, Deborah L. *Controlling Readers: Guillaume de Machaut and His Late Medieval Audience*. Studies in Book and Print Culture. Toronto: University of Toronto Press, 2006.

– "Reading for Authority: Portraits of Christine de Pizan and Her Readers." In *Medieval Authorship: Theory and Practice*, edited by Steve Partridge and Erik Kwakkel, 154–77. Toronto: University of Toronto Press, 2012.

McGurk, Patrick. "La Bible au Moyen Âge." *The Journal of Ecclesiastical History* 56, no. 2 (April 2005): 351–2.

Meiller, Albert, ed. *La pacience de Job, mystère anonyme du XVe siècle (ms. fr. 1774)*. Paris: Klincksieck, 1971.

Meyer, Wilhelm. "Die *Geschichte des Kreuzholzes vor Christus*." *Abhandlungen der Philosophisch-Philologischen Classe der Königlich Bayerischen Akademie der Wissenschaften* 15 (1882): 103–60.

Morand, François. "Un opuscule de Guiard des Moulins." *Revue des Sociétés Savantes* (1861): 490–511.

Morey, James H. *Book and Verse: A Guide to Middle English Biblical Literature*. Urbana: University of Illinois Press, 2000.

– "Peter Comestor, Biblical Paraphrase, and the Medieval Popular Bible." *Speculum* 68, no. 1 (1993): 6–35.

Murdoch, Brian. *The Apocryphal Adam and Eve in Medieval Europe: Vernacular Translations and Adaptations of the* Vita Adae et Evae. Oxford: Oxford University Press, 2009.

Newman, Barbara. *Medieval Crossover: Reading the Secular against the Sacred.* Notre Dame, IN: University of Notre Dame Press, 2013.

Nichols, Stephen G. *From Parchment to Cyberspace: Medieval Literature in the Digital Age.* New York: Peter Lang, 2016.

– "Introduction: Philology in a Manuscript Culture." *Speculum* 65, no. 1 (1990): 1–10.

– "Prophetic Discourse: St. Augustine to Christine De Pizan." In *The Bible in the Middle Ages: Its Influence on Literature and Art*, edited by Bernard S. Levy, 51–76. Binghamton, NY: Medieval and Renaissance Texts and Studies, 1992.

– *Romanesque Signs: Early Medieval Narrative and Iconography.* New Haven, CT: Yale University Press, 1983.

Nida, Eugene. *Toward a Science of Translating: With Special Reference to Principles and Procedures Involved in Bible Translating.* Leiden: Brill, 1964.

Nobel, Pierre. "Early Biblical Translators and Their Readers: The Example of the *Bible d'Acre* and the *Bible Anglo-Normande.*" *Revue de linguistique romane* 66, no. 263–4 (2002): 451–72.

O'Gorman, Richard. "The *Gospel of Nicodemus* in the Vernacular Literature of Medieval France." In *The Medieval Gospel of Nicodemus: Texts, Intertexts and Contexts*, edited by Zbignieu Izydorczyk, 103–32. Binghamton, NY: Medieval and Renaissance Texts and Studies, 1997.

Ong, Walter J. "Orality, Literacy, and Medieval Textualization." *New Literary History* 16, no. 1 (1984), 1–12.

Orlemanski, Julie. "Who Has Fiction? Modernity, Fictionality, and the Middle Ages." *New Literary History* 50, no. 2 (Spring 2019): 145–70.

Palmer, Andrew, Sebastian P. Brock, and Robert Hoyland. *The Seventh Century in the West-Syrian Chronicles.* Translated Texts for Historians 15. Liverpool: Liverpool University Press, 1993.

Patschovsky, Alexander. "The Literacy of Waldensianism from Valdes to c. 1400." In *Heresy and Literacy, 1000–1530*, edited by Peter Biller and Anne Hudson, 112–36. Cambridge Studies in Medieval Literature 23. Cambridge: Cambridge University Press, 1994.

Patterson, Jeanette. "Christine de Pizan, Translator and Translation Critic." In *A Companion to Medieval Translation*, edited by Jeanette Beer, 85–96. Leeds: Arc Humanities Press, 2019.

– "Interpreting Job's Silence in the *Bible historiale.*" Supplement, *Modern Language Notes* 127, no. 5 (December 2012): S217–42.

– "La Bible française du moyen âge comme expérience multimédia: Texte, image, voix." In *Paroles et images sur le commencement: Le discours des peintures de la chapelle de Merléac,* edited by Xavier-Laurent Salvador and Jeanette Patterson, 117–34. Orléans: Paradigme, 2019.

– "Solomon *au feminin*: (Re)translating Proverbs 31 in Christine de Pizan's *Cité des dames.*" In "Medieval Futures," edited by Marilynn Desmond. Special issue, *Mediaevalia* 36/37 (2015/2016): 353–92.

– "Stolen Scriptures: The *Bible historiale* and the Hundred Years' War." In "Rethinking the Boundaries of Patronage," edited by Deborah L. McGrady. Special issue, *Digital Philology: A Journal of Medieval Cultures* 2, no. 2 (Fall 2013): 155–80.

Peignot, Gabriel. *Catalogue d'une partie des livres composant la bibliothèque des Ducs de Bourgogne.* Dijon: Lagier, 1830.

Perdue, Leo G., and W. Clark Gilpin. *The Voice from the Whirlwind: Interpreting the Book of Job.* Nashville: Abingdon Press, 1992.

Peter Comestor. *Historia scholastica. Patrologia Latina.* Edited by J.-P. Migne, 128.1049–1722. Alexandria, VA: Chadwyck-Healey, 1996. http://pld .chadwyck.com/.

Peter Lombard. "Pauli Apostoli Epistolas." *Patrologia Latina.* Edited by J.-P. Migne, 191.1297–1696. Alexandria, VA: Chadwyck-Healey, 1996. http://pld .chadwyck.com/.

Philippe de Mézières. *Le Songe du vieil pelerin.* Edited by G.W. Coopland. 2 vols. Cambridge: Cambridge University Press, 1969.

Pierre de Nesson. *Les vigiles des morts (XVe s.).* Edited by Alain Collet. Classiques français du Moyen Âge 141. Paris: Champion, 2002.

Pinsky, Robert. "On Translation." *The Literary Review* 50, no. 1 (Fall 2006). www.theliteraryreview.org.

Quéreuil, Michel. *La Bible française du XIIIe siècle: Édition critique de la Genèse.* Publications romanes et françaises 183. Geneva: Droz, 1988.

Quinn, Esther Casier. *The Quest of Seth for the Oil of Life.* Chicago: University of Chicago Press, 1962.

Rabinowitz, Peter J. "Truth in Fiction: A Reexamination of Audiences." *Critical Inquiry* 4 (1977): 121–41.

Randall, Lilian M.C., and Judith Oliver. *Medieval and Renaissance Manuscripts in the Walters Art Gallery.* 3 vols. Baltimore: Johns Hopkins University Press in association with the Walters Art Gallery, 1989–97.

Reiss, Katharina, and Hans Vermeer. *Towards a General Theory of Translational Action: Skopos Theory Explained.* Translated by Christine Nord. London: Routledge, 2014.

Reuss, E.W.E. "Fragments littéraires et critiques relatifs à l'histoire de la Bible française. Seconde série. Les Bibles du quatorzième et du quinzième siècle et les premières éditions imprimées." *Revue de théologie et de philosophie chrétienne* 14 (1857): 1–104.

Ricoeur, Paul. *Temps et récit*. 3 vols. Ordre philosophique. Paris: Seuil, 1983.

Robertson, Duncan. *Lectio divina: The Medieval Experience of Reading*. Trappist, KY: Cistercian Publications, 2011.

Robinson, Douglas. *Translation and Taboo*. Dekalb: Northern Illinois University Press, 1996.

Robson, C.A. "Vernacular Scriptures in France." In *The Cambridge History of the Bible*, vol. 2: *The West from the Fathers to the Reformation*, edited by G.W.H. Lampe, 437–43. Cambridge: Cambridge University Press, 1969.

Rolin, Kristina, "Standpoint Theory as a Methodology for the Study of Power Relations." *Hypatia* 24, no. 4 (2009): 218–26.

Rosenberg, Joel. "Meanings, Morals, and Mysteries: Literary Approaches to the Torah." *Response* 9, no. 2 (Summer 1975): 67–94.

Rouse, R.H., and M.A. Rouse. "The Commercial Production of Manuscript Books in Late Thirteenth-Century and Early Fourteenth-Century Paris." In *Medieval Book Production: Assessing the Evidence. Proceedings of the Second Conference of the Seminar in the History of the Book to 1500, Oxford, July 1988*, edited by L.L. Brownrigg, 103–16. Los Altos Hill, CA: Anderson-Lovelace, 1990.

Rouyer, Jules. *Recherches historiques sur le chapitre et l'église collégiale de Saint-Pierre d'Aire-sur-la-Lys*. Saint-Omer: Fleury-Lemaire, 1860.

Salvador, Xavier-Laurent. *Archéologie et étymologie sémantiques: La traduction du Livre de l'Exode de la Bible Historiale (1295)*. Bucharest: Zeta Books, 2017.

– "Les 'biblismes,' un système de définition original du lexique dans le discours pédagogique de la Bible Historiale." *Quaderni del CIRSIL* 2 (2003). http://halshs.archives-ouvertes.fr/halshs-00418571/en/.

– "Une autre définition de l'étymologie: Dire le vrai dans la Bible." In *Par les mots et les textes, mélanges de langue, de littérature et d'histoire des sciences médiévales offerts à Claude Thomasset*, edited by Danièle James-Raoul and Olivier Soutet, 663–77. Paris: Presses universitaires de France, 2005.

– *Vérité et Écriture(s)*. Bibliothèque de grammaire et de linguistique 25. Paris: Champion, 2007.

Salvador, Xavier-Laurent, and Jeanette Patterson, eds. *Paroles et images sur le commencement: Le discours des peintures de la chapelle de Merléac*. Orléans: Paradigme, 2019.

Salvador, Xavier-Laurent, Jeannette Patterson, Céline Guillemet, Christine Jablonski, Michel Bernard, François Ploton-Nicollet, and Juliette Vion-Dury et al. *Biblehistoriale.fr: Histoire de la Bible Historiale dans l'Europe Médiévale*. http://www.biblehistoriale.fr.

Sargent-Baur, Barbara Nelson. *Brothers of Dragons: Job Dolens and François Villon*. New York: Garland, 1990.

Seybolt, Robert Francis. "The *Legenda aurea*, Bible, and *Historia scholastica*." *Speculum* 21, no. 3 (1946): 339–42.

Sherman, Claire Richter. *The Portraits of Charles V of France (1338–1380)*. New York: New York University Press, 1969.

Simonetti, Manlio, and Marco Conti. *Job*. Edited by Thomas C. Oden. Ancient Christian Commentary on Scripture 6. Downers Grove, IL: InterVarsity Press, 2006.

Smalley, Beryl. *The Study of the Bible in the Middle Ages*. 2nd ed. Oxford: Blackwell, 1952.

Smeets, J.R., ed. *La Chevalerie de Judas Macabé*. Assen: Van Gorcum, 1955.

Sneddon, Clive R. "The 'Bible du XIIIᵉ siècle': Its Medieval Public in Light of its Manuscript Tradition." In *The Bible and Medieval Culture*, edited by W. Lourdaux and D. Verhelst, 127–40. Mediaevalia Lovaniensia ser. 1, studia 7. Leuven: Leuven University Press, 1979.

– "A Critical Edition of the Four Gospels in the Thirteenth-Century Old French Translation of the Bible." PhD diss., Oxford University, 1978.

– "Translation Technique and the *Old French Bible*." *Forum for Modern Language Studies* 35, no. 4 (1999): 339–48.

Somerset, Fiona, Jill C. Havens, and Derreck G. Pitard, eds. *Lollards and Their Influence in Late Medieval England*. Woodbridge, UK: Boydell, 2003.

Spacey, Beth C. *The Miraculous and the Writing of Crusade Narrative*. Crusading in Context. Woodbridge, UK: Boydell, 2020.

Spiegel, Gabrielle. "Memory and History: Liturgical Time and Historical Time." *History and Theory* 41, no. 2 (2002): 149–62.

– *The Past as Text: The Theory and Practice of Historiography*. Baltimore: Johns Hopkins University Press, 1997.

Spivak, Guyatri Chakravorty. "Can the Subaltern Speak?" In *Marxism and the Interpretation of Culture*, edited by Cary Nelson and Lawrence Grossberg, 271–313. Basingstoke, UK: Macmillan, 1988.

St.-Jacques, Raymond. "French Translations of the Bible in the Fourteenth and Fifteenth Centuries: Guyart des Moulins and His Contemporaries." *Revue de l'Universite d'Ottawa/University of Ottawa Quarterly* 55, no. 1 (1985): 75–86.

Stahuljak, Zrinka. "An Epistemology of Tension." *The Translator* 10, no. 1 (2004): 33–57.

Stephenson, Barbara. *The Power and Patronage of Marguerite De Navarre*. Women and Gender in the Early Modern World. Aldershot, UK: Ashgate, 2004.

Stock, Brian. *After Augustine: The Meditative Reader and the Text*. Material Texts. Philadelphia: University of Pennsylvania Press, 2001.

– *Augustine the Reader: Meditation, Self-Knowledge, and the Ethics of Interpretation*. Cambridge, MA: The Belknap Press of Harvard University Press, 1996.

– *The Implications of Literacy: Written Language and Models of Interpretation in the Eleventh and Twelfth Centuries*. Princeton, NJ: Princeton University Press, 1983.

Sturges, Robert Stuart. *Medieval Interpretation: Models of Reading in Literary Narrative, 1100–1500.* Carbondale: Southern Illinois University Press, 1991.

Taguchi, Mayumi. *The Historye of the Patriarks: Edited from Cambridge, St John's College, MS G.31. With Parallel Texts of* The Historia scholastica *and the* Bible historiale. Middle English Texts 42. Heidelberg: Universitätsverlag Winter, 2010.

Tertullian. "Of Patience." Translated by S. Thelwall. In *The Ante-Nicene Fathers*, edited by Alexander Roberts and James Donaldson. Vol. 3, 707–17. Buffalo: Christian Literature Publishing, 1887.

Thiesse, Anne-Marie. *La création des identités nationales. Europe XVIIIe–XXe siècle.* 2nd ed. Paris: Seuil, 2001.

Thomas Aquinas. *Expositio super Iob ad litteram.* Textum Leoninum. Rome, 1965.

– *Literal Exposition on Job: A Scriptural Commentary Concerning Providence.* Translated by Anthony Damico with interpretive essay and notes by Martin D. Yaffe. Oxford: Oxford University Press, 1989.

– *The* Summa Theologica *of St. Thomas Aquinas.* Translated by Fathers of the English Dominican Province. 2nd ed. London: Burns, Oates & Washbourne, 1920. Online edition by Kevin Knight. New Advent, 2017. https://www.newadvent.org/summa/.

Thouzellier, Christine. *Catharisme et valdéisme en Languedoc à la fin du XIIe et au début du XIIIe siècle.* 2nd ed. Louvain: Éditions Nauwelaerts, 1969.

– "L'emploi de la Bible par les Cathares (XIIIe s.)." In *The Bible and Medieval Culture*, edited by W. Lourdaux and D. Verhelst. Mediaevalia Lovaniensia, ser. 1, vol. 7, 141–56. Leuven: Leuven University Press, 1979.

Tóth, Péter. "Way Out of the Tunnel? Three Hundred Years of Research on the Apocrypha: A Preliminary Approach." In *Retelling the Bible: Literary, Historical, and Social* Contexts, edited by Lucie Doležalová and Tamás Visi, 47–86. Frankfurt: Peter Lang, 2011.

Tymoczko, Maria. *Enlarging Translation, Empowering Translators.* Manchester: St. Jerome, 2007.

– "Ideology and the Position of the Translator: In What Sense Is the Translator 'In Between'?" In *Apropos of Ideology: Translation Studies on Ideology – Ideologies in Translation Studies*, edited by María Caldaza Pérez, 181–201. Manchester: St. Jerome, 2003.

– "Western Metaphorical Discourses Implicit in Translation Studies." In *Thinking Through Translation with Metaphors*, edited by James St. André, 109–43. Manchester: St. Jerome, 2014.

Uhlenbruch, Frauke, and Sonja Ammann, eds. "Fan Fiction and Ancient Scribal Cultures." Special issue, *Transformative Works and Cultures* 31 (2019).

United Church of Christ. "Lectio divina." https://www.ucc.org/feed -your-spirit_practices_lectio-divina.

Vance, Eugene. *Mervelous Signals: Poetics and Sign Theory in the Middle Ages.* Lincoln: University of Nebraska Press, 1986.

Van Liere, Frans. *An Introduction to the Medieval Bible.* Cambridge: Cambridge University Press, 2014.

Venuti, Lawrence. *The Scandals of Translation.* New York: Routledge, 1998.

– *The Translator's Invisibility: A History of Translation.* London: Routledge, 2008.

Villon, François. *Le Testament Villon.* Edited by Jean Rychner and Albert Henry. 2 vols. Geneva: Droz, 1974.

Walsh, Katherine, and Diana Wood, eds. *The Bible in the Medieval World: Essays in Memory of Beryl Smalley.* Studies in Church History. Oxford: Published for the Ecclesiastical History Society by Blackwell, 1985.

White, James R. *The King James Only Controversy.* Minneapolis: Bethany House, 1995.

Wilkins, David. *Concilia Magnae Britanniae et Hiberniae, ab Anno MCCCL ad Annum MDXLV.* Vol. 3. London: 1737.

Winn, Mary Beth. *Anthoine Vérard: Parisian Publisher 1485–1512: Prologues, Poems, and Presentations.* Travaux d'Humanisme et Renaissance 313. Geneva: Droz, 1997.

Yaffe, Martin. "Providence in Medieval Aristotelianism: Moses Maimonides and Thomas Aquinas on the Book of Job." In *The Voice from the Whirlwind: Interpreting the Book of Job.* Edited by Leo G. Perdue and W. Clark Gilpin, 111–28. Nashville: Abingdon, 1992.

Yocum, John. "Aquinas's *Literal Exposition on Job.*" In *Aquinas on Scripture: An Introduction to His Biblical Commentaries,* edited by Thomas Gerard Weinandy, Daniel A. Keating, and John Yocum, 21–42. New York: T & T Clark, 2005.

Zumthor, Paul. *Essai de poétique médiévale.* Collection Poétique. Paris: Seuil, 1972.

– *La poésie et la voix dans la civilization médiévale.* Paris: Presses universitaires de France, 1984.

Index

authority (*continued*)
   or translation, 13, 20, 24, 57, 81,
   134–5, 147, 197n8; of university
   masters, 50, 83, 133–6, 197n8; of
   Vulgate Bible, 13, 20, 50–1, 73

Bacon, Roger, 81–2, 191n26
Barlaam and Josaphat, 68–9, 186n41
Bede, 94–5, 98, 134, 144, 196n69
Beer, Jeanette, 5, 26–7
belief. *See* faith
Berger, Samuel, 10, 15–16, 37–8,
   41, 113, 118, 145, 163–6, 169n15,
   175nn37–8, 178n59, 179n62,
   188n6, 203n50, 213n43, 216n1
Bibb, Bryan, 152–5
Bible: culturally contingent
   definitions of, 3–5, 13, 18–19, 22,
   26–7, 37, 152–62; formats and
   technologies for reading, 6, 13, 41,
   61, 129–30, 132–3, 136, 152–62;
   political or ideological uses of,
   3, 6, 9, 25–7, 39–40, 64–5, 67–8,
   85, 140–3, 162; social and literary
   functions of, 3–4, 18–19, 25–7,
   39–42, 67–70, 88, 153–5, 162,
   167nn2–3; textual criticism and
   history of, 10–11, 43, 114, 153–8;
   unity of Old and New Testaments
   in Christian Bible(s), 12, 46, 64,
   73, 75, 79–80, 128, 142–6, 157,
   159. See also *Bible historiale*; Bible
   translation(s); canon; *and individual
   parts and books of the Bible*
Bible du XIIIe siècle, 4, 15, 26, 37–8, 44,
   49, 67, 179n67; combined with the
   Bible historiale, 4, 15, 37–9, 74, 112–14,
   117–18, 145, 161–6, 168n6, 171n8
Bible historiale: authorship of, 4, 13–14,
   27, 31, 74, 140–2; classification
   of manuscripts, 15–16, 37–8, 41,
   113–14, 145, 163–6, 167n5, 175n44,
   213n43; contents and structure of,
   18, 28–44, 105–6, 112–14, 129–30,
   137, 139, 144–5, 160–6, 178n59;
   customization of manuscripts, 4–5,

10, 38–41, 113, 116–19, 125–6,
   145, 150–1, 156–7, 160–2, 175n39,
   184n26; expansions of, 4–5, 15–16,
   31, 37–44, 112–14, 117–18, 126,
   129–30, 145, 149, 156, 160–6;
   and French literature, 5–6, 9–12,
   54–5, 67–72, 97, 100–1, 121–2,
   161–2; and "historical Bibles" in
   other vernacular languages, 18,
   171n7, 176n45, 190n19; manuscript
   layouts of, 29–30, 55, 68, 125, 127,
   130, 135–6; in miscellanies, 67–8,
   168n6, 175n44; misrepresentations
   of, 19–20, 171n7, 172n9, 173n20;
   patrons and owners of, 4, 9, 21, 25,
   37–41, 114, 117–18, 130, 157–60,
   169n14; printed editions of, 4, 10,
   28, 29, 41–4, 113, 162, 174n27,
   175n39; translation style of, 33–7,
   52–5, 182n13, 183n16, 184n17. *See
   also* manuscripts; printed books
*Bible historiale complétée. See Bible
   du XIIIe siècle*: combined with
   the *Bible historiale*; *Bible historiale*:
   classification of manuscripts; *Bible
   historiale*: expansions of
Bible, King James Version, 20, 172n13
Bible moralisée, 6, 12, 19, 38, 127–30,
   136–7, 145, 149, 154, 158–61, 166,
   207n4, 216n16; combined with the
   Bible historiale in some manuscripts,
   127, 129–30, 161, 165–6
Bibles for America, 20, 172n12
Bible translation(s): and adaptability to
   readers' needs, 4–6, 9–13, 18, 27–8,
   36–43, 57, 114, 125–33, 149–51,
   156–8, 162; and church control
   over, 6–9, 21–5, 43, 124–5, 135, 160;
   comparative study of, 49–55, 162–3;
   medieval translations in French,
   22, 25–6, 37–9, 49–55, 127–30; in
   other vernacular languages, 17, 24,
   170n2, 171n7, 174n27; outside of
   books, 17–18, 25–6; and preaching,
   4, 13, 17, 25–6, 31–2, 35–6, 73, 87,
   160, 170n3, 177n54; in prose, 8, 10,

Jesus: and apostles, 75–6, 78, 85;
chasing moneylenders from
Temple, 62, 147; childhood of, 85;
dual human and divine nature of,
146; as an infant, 40, 62, 79, 91; life
of, 67, 75–9, 92, 95, 100, 119, 139;
prophecy about, 64, 79, 109–10,
119, 139; quotations of, 7; return of,
131. *See also* Crucifixion; Gospels;
Nativity; parables; Resurrection
Jeu d'Adam, 47
Jews, 9, 57–9, 64–5, 79–80, 89, 105;
and anti-Semitism, 64–5, 80, 191n21,
211n36; and supersessionism, 3, 9,
46, 64–5, 79–80, 143, 146, 179n68.
See also exegesis: Jewish; history:
Jewish; Judaism
Job, Book of, 101–25, 139; allegorical
versus literal readings of, 70,
109–11, 117; ambivalent ending
of, 107, 198n13; art based on, 107;
commentaries about, 70, 103,
107–12; as critique of conservative
theologies, 107, 148; Grand Job,
68, 112–21, 201n34, 201n36; as
hagiography, 68, 107–10, 116,
119–21; and heresy, 110–11, 148,
204n57; and its interpretation
of itself, 103–4, 107–8, 110–12;
Jerome's prologue and translation
of, 109, 199n18; Jewish readings
of, 108–11, 198n15, 199n18;
literature inspired by, 121–2; as
moral example of patience, 101,
103, 107, 109, 116–17, 121, 126, 131,
136; Petit Job, 29, 106–7, 112–22,
136, 148, 201n34, 203n45; use of
in Office of the Dead, 121; other
vernacular versions of, 22, 26, 106–7;
as prefiguring or prophesying
Christ, 109–10, 117, 121, 199n18;
as problematic model for laity, 111,
120, 132; as secular social critique,
121; self-censorship of in the *Bible
historiale*, 12, 90, 101–6, 126–7,
136, 148–9; as theological debate,

107–11, 116; two-part composition
of, 103–4, 107–8; varied treatment
in manuscripts, 68, 101, 112–20.
See also *Moralia in Job*; Maimonides,
Moses; Thomas Aquinas
John, Gospel According to, 66, 79,
119, 154–5, 214n6
John Hyrcanus, 29, 64–5, 146, 179n68
Johns, Adrian, 158
Jonah, 139
Josephus, Flavius, 29, 38, 94, 118, 134,
140, 143–4, 146–7
Judaism, 58, 62, 105, 108–9; and
relationship to Christianity, 62–5,
136, 139. *See also* exegesis: Jewish;
Hebrew Bible; Jews
Judas Iscariot, 69, 73–9, 83, 85–6, 92,
95, 99–100
Julian the Apostate, 73–7, 79, 94, 100
justice: divine, 12, 77–8, 91, 103–4,
108, 110, 142, 148; as human virtue,
121, 204n55; and injustice, 108,
121–2; legal, 99, 121; poetic, 100
Justice, Stephen, 97, 206
Justine, Saint, 77–8

Karnes, Michelle, 97, 196n63
Kelly, Henry Ansgar, 24, 174n26
Kings, Books of, 29, 67, 98

laity: and access to translated Bibles,
19–28, 42–3; aristocratic, 25–5,
126, 162; clerical assumptions
about, 22–3, 116, 126, 132–6, 162;
as curious, 22–3, 37, 116, 133,
145–9; diverse literacies and needs
of, 25–8, 101–7, 112–20, 125, 128,
132–3, 135, 150, 156–61; educated
among, 115–16, 133, 136; Guyart's
comments about, 4, 7, 10–11, 28,
57, 59–60, 62, 90, 104–5, 124, 126,
132–3, 149–50, 160; as "impatient,"
126, 128–30, 132–6; and modern
"non-professional" readers, 8, 152–4;
as needing clerical mediation,
6–7, 11–12, 22–4, 31–7, 82, 102–5,